MUSICIANS GUIDE

TO

EVANGELICAL LUTHERAN WORSHIP

Augsburg Fortress

Musicians Guide to Evangelical Lutheran Worship

Copyright © 2007 Augsburg Fortress

Portions of this book were previously published in *Leading the Church's Song* (Augsburg Fortress, 1998)

Evangelical Lutheran Worship Leader Guides
The Sunday Assembly
The Christian Life: Baptism and Life Passages
Keeping Time: The Church's Years
Indexes to Evangelical Lutheran Worship
Musicians Guide to Evangelical Lutheran Worship
Hymnal Companion to Evangelical Lutheran Worship

Manufactured in the U.S.A.

ISBN 978-0-8066-5389-1

15   14   13   12   11   10   09   08   07   1   2   3   4   5   6   7   8   9   10

CONTENTS

FOREWORD

Evangelical Lutheran Worship is a book for the whole church. For all its wealth of resources, though, it was never imagined that *Evangelical Lutheran Worship* would contain all the hymns and songs for all worshiping assemblies and all circumstances among Lutherans. It is understood to be a *core* and a *primary* resource for worshiping assemblies. With each generation, the diversity of music within that core is growing. This *Musicians Guide to Evangelical Lutheran Worship* reflects the diversity of music in the church—with different approaches to the music of the church's song, the array of musical styles, and perspectives among us. The purpose of this book is to help musicians to lead and the church to sing the song it has been given. Yes, most of us at times probably find the ever-increasing variety of our music confusing and bewildering. However, before we turn away in frustration, it helps to step back far enough from the individual trees in order to see the forest and our place within it. Here are some suggestions for doing that:

Focus on the possible. Leaders of the church's music and members of their communities of faith will, ideally, learn as much as possible about as many liturgical and musical options as possible, but they still have to reckon with the implications of the first commandment. God is God, not they or the communities they serve. The leaders and members of particular communities are finite creatures in one time and place. None of us can be or know everything or be proficient at everything. You and your people will know some styles better than others and be able to sing those styles more easily than others. That's the way the world is. This does not mean there is only one way you can sing, but grasping for more than is humanly possible—trying to be God—is not good. Said another way, neither you nor your community can sing everything.

Greater than the sum. You and your *community* can sing far more than any of you *individually* could sing or imagine possible. A community of Christians who sing around word, font, and table is not a trained choir, but they're like a choir in that the whole is greater than the sum of its parts. The parts contribute in various ways with surprising gifts that together enable the song to take more shapes and contours than you can anticipate. We are not God, but we are gifted by God with talents that are not to be buried. This is as true where two or three are gathered together as where there are twenty or thirty, two or three hundred, or two or three thousand. Do not underestimate what is possible. Do not sell yourself or your people short.

Start with what you know. We are called to be stewards of the resources we have been given. That begins with discovering and knowing our own idioms well. They cannot be slighted without serious damage to ourselves and to the body of Christ beyond us. To neglect them is to lose our memory. But our own idioms are healthiest when they are balanced by those of others, lest we forget that our own dearly loved songs are not the only ones in the world. Other songs tht may be unfamiliar to us also reflect parts of God's great creation and help bring that creation into our worship. The key is to work outward gradually and explore the wealth with which God has graced this creation and its many creatures.

It takes work. There is no quick fix, in this book or anywhere else. As in all worthwhile pursuits, we learn to lead by leading and to sing by singing. A community learns to sing together through the discipline of singing together, but—and this is important—doing so within the love that binds us to one another and to the service of the neighbor and the whole creation. That can't happen overnight. Nor will it be helped by the intrusion of a prerecorded sonic environment that may give the impression a community is singing when in fact it is silent or, at best, singing along. The Christian church sings naturally in response to the grace of God. But once the song has been sensed, it takes shape by hard work, just like all other worthwhile human endeavors. John Wesley was blunt when he admonished the people to sing even if they found it a burden at first. They would, he correctly predicted, eventually find it a blessing. That admonition stands against an expectation of immediate gratification found in our culture, but the church's message is deeper than quickly disappearing superficialities.

Make careful choices. We hope this book will serve you in all sorts of helpful ways, but it increases rather than decreases your responsibilities. The more possibilities there are, the more you have to make distinctions. The song of the church is for the long haul, not the short run. Not everything is worth its time and effort. Not everything is congregational. There are standards of musical craft and fittingness for worship, and we flout them at our peril. Since we are finite and cannot sing everything, appropriate choices have to be made in loving respect for the people of God who sing. Leaders have to make choices as thoughtfully and lovingly as possible.

Start with the simple. The goal is not complexity. The goal is a song that sings around word, font, and table. A simple unison line sung by an assembly is far superior to complex confusion and a silent assembly of worshipers. Complexity has its place. Choirs and instruments can embody more complexity than an assembly. They should sound alone at times and they can lead and enliven the assembly's song in splendid ways. But the ideal is not some imaginary complex intrusion. The ideal is the sound you and your people make, which will vary in complexity depending upon available resources.

We are one body. In our atomized world of isolated groups, it is easy to see an array of resources as a menu to be dished up for various segments of society—for young, old, rich, poor, men, women, certain ethnic backgrounds, this taste, that taste, this class, that class, urban, rural, and so forth. A discriminatory presumption often accompanies such a perspective and assumes that a given slice of the population is only capable of, deserving of, responds to, or

likes a narrowly defined kind of music. The analysis often is faulty, as poor people who like art music, rich people who like folk music, and the inquisitive spirit of the human race amply demonstrate.

As it proclaimed in its first century, the Christian church at its essence knows another reality, that we are one in Christ and sing with one voice. To be sure, the reality is broken in this world, but the church remembers that the foretaste of the feast to come already is present among us. We deny our nature as one body of Christ when we allow the world's divisions to keep us from singing together. How to sing together in our age is no easy matter. But the riches in *Evangelical Lutheran Worship* challenge us to work toward that goal, providing the church musician with both tools and increased responsibility. In the church and its song there is no distinction between high or low, rich or poor, male or female, old or young, slave or free, suburban or rural, one ethnicity or another. Nor is anybody in one of these segments merely a statistic on a spreadsheet, no matter how helpful such charts may be. We are all human beings rescued in Christ, all freed to sing together, and all worthy of the best and most fitting music.

Rejoice then in the freedom you have been given, the song you have to sing, and the multiple ways you can embody it. Savor the array with which we are graced and to which this book seeks to give you access. If details become too heavy, back off for perspective and recall your place in God's good creation. Then sing as the Spirit bids and remember to delight in the song of the one who said, "My yoke is easy, and my burden is light." (Matt. 11:30)

Using this resource

This book is intended to be one resource among many in the process of learning to lead God's people in song with confidence and integrity. In it, you will find—

- an introduction to the role of music in Christian worship;
- a brief look at the way music can be used in the liturgies of *Evangelical Lutheran Worship*;
- an exploration of key skills in leading all forms of communal song;

- a brief survey of musical elements and possibilities for leading specific musical styles; and
- in the largest section of this book, assistance in understanding how to lead each hymn, song, or piece of liturgical and service music in *Evangelical Lutheran Worship*.

This resource is a compilation of helpful suggestions by many knowledgeable musicians.

As a companion to *Evangelical Lutheran Worship*, it will often assume a Lutheran readership, but it is intended also to be useful beyond the Lutheran community. It is not exhaustive. It is not intended to prescribe how the assembly and the leader *must* do things. Rather, it is an invitation: "Give this song a try." "Attempt this style that may be unfamiliar to you." "This technique may help your assembly sing more confidently."

Contributors

Compilers and editors of this volume:
Jennifer Baker-Trinity, Scott Weidler, Robert Buckley Farlee

Mark Bangert	Rawn Harbor	Thomas Pavlechko
Marie Rubis Bauer	Marty Haugen	William Dexheimer Pharris
Michael Bauer	Gayle Hill	Mary Preus
Jay Beech	Richard Hillert	William Bradley Roberts
Lorraine Brugh	Robert Hobby	Carl Schalk
Mellonee Burnim	Barbara Hoffman	Thomas Schmidt
James Capers	Amanda Husberg	Russell Schulz
Gerhard Cartford	Carolyn Jennings	Daniel Schwandt
David Cherwien	Linda Kempke	May Schwarz
Jayne Southwick Cool	Karen Johnson-Lefsrud	Mark Sedio
Rusty Edwards	Larry Long	Timothy Strand
Kathy Eggleston	José Antonio Machado	Kwamise Taylor
Rick Erickson	Angel Mattos	Robin Knowles Wallace
John Ferguson	Ray Makeever	Richard Webb
Erik Floan	Joel Martinson	Paul Weber
Dennis Friesen-Carper	Donald Meineke	Richard R. Webster
Robert Gallagher	Mark Mummert	Paul Westermeyer
Diane Gilbert	James Notebaart	Wayne Wold
Mark Glaeser	Charles Ore	John Ylvisaker
Handt Hanson	Anne Krentz Organ	Jeremy Young

1

ESSAYS ON
STYLES AND PRACTICES

CHAPTER ONE

INTRODUCTION

gather, unite, and bind individuals together. This is indeed a high and holy calling.

The Heart of Music for Lutherans

At the heart of a Lutheran musical practice is the song of the people. Music that embodies this Lutheran emphasis focuses on God's activity in, among, and through the worshiping assembly gathered around word and sacrament. A primary contribution of Luther to the Reformation was the restoration of the people's song proclaimed in their own language. Even most choral and instrumental music from Lutheran composers has been based on congregational melodies and texts.

Dietrich Bonhoeffer, in *Life Together,* writes: "It is not you that sing, it is the church that is singing, and you, as a member of it, may share in its song." When Lutherans assemble for worship, they sing not as individuals, but as the church. Indeed, the individual faith experience is important. Many of the songs in the book of Psalms are expressed in the first person singular. But when Christians, when Lutherans in particular, sing together in worship, it is primarily community song. The song of the church provides a balance with the song of the culture. In this day and age, an emphasis on *we* helps to balance society's emphasis on *me.*

In the early years of the Reformation, Lutheran composers used German folk melodies in worship, but only after they broke open the musical idioms and ideas of their day and transformed them into vehicles through which God's grace was communicated. The task is similar today. More and more composers for Lutheran worship are accepting the challenge of beginning with elements of jazz, blues, rap, and other musical styles from within our culture and transforming them for use in the church.

Lutherans expect music clearly to proclaim the message of salvation by grace through faith. The focus is always on God's saving activity. While these specific words are not included in

As the church, we possess a large and wonderful treasure chest of hymns, songs, chants, psalms, and canticles. In singing them, by participating and adding our own voice to the song, we make them our own. We join the song of all creation, the song of the church of all times and places, of Hannah, of Miriam and Moses, of Zechariah, of Simeon, of Anna, of Mary, of Christ Jesus.

Something happens to us when we sing. On a communal level we become more conscious of how we fit into the group, of our role in the larger gathering. On a spiritual level, tune, text, and the sound of our singing can transport us to places we never thought possible. Catechetically, we internalize what we sing. Propelled by the wings of melody, rhythm, and perhaps harmony, the message and images of the text pass through our lips, finding ways into our memories as well as our hearts. The kernel of faith is nurtured. It has often been said that the way we pray *(lex orandi)* has great bearing on what we believe *(lex credendi).* It is probably just as valid to say that what we sing also shapes our faith—*lex cantandi, lex credendi.* We who lead that song are by nature servants of God's people, and serving them well requires work. The task calls us to continuously study things churchly: scripture, historical models and the function of liturgy, the cycles of the church year. It requires of us to constantly study and practice, to keep musical skills—instrumental, vocal, choral, conducting—at sufficiently high levels. And it often challenges us to risk doing something we have never done before.

The calling of the church musician is also pastoral, functioning in and serving a community. We are among the means by which the Holy Spirit creates community, as we help every song, that grace-faith message weaves its way through the whole of the repertoire that we sing. Thus, music always seeks a balance—

- between law and gospel, never losing sight of Luther's emphasis on the theology of the cross, even in a current culture that may not want to hear it;
- between the new and the familiar, allowing music to express the timeless nature of the communion of saints;
- between community and individual; and
- between simple texts and melodies and challenging ones. The simple may be nurturing and faith-forming for some; the more complex may endure through the ages, express the strength of our faith, and form faith for others.

At the heart of a Lutheran understanding of the role of music in worship is the conviction that music invites those who seek the message of God's love to witness the depth of our faith, and it provides opportunities for faith to be sown in them.

Assembly Song: A Lesson in Community

Throughout history, the arts—and especially music—have played a vital role in the rituals of humankind. There is evidence of this in every culture, in every religious community. Most often, though not always, worship is a community event. Music, through its intimate connection with human emotion, helps heighten individual responses; but it also nurtures community in the deepest sense. Music, by nature, usually requires some sort of community. It does not and cannot exist in a vacuum. Music unites—it is an important aspect of communal worship, of being an assembly gathered around word and sacrament. Singing together is the quickest way to unite a gathering of individuals, no matter how large or small, into one corporate worshiping body, the body of Christ. Something happens when we sing!

The Primacy of the People's Song

Assembly singing of any sort requires leadership—people don't often just begin to sing spontaneously—but this leadership should never overshadow the song of the people. Simply expecting the assembly to "sing along"

with the leaders is not good enough. The assembly's voice is primary. The vocalist who "leads" the assembly by means of a microphone connected to a too-loud sound system, the organist who employs harsh detachments in articulation and overpowering registrations to beat the assembly into submission, and pastors who sing so loudly that they cannot hear the assembly's voice above their own are all guilty of replacing rather than nurturing the song of the people.

If the voice of the assembly is not primary in the music of worship, then simple, profound silence would be preferable. Leaders need to consider ways they can help assemblies find their collective voice, not fill in for them, taking their place. The key is facilitation—*helping* it happen, not *making* it happen. This should be the starting point for any decisions regarding the leadership of assembly song.

For leaders of the church's song, it means—

- choosing music that is assembly-based, having the characteristics necessary for ease in group singing;
- selecting tunes that sing well for your unique assembly, are sufficiently predictable as well as interesting, are both memorable and worthy of memory, bring the text to life, and embrace textual accents in a natural way;
- selecting texts that sing well, texts with chains of vowel patterns that flow, that follow predictable rhythmic structures from one stanza to the next; that do not overreach in their rhythmic schemes, that are worthy (poetically and theologically) of being sung by the assembly;
- nurturing the development of the assembly's collective voice so that, on occasion, they may sing unaccompanied—a great way to allow them to really hear themselves;
- cultivating an awareness of placing those musical entities in the service so they are meaningful and contribute to the flow of worship rather than attracting attention to themselves;
- introducing the hymn, song, or liturgical piece in such a way that there is no question in the mind of the participant as to what his or her part is to be, and in a way that sparks that participation;
- taking time to analyze both tune and text,

ascertaining where the difficulties in singing may lie, and determining how the
assembly might best encounter them;

- researching the origins of both text and
tune, learning what fostered their creation,
to better communicate what is essential;
- learning the musical languages of cultures other than your own to enhance the
assembly's awareness of its place within the
worldwide church;
- varying the instrumentation appropriate to
the musical style and—for organists—not
always using the same registration; and
- making friends with the element of surprise.

Assembly song is often based on *repetition*.
Repetition of stanzas or refrains can facilitate
the process of familiarization, thereby increas-
ing the assembly's comfort zone. In singing
each successive stanza, the singer becomes
more comfortable with the natural twists of
melody and rhythm. The text is able to unfold.
A good marriage of text and tune allows this to
happen with some degree of both expectancy
and surprise. A good music leader is both sup-
porter and guide.

Helping the Assembly Find Its Voice

The musician, in facilitating the song of the
people, must take into account a multitude of
factors: Who will make up the assembly? This
obvious question deserves careful attention.
The size of the assembly, for example, has bearing on decisions regarding instruments used,
organ registration, and the choice of the music
itself. What is the assembly's age range? What
are they used to singing in church? What is
the purpose of this particular gathering? What
part does music play in the flow of the service?
How might the musician facilitate not only
mood but also drama and flow? How musically
literate is the assembly?

No two assemblies sing exactly alike.
While there is likely some degree of predictability from week to week and from service
to service, the musician constantly needs to be
aware of the current disposition of the people
gathered. Are they singing well today? How
can I best encourage their participation? What
can I do to help the assembly gel as a worshiping unit? While the fundamental patterns of
the liturgy—combined with elements such

as expectancy and anticipation on the part of
those gathered—foster at least a fundamental base, the question still must be addressed:
What can I do to help expand and uplift?

Leaders of assembly song who tend to be
most effective understand the importance of
working together—of leading through the
building of relationship, of working from
within as part of the assembly, of keeping one
eye toward beauty of tone and color and one
eye toward meeting the people where they are
on this particular day. Anticipate musical prob-
lems before they arise and learn to deal with
them as they come up. Know the worshiping
community you serve. Familiarize yourself
with their existing repertoire, their cultural
heritage, their likes and dislikes. Then build on
this base. Set a vision for incorporating areas of
growth: new literature, hymns and songs from
unfamiliar traditions. At the same time, remain
respectful of the songs they love.

The one who facilitates the church's song
also needs to consider the environment in
which the community worships. This includes
instruments available, acoustics, visual lines,
seating design, amplification system, light-
ing, tone of intimacy or grandeur, as well as
the positioning of the choir and other worship
leaders. Consult with others who plan and lead
worship to determine how such factors can be
used together to enhance not just the song but
the entire worship service.

In a time when convergence of various musical, liturgical, and theological traditions within
Lutheran and other denominations is on the rise,
musicians need to explore and familiarize themselves with the music and performance practice
of other congregations and churches. Church
musicians need to be familiar with the German
chorale, the tunes from the Genevan Psalter,
the hymns of the English and Welsh traditions,
white spirituals, Black gospel, revival hymnody,
music from Africa, Asia, Latin America, and
so on. Make use of books, articles, recordings,
telephone calls to friends, seminars—our learning should never cease.

How Much Diversity Can Your Assembly Handle?

In using *Evangelical Lutheran Worship,* with
its ten musical settings for Holy Communion

and a diverse repertoire of liturgical music, hymns, and songs, the goal is *not* for every worshiping assembly to learn everything within its pages. The intent of liturgical music is to carry the *texts* of the liturgy, themselves grounded in biblical language, rather than to draw attention to the music itself. The music, used regularly over long periods of time, should help instill these texts of our faith deeply into the hearts of worshipers who, thereby, offer praise to God. Constantly changing music does not help attain this goal.

However, challenging an assembly with new music can also be an effective way to enliven old texts and express new images and ideas with refreshing musical expressions. The difficult task for worship planners is to the find the right balance for each worshiping assembly.

The question of how much repertoire an assembly can handle must be answered locally for and by each community. Leaders may want to start with genres rather than individual hymns or songs, such as German, Scandinavian, English, contemporary, folk, world-global, and so forth. What genres are nearest and dearest to the core of your congregation? If you have several services each week, that core may vary for these different assemblies. What genres are known but not loved as deeply? Chart these out, mapping the dearly held core surrounded by a swirl of all the music your assemblies know. Surround that familiar repertoire with styles that some may know and wish would become part of the core. What styles may you need to introduce for the sake of mission in your community? You get the picture. As worship planners, you now have a visual idea of where you may go—or choose not to go—with the task of introducing new music.

Most assemblies need to repeat a new hymn every week for a while in order to learn it well. It is also important to bring that new melody back several times over the coming months for it to become deeply engrained in a community. Only by planning your liturgical music and hymns far in advance—perhaps an entire church year in advance—can you begin to see important patterns emerge. Important questions for worship planners to ask themselves include:

- Is this a new tune the assembly will need repeated Sundays to learn, or can they sing it easily on sight?
- If it will require substantial work to learn, is it a tune worthy of our time and effort?
- If yes, on what Sundays and in which season can we sing this hymn for several weeks in a row?
- Are there other times throughout the year for which this new tune and text will also work?
- Does this tune appear in *Evangelical Lutheran Worship* with other texts, so we can reinforce the new tune while singing words that may fit better elsewhere in the church year?

Remember that Lutherans understand assembly singing to be a part of the proclamation of God's word. It deserves our careful attention and time.

Even when you plan far in advance, particular events in the community or in the world may change the atmosphere in a congregation on short notice. Pastoral sensibilities may call on leaders to adjust plans. You may discover that you were a bit ambitious in learning new music and your people simply need a few weeks to catch their breath with more familiar repertoire. Or you may have underestimated their abilities and want to challenge them a bit more. Planning well in advance is a great blessing, but only if you are also prepared to adjust those plans as the year unfolds.

Be alert to your community. Don't be afraid to challenge them, but be aware of their feelings. Always be prepared with appropriate assembly song that is both familiar and new.

CHAPTER TWO

THE PLACE OF MUSIC
IN THE SERVICES OF EVANGELICAL LUTHERAN WORSHIP

Music plays an important role in the worship of the Lutheran church. Although it is possible to worship without music, and at times the absence of music can be quite powerful, Lutherans expect music. They want to sing. Their song is integral to the liturgies of the church, not just an add-on to make it more beautiful. Lutherans believe that God's word can be proclaimed through song. Musicians participate in that proclamation. Planning for and leading music in worship is not a responsibility to be taken lightly. Those who prepare for worship need to know the expectations and possibilities. This chapter walks through the liturgical portions of *Evangelical Lutheran Worship,* highlighting the places where music can play a role, helping unpack some of the intent behind the rubrics—the service notes in red italic type—within the services and other explanatory materials, and beginning an exploration of the possibilities that lie within them.

Throughout the services in *Evangelical Lutheran Worship,* one finds many rubrics about music. Many are quite flexible, allowing for a variety of ways to form that part of the service. This is especially true in the Gathering of Holy Communion and Service of the Word. Other parts are more straightforward. Although there is room for variety of music and prayers, the fundamental shape is more common between congregations. This is seen in the Meal portion of Holy Communion. As you study *Evangelical Lutheran Worship,* pay close attention to the words of these rubrics. They can be a helpful guide in planning worship.

Every musician with responsibilities for worship planning should also know well the Notes on the Services in the Leaders Desk Edition (pp. 9–52), as well as these other *Evangelical Lutheran Worship* leader guides: *The Sunday Assembly, The Christian Life,* and *Keeping Time.* Music should never be isolated from other parts of the service. Music works hand-in-hand with the liturgical texts, the shape of the liturgy, scripture readings for the day, preaching, visual arts, ministries of hospitality, and more, to create a cohesive worship experience. It's crucial that local planners both understand the intent of the services in *Evangelical Lutheran Worship* and contextualize and breathe life into them in their own location. These suggestions are just the beginning of a process of discovery that will lead to many more possibilities to enliven the use of *Evangelical Lutheran Worship.*

Appropriate

A recurring phrase in the rubrics is "or another appropriate hymn or song," or something similar. The key word is *appropriate.* The texts and music that are included in the services have been included for excellent reasons. Many have been formed throughout centuries of use by Christian assemblies. Certainly, there is value and a need for new expressions to be shaped for use in worship today. Planners must be careful to understand the ritual (experiential) and theological functions that any particular piece of music plays in the liturgy. For instance, "Glory to God," the canticle of praise, grounded in a biblical text, presents a clearly Christological shout of praise. A song such as "Amen, We Praise Your Name/*Amen, siakudumisa*" (#846), while certainly a song of praise, does not carry the same depth of meaning as "Glory to God." It may be an appropriate choice in some contexts, but worship planners need to be intentional about the substitutions they make. On the other hand, the alleluias, with a verse of scripture, function as a brief acclamation, introducing the proclamation of the gospel. A canticle, such as "Glory to God," would not serve well at that moment in the rite.

Canticle

A canticle is a hymn or song from the early church, usually rooted in a biblical text. The best known include "Glory to God" (*Gloria in excelsis*), "My soul proclaims the greatness of the Lord" (*Magnificat*), "Now, Lord, you let your servant go in peace" (*Nunc dimittis*), "Blessed are you, Lord" (*Benedictus*), "We praise you, O God" (*Te Deum*) and "This is the feast." Care must be taken when making a decision to substitute another hymn or song when one of the canticles is suggested. Certainly, there are other texts that may be a fine substitute on occasion, but these canticle texts carry with them a long history of valued use in the church and must not be forgotten. These ancient texts continue to inspire composers writing in many musical styles.

Speak or Sing?

Any of the texts that appear with music may be spoken. It isn't likely, or very edifying, that an assembly would recite long portions of canticles that were intended to be sung, any more than they would speak hymn texts. However, shorter acclamations and brief moments of liturgical dialogue may effectively be spoken when a minister does not sing. If one part (presiding minister or leader) is spoken, the response should be spoken as well. (This would be the case, for example, in the opening dialogue of the great thanksgiving.)

On the other hand, there are many examples where a text appears without music. Some assemblies, in some contexts, may want to chant these portions. This can be done quite simply by teaching an assembly to sing their response on the same pitches that were sung to them. For example, the greeting near the beginning of the Holy Communion service could be sung:

The grace of our Lord Jesus Christ,
the love of God and the communion
of the Holy Spirit be   with you all.

And al - so with you.

. . . or:

The grace of our Lord Jesus
Christ, the love of God, and the
communion of the Holy Spirit be with you all.

And al - so with you.

Be careful to use pitches that correspond to other music sung before or after, and be sure that text changes pitches with its natural accents.

The dismissal might be sung as follows:

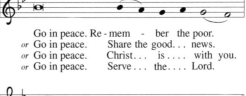

Go in peace. Re - mem - ber the poor.
or Go in peace.   Share the good. . . news.
or Go in peace.   Christ. . . is . . . . with you.
or Go in peace.   Serve . . . the . . . . Lord.

Thanks be to God.

The opening dialogues of the Evening Prayer service demonstrate this principle nicely. On pages 309–310, the first general dialogue is set to a simple tone, with the assembly singing their responses to the same melody as the leader. The other general and seasonal options that follow are simply pointed, alerting the singer when to change pitches. These dialogues could be sung to the same or different tones, with the assembly echoing back the melody. For example, the second dialogue could be sung with a different melody, such as:

God is light and our sal - vation,

our refuge and our stronghold.

More elaborate possibilities could be explored. Numerous places in the seasonal rites could be enhanced using this simple system as well. Consider the acclamation before and after the procession of palms at the beginning of the Passion Sunday liturgy. It could be sung:

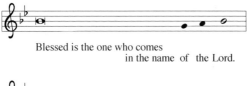

Blessed is the one who comes
in the name of the Lord.

Hosanna in the highest.

This coordinates well with the melody of "All Glory, Laud, and Honor," which is often sung between these two acclamations. If the sung acclamation is followed by a prayer, it prayer may be sung (chanted) as well. This simple method of echo dialogue can be adapted and used with many liturgical texts.

Chanting Prayers

Certain contexts may call for worship leaders to sing prayers rather than speak them. There is no absolute right or wrong way to chant prayers. The best advice is to keep it simple and be certain to conclude in a way that leads the assembly confidently to their sung "Amen." Pages 705 and 724 in the leaders edition provide two good examples. Again, be certain to change pitches at natural places, using the accents of the text. This may mean singing several syllables on a pitch before moving on, or adding an extra syllable or two to the final pitch:

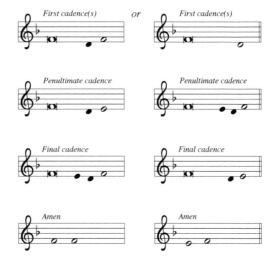

First cadence(s)   or   First cadence(s)

Penultimate cadence   Penultimate cadence

Final cadence   Final cadence

Amen   Amen

Psalms

Many of the services in *Evangelical Lutheran Worship* call for the singing of psalms. Although there are numerous systems for singing the psalms and many musical resources available from publishers, this resource will only address the simple system that is included in *Evangelical Lutheran Worship* (see page 33). But worship planners should never feel limited to the system included in the book.

How Much Can We Handle?

The liturgical music in *Evangelical Lutheran Worship* is diverse, especially within the ten musical settings of Holy Communion, in addition to the Service of the Word, the Daily Prayer services and all the possibilities in the service music section. The diverse musical styles allow for greater variety within our assemblies. Whether most of the people in a given assembly share an ethnic identity or the assembly is broadly diverse, an ever-widening repertoire of song is encouraged. The incarnation is heard and confessed as a more astounding reality when we sing songs that connect us to the many people and places of the world that are also claimed and blessed by God. However, it is likely, and probably wise, that most congregations will only learn a few settings of the liturgy. With historic texts that are repeated week after week, year after year, century after century, the purpose of the music is to carry the text, not distract from it. Determining how many settings to learn and which ones will work best in your setting will be a critical decision for each congregation.

Holy Communion

Although the rubrics are the same in each musical setting of Holy Communion, the page numbers here refer to Setting One.

GATHERING

Although not specifically mentioned in the rite itself, there may be gathering music before the liturgy actually begins. This may include instrumental music, vocal music, and assembly song. This may be a valuable time used for teaching the assembly music to be used in the liturgy that day. This is especially helpful when learning something new or when there are many visitors in the assembly. In a day when keeping silence is not a natural part of life for many, gathering an assembly with communal singing and then drawing them into a time of intentional silence may be a positive way to prepare for worship. Never underestimate the power of silence as a musical element—or assume that members of an assembly know how to keep silence effectively.

The gathering section has more options for shaping the pattern of worship than any other part of the liturgy. Rather than prescribing a set order, *Evangelical Lutheran Worship* gives possible components that may be shaped in different ways. These include confession and forgiveness or thanksgiving for baptism, a Kyrie, canticles of praise, "Glory to God" or "This is the feast" or other hymns and songs, and a greeting. Use as many or few of these elements as may be needed to gather a particular assembly on a certain day. This may vary based on the size of the assembly, the architecture, the season or day in the church year, the musical repertoire of an assembly, and more. All the elements are present for those desiring a full historic gathering rite. The freedom for those using more contemporary musical styles and models is also there. Consider the following possibilities or other combinations of these musical and liturgical elements:

Hymn
Greeting
Prayer of the Day

Greeting
Hymn
Prayer of the Day

Confession and Forgiveness
Kyrie
Greeting
Prayer of the Day

Medley of Gathering Songs
Greeting
Prayer of the Day

Confession and Forgiveness
Hymn
Greeting
Kyrie
Prayer of the Day

Medley of Gathering Songs
Confession and Forgiveness
Kyrie
Greeting
Prayer of the Day

Thanksgiving for Baptism
Hymn
Greeting
Canticle of Praise
Prayer of the Day

Thanksgiving for Baptism
Hymn
Greeting
Kyrie
Canticle of Praise
Prayer of the Day

Medley of Gathering Songs
Thanksgiving for Baptism
Canticle of Praise
Greeting
Prayer of the Day

Unique architectural settings or other factors may encourage yet greater flexibility, even when not specifically mentioned in *Evangelical Lutheran Worship.* Consider the following if a procession to the baptismal font, for either confession and forgiveness or thanksgiving for baptism, is desired:

Hymn
Confession and Forgiveness or
Thanksgiving for Baptism
Kyrie and/or Canticle of Praise
Greeting
Prayer of the Day

In some informal settings and on a few occasions, there may be no music at all, simply:

Greeting
Prayer of the Day

Especially in Advent or Lent, the Kyrie may stand alone. During Christmas and throughout the Sundays after Epiphany, the canticle "Glory to God" may have a prominent role, while "This is the feast" is best sung for communion services during the season of Easter and on other festival days related to resurrection, such as All Saints Day. Whatever is sung, gathering songs are best when they surround and support people who come to worship with different frames of reference and different emotions, moving each individual into the communal experience and purpose of worship. Gathering songs should welcome the assembly to the mercy of the triune God, and not only speak to our individual needs or desires. Especially those who plan worship in more global or popular styles may find new expressions and combinations of songs that would work well.

In some musical settings of the liturgy, there are portions designated for singing by an assisting minister. That person may be someone who is vested and leading alongside the presiding minister, someone in the choir, the entire choir singing the part together, or another person in the assembly. The term assisting minister—one who assists the assembly in worship—should be understood broadly.

Incidentally, as the traditional title of cantor for the church musician is being rediscovered in the Lutheran church, it is worth pointing out that it *may,* but need not, indicate someone who sings leader parts in the services. The title has more to do with clarifying the role of the musician as the person who leads the assembly's song.

WORD

The reading of scripture is surrounded by song. This pattern of proclaiming the word is as ancient as the synagogue worship of the Jewish people. Christians have inherited the practice of publicly reciting the appointed biblical texts and responding to the recitation with singing. This read-sing-read-sing sequence continues: we respond to the first reading with the singing of a psalm. After the second reading, we stand to greet the gospel and sing an acclamation. Retaining this sequence will help all assemblies fall into a rhythm of proclamation.

Psalm

Traditionally, after the first reading (usually from the Old Testament) a psalm is sung. See page 33 for information about singing the psalms using the simple method.

Gospel Acclamation

After the second reading, the assembly stands and sings to welcome and honor the living Christ, who is among us. In *Evangelical Lutheran Worship,* the gospel acclamation holds a place of prominence as one of the chief acclamations in the liturgy.

The gospel acclamation consists of two parts: alleluia and a verse of scripture. On some occasions, singing just the alleluia is appropriate, and on others, such as during Lent, singing just the verse is appropriate.

On page 102 of the pew edition is an alleluia refrain that can be sung by the assembly. It would be appropriate—and perhaps wise, especially when learning something new—for the refrain to be sung first by a cantor (soloist) or choir, then repeated by the assembly. Then follows a verse from scripture. Then the alleluia refrain is repeated by all.

In order that more scripture is heard and for greater continuity between readings, biblical verses appointed for each day and festival are intended to be sung at this point. These texts are printed in the leaders edition (pp. 60–137) and the liturgies accompaniment edition (pp. 217–226). They are pointed like the psalms, so they will work with any setting. Alternatively, the verse printed in Setting One ("Lord, to whom shall we go? . . .") could be sung at most anytime in the church year (except Lent), by the entire assembly or by a soloist or choir.

If the pointed text were printed out each Sunday for all worshipers, the assembly could learn to sing these texts that change weekly. An easier alternative is for a cantor, choir, or praise ensemble to sing it, surrounded by the assembly's alleluias.

This is how the verse for Epiphany would look when sung to the gospel acclamation in Setting One:

desired. Some choir anthems that include many alleluias and an appropriate text could be sung. Instrumental introductions to festive alleluias sung by the assembly could be used. There are many possibilities. Planners must be certain the music does not overshadow the proclamation of the gospel to follow. A reprise of the alleluias or a portion of the music played before the gospel may be repeated after the gospel is proclaimed to bracket the reading with alleluias and to accompany the procession back to the chancel.

Hymn of the Day

The hymn of the day is the principal hymn of the service and is a distinctively Lutheran element in the liturgy. The assembly participates in proclaiming and responding to the

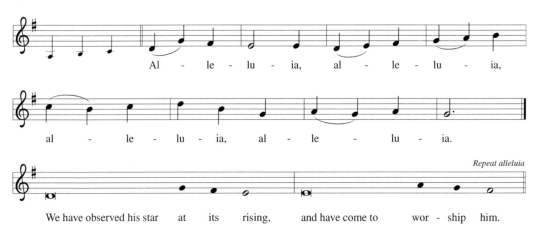

With verses like this, it is important that the singers keep the accents in their natural place. In this example, do not accent the word "at" just because it occurs on the moving note. Rather, stress "star" before moving on with the text.

Most of the settings include a verse of scripture set to a melody that can be used throughout the Lenten season. It will be a local decision whether to use that, or instead the appointed verse for the particular Sunday sung to an appropriate psalm tone. These short verses provide perfect material for local compositions or improvisations.

The rubric at this point includes the possibilities of using "another appropriate song." Especially on festival days, when the sung acclamation may be accompanying a gospel procession, additional music may be needed and

word of God with a common voice. This particular hymn must be chosen carefully in relation to the season or day, the readings, and the preaching. It carries theological weight unlike any other music in the liturgy. Suggestions for the hymn of the day are in *Indexes to Evangelical Lutheran Worship*.

To signify its importance in the liturgy, the hymn of the day may be highlighted with an extended instrumental introduction, alternation (see pages 45–46), descants, and so forth. Other hymns and songs sung in the liturgy should not overshadow this hymn, with the possible exception of the gospel acclamation and music during the great thanksgiving.

Prayers of Intercession

Although the prayers of intercession are usually spoken by an assisting minister with a spoken response by the assembly, they may be sung. The litany in the Evening Prayer service (pew edition, pp. 316–317) provides one model. Simple refrains, such as #178–180 in the service music section, could be sung instead of a spoken response by the assembly. To do this well requires careful coordination between the assisting minister and the music leader.

MEAL

The Meal portion of the liturgy usually begins with two elements: the offering and setting the table. You'll notice that no specific music is provided at the offering. A rubric (p. 106) says: *Assembly song or other music may accompany or follow the gathering of the offering.* The intent here is to acknowledge the wide variety of practice in our church.

Consider which of these or other alternatives might best suit your context and practice:

- Choir, soloist, band, or instrumentalist offers music as the offering is received. This music also accompanies the gifts being brought forward. The table is set simply, with bread and wine brought from a side table.
- Music is offered as the offering is received and the table is set. After the music is complete, the gifts are brought forward as a brief psalm or single stanza of a hymn is sung by the assembly.
- Music is offered as the offering is received. After the music is complete, the gifts of money, bread and wine are brought forward as a complete hymn is sung by the assembly. The table is set as the hymn continues.
- Music is offered by a choir, band, or soloist as the entire assembly processes forward with their gifts. Part of this procession may include the bread and wine and the setting of the table. Music that includes a refrain can also include assembly singing, even as they participate in the offering procession.

Ideally, the text of anything sung at this point will focus on either our grateful response to the gifts of God and/or God's grace to be received in the sacrament to follow. The season, the day, the assembly, and the musicians

available are all factors in making an appropriate selection.

If assembly song, in addition to what may be played or sung by musicians during the offering, is desired, consider the following:

Shorter, general possibilities
> Let the Vineyards Be Fruitful (#181–184)
> Create in Me a Clean Heart (#185–188, especially during Lent)

Seasonal possibilities
> Come Now, O Prince of Peace (#247)
> Let All Mortal Flesh Keep Silence (#490, especially st. 2 during Advent)
> In the Bleak Midwinter (#294, especially st. 3)
> What Child Is This (#296, especially st. 3)
> Seed That in Earth Is Dying (#330)
> At the Lamb's High Feast We Sing (#362, especially sts. 2 and 4)
> Christ Jesus Lay in Death's Strong Bands (#370, especially st. 5)
> Alleluia! Sing to Jesus (#392, especially st. 3)
> Like the Murmur of the Dove's Song (#403)

Possibilities focusing more on communion
> Now the Silence (#460)
> All Who Hunger, Gather Gladly (#461)
> Now We Join in Celebration (#462)
> Bread of Life, Our Host and Meal (#464)
> As the Grains of Wheat (#465)
> We Place upon Your Table, Lord (#467)
> Around You, O Lord Jesus (#468)
> I Come with Joy (#482)
> God Extends an Invitation/*Nuestro Padre nos invita* (#486)
> Come, Let Us Eat (#491)

Possibilities focusing more on response to God's gifts
> Take My Life, That I May Be (#685)
> We Give Thee but Thine Own (#686)
> Come to Us, Creative Spirit (#687)
> Praise and Thanksgiving (#689)
> Accept, O Lord, the Gifts We Bring (#691)
> We Are an Offering (#692)

Great Thanksgiving

The classic dialogue ("The Lord be with you . . .") begins the great thanksgiving. Although this dialogue and the proper preface ("It is indeed right . . .") that follows can be spoken, they appear with the simple melody that has accompanied these texts for centuries (although the keys have been changed to coordinate with the "Holy, holy, holy"). The melody itself communicates to many worshipers around the world. Notice that the same melody is used in all settings. This has been done both for historic reasons and to make it more consistent for presiding ministers. Since these chants are best sung with melody alone, no keyboard accompaniment is provided. If one is necessary to support the assembly, the melody may be played on the organ, piano, or other instrument. However, music leaders are encouraged to challenge their assemblies with at least a small bit of unaccompanied singing each week. Achieving that goal will strengthen all assembly singing. If a presiding minister is unable to sing the dialogue and proper preface, it is best that the entire dialogue, including the assembly's responses, be spoken. But the "Holy, holy, holy" may be sung even when dialogue and preface are spoken.

The style of music for the "Holy, holy, holy…" "Christ has died . . ." and "Amen . . ." within the great thanksgiving varies throughout the ten settings. Music leaders will do well to consider the setting when determining how it should be led. Some are jubilant and festive; others are ethereal and mystical. As with all liturgical music that grows out of a sung or spoken text by the presiding minister, the music leader must be aware of the natural rhythm between presiding minister and sung response. The rhythm must flow naturally in and out of one another.

If a sung version of the Lord's Prayer is desired, a traditional chant version is in Setting Five, on page 163.

Communion

The historic text "Lamb of God" may be sung as the first communion song, immediately following the invitation ("Taste and see . . ." or "Come to the banquet . . ."). Depending on communion procedures, this can sometimes be an awkward moment of silence as ministers move to their places to serve communion. Singing "Lamb of God" can help worshipers focus on something more important. On occasion, other appropriate songs may be substituted, but this text holds an important place in historic practice and should not be eliminated

from a congregation's repertoire.

Other music may follow as communion proceeds. This may be instrumental, choral, solo, or assembly song. Songs with an appropriate refrain maybe be especially helpful, allowing individuals to sing even as they move forward to receive communion. See #466, 472, 473, 474, 477, and 483 as examples. A hymn with more text may best be sung after a good portion of the assembly have communed and returned to their seats. The rubrics are flexible at this point, allowing for a variety of practice. The season, the day, the assembly, and the communion procedures in your unique architecture are all factors in making good local decisions for music during communion. Whatever is chosen, the music should contribute to an understanding of communion as a joyful meal of reconciliation, without overshadowing the reception of the sacrament itself. Balance, appropriate to the season or day, is key.

Another distinctively Lutheran contribution to the liturgy is to sing the song of Simeon ("Now, Lord, you let your servant go in peace") at the end of communion. Again, notice the flexibility of the rubric (p. 113): "The assembly *may* sing the following *or another suitable song.*" This canticle, or another song, may be sung either at the end of communion or as part of the Sending.

SENDING

Sending Song

Although not necessary, a song at the end of the liturgy is a common way to conclude. If not sung at the end of communion, "Now, Lord, you let your servant go in peace" may be sung. If a sending song is included, it may best precede the dismissal, allowing the assisting minister's charge to the assembly to be the final words of the liturgy.

There are many opinions about the value of a postlude, instrumental music played at the end of the liturgy or after the liturgy concludes. Many organists play music while the assembly disperses and talks. To some this seems as though the music is just background filler. To others, the music accompanies the assembly into the world, where the liturgy continues in their daily lives. In some assemblies, organists or other instrumentalists play a postlude while the assembly sits and listens. To some, this shows respect for the music and musicians. For others, it unduly delays the sending of the assembly into mission. In some settings it may be best to delay the dismissal ("Go in peace . . .") until after the postlude. There is no one correct answer to this matter. Worship planners, musicians, and assemblies in a particular place should come to a common understanding and agreed upon practice, or a plan for varying it by season.

Service of the Word

The Gathering, Word, and Sending portions of this service are the same as Holy Communion and the musical opportunities are similar. Note, though, that in the absence of a meal, the canticle "This is the feast" may not be appropriate. One additional difference regards decisions about the music to be sung as the offering is brought forward, since it doesn't relate to a following meal. It may be most appropriate that the offering be brought forward during whatever music accompanies the offering itself or during the canticle of thanksgiving that follows.

Canticle of Thanksgiving

A canticle of thanksgiving follows the offering. Its text focuses specifically on the word of God (". . . blessed is the one whose name is the Word of God . . ."). If substitutions are made, be sure the emphasis is appropriate. Hymns and songs in the Word section (#503–519) provide some good options.

Holy Baptism

Each of the rites within this section—Holy Baptism, Welcome to Baptism, Affirmation of Baptism, and Corporate Confession and Forgiveness—share primary characteristics. Since all are usually celebrated within another service, such as Holy Communion, most decisions concerning music are covered in that section. However, *Evangelical Lutheran Worship* does include suggestions for using music within the rites themselves. These rites are celebrated occasionally rather than weekly, so assembly song that will work with less preparation must be chosen carefully.

Holy Baptism

Since baptisms normally follow the hymn of the day, those gathering at the font can do so during the final stanza of that hymn. Depending on the season or day, the hymn selected may reflect themes of baptism but should not overshadow the themes presented in the scripture readings for the day. Ideally, baptisms are on a day when baptismal connections are already present in the reading, so there shouldn't be a conflict. If baptisms are at the beginning of the service, a brief hymn or refrain may be sung as the baptismal party gathers at the font.

After the actual baptism, as the newly-baptized comes out of the water and is dried off and, perhaps, clothed in a white garment, is the perfect time for the assembly to offer their acclamation. Most people in the assembly will want to see what is going on, so repeating a brief refrain may be the best choice. There are several possibilities in the service music section, including #209–213. Since baptisms would usually not be celebrated during Lent, any refrain with Alleluias would be appropriate. The refrains from hymns, such as #366, 385, 386, 422, 424 or any gospel acclamation refrain (without the verse) from the service music section (#168–175), would work well. If there is more than one baptism, the chosen refrain could be repeated several times following each baptism. Including bells and other instruments, as available, would add to the festivity.

At the conclusion of the rite, as those gathered at the font return to their places and the ministers move to their places for prayers of intercession, an acclamation, psalm, or hymn may be sung. Service music canticles #209–215 are possibilities. Whatever is chosen should reflect baptism and be appropriate to the length of time needed to accompany the movement. Unduly delaying the liturgy at this point is not desirable. Perhaps a refrain sung earlier could be reprised and repeated as long as needed.

Welcome to Baptism

This rite includes two parts, the first at the start of the liturgy, the second following the hymn of the day. The only music needed at the beginning is whatever hymn or song has been chosen for the gathering. Those being welcomed may enter with a procession during the singing.

Ministers, those being welcomed, and their sponsors may gather before the assembly during the final stanza of the hymn of the day. The assembly responses "Praise to you, O Christ" and "May the God of all grace" (#216 and 217) may both be sung if desired. There is an option in the leaders edition for multiple signings of the cross to be made, in which case the first response would be repeated numerous times. If this option is used, it is particularly effective for the response to be sung, creating a natural rhythm between the spoken words of the presiding minister and the assembly response. One of these responses, first sung when someone is welcomed into a journey toward baptism, may be repeated by the assembly each Sunday, perhaps during the intercessions when the candidate is held in prayer, until the day of their baptism. The short texts of these responses also are ideal for local composers to craft a melody unique to the worshiping community.

Affirmation of Baptism

The choices for music during Affirmation of Baptism are similar to those for Holy Baptism

or Welcome to Baptism. Those gathering before the assembly may do so during the last stanza of the hymn of the day. After the spoken acclamation by the assembly ("We rejoice with you . . ."), a hymn, song, or refrain may be sung. Any of the possibilities mentioned for baptism may work here as well. If a visible reminder of baptism is used, such as sprinkling the assembly or inviting them to the font, the music chosen will need to be of appropriate length. Especially when coming to the font while singing, a repeated refrain may be most effective.

Corporate Confession and Forgiveness

This rite may be incorporated into another service or may be a service by itself. If it is a separate service, Psalm 25:1-17, Psalm 51:1-15, Psalm 103, another psalm, or an appropriate hymn or canticle may be sung as the assembly gathers. Hymns from the confession section (#600–609) may be sung. Music during the Word section would be similar to what would be prepared for any service of holy communion.

The prayer of confession (p. 240) includes a refrain: "Holy God, holy and mighty, holy and immortal, have mercy on us." This text— the Trisagion, Greek for "thrice holy"—may be sung, rather than spoken, by the assembly. Three settings are included in the service music section (#159–161). The presiding minister's texts also could be chanted, on a pitch that would lead the assembly into their refrain.

Following the announcement of forgiveness, a hymn of praise and thanksgiving may be sung. When celebrating God's forgiveness, time is not an issue. This may be a time for the assembly to stand and sing a hymn or song reflecting this joy.

Lent and the Three Days

The services for Ash Wednesday, Passion Sunday, Maundy Thursday, Good Friday, and the Vigil of Easter are full of musical possibilities. What follows is a brief overview of options to explore.

Ash Wednesday

Psalm 51 holds a historic place of prominence in this liturgy. It may be sung at the gathering, as the psalm during the word, or during the imposition of ashes. Worship planners should make certain that a musical setting of this psalm is included somewhere in the liturgy.

A primary musical element in this service is *silence*. Music is not played or sung before the liturgy. After gathering in silence, the assembly sings a psalm, hymn, Kyrie, or other litany. Any appropriate Kyrie, from the ten settings of Holy Communion, the Service of the Word, service music #151–158, or another source may be sung. The Great Litany (#238) may be sung here or at its traditional place as the gathering music on the First Sunday in Lent.

The Word section of the service continues in the familiar pattern. For the gospel acclamation, a pointed text is provided and pointed so it can be sung to any psalm tone or the tone provided with any gospel acclamation in the Holy Communion settings. Local composers may craft a melody for this brief text.

During the imposition of ashes, hymns or penitential psalms may be sung or silence kept. Many hymns or refrains in the confession, forgiveness, grace, faith, Lent, and healing sections of assembly song may be appropriate. The focus should be on the reception of ashes. Music should accompany, not overshadow, the primary event.

The service concludes simply, with or without communion. "Create in me" (a portion of Psalm 51) is especially appropriate at the setting of the table on this day and throughout Lent. Silence may replace a postlude at this service and perhaps through the season of Lent.

Sunday of the Passion

This service begins with a glimpse of the entry into Jerusalem, then makes a sharp turn into the Passion of Christ. Music can be helpful in highlighting this dramatic shift. The service begins with the procession of palms, which can happen in very different ways. It may include the entire assembly in a lengthy procession, perhaps outside around the building or even around the block. The whole assembly may process around the interior of the church or gather in one part of the building and process into the worship space. Or most of the assembly may stand in their places during a procession of cross, candles, ministers, and perhaps choir throughout the church. However it is done, festive music, appropriate to the logistics, should be included. Away from the worship space this may mean

instrumental or choral music without piano or organ. The hymn "All Glory, Laud, and Honor" (#344) has a traditional place in this procession. It can be difficult for an assembly to sing a hymn while in procession. It may be best to accompany the procession with instrumental or choral music, refrains, or shouts of Hosanna! until most worshipers are in the church. Then proceed with the hymn. The acclamations ("Blessed is the one . . .") may be sung (see page 7).

Following the prayer of the day, the focus of the service shifts to the suffering and death of Christ. Music from this point on should reflect that shift. The service continues with Word, Meal, and Sending. The primary reading on this day is the lengthy passion gospel from Matthew in year A; Mark in year B; or Luke in year C. Numerous musical versions of these passions are available and may be considered for liturgical use, if not too lengthy. Otherwise, single stanzas of appropriate Lenten and Holy Week hymns could be interspersed at appropriate moments in the reading to help the assembly connect with the reading.

Maundy Thursday

The evening services of Thursday, Friday, and Saturday form one continuous liturgy. Worship planners may consider ways that music may help to provide continuity throughout. On this night, simplicity is key. The assembly may gather in silence.

Confession and Forgiveness

Assembly song, other music, or silence may accompany the laying on of hands. Since worshipers will be going forward during this time, a repeated refrain may be most effective if assembly song is desired. This time may conclude with a hymn, as most worshipers will have returned to their places.

Word

The Word section continues in the familiar pattern. For the gospel acclamation, a pointed text is provided and can be sung to any psalm tone or the tone provided with any gospel acclamation in one of the Holy Communion settings (but without alleluias). A local composer might create a melody for this brief text.

Footwashing

Methods of footwashing vary widely, including only representatives or the entire assembly. Choral or instrumental music may accompany this action. If assembly song is desired, a song with a refrain, such as "Where True Charity and Love Abide" (#642 or 653), is especially appropriate.

Stripping of the Altar

Following the communion, if the altar is stripped, Psalm 88 or Psalm 22 may be sung by a cantor, the choir, or the assembly. To allow the assembly to pray or meditate during this time, the psalm may best be sung by cantor or choir. No matter who sings, simplicity is the key. Choose an appropriate psalm tone, such as 2, 8, 9, or 11 (pp. 337–338). If using Psalm 22, singers may change to a brighter tone at verse 25. The assembly departs in silence and the service will continue on Friday.

Good Friday

It is an ancient tradition that the only instrument used on Good Friday is the human voice. If your assembly can sing unaccompanied, the contrast with most liturgies accompanied by instruments is powerful. If instrumental support is required, it should be kept to a minimum.

There is no prelude or pre-service music. All gather in silence. The psalm and gospel acclamations are sung to simple tones.

The primary reading on this day is the Passion according to John. Simple settings of this passion for cantors or choir may replace the reading, but clear proclamation is the goal. This is not the time for extended musical treatments of this reading.

Silence is a profound musical element and should be used in abundance throughout this liturgy.

Procession of the Cross

Using the technique in which the same tone is sung by the leader and then echoed by the assembly (see pages 6–7), the dialogue during the procession of the cross could be chanted. For example:

This text is sung three times throughout the procession. It is best sung by the minister carrying the cross. If this is not possible, a cantor may accompany the minister in the procession, singing the text.

Two primary texts are provided for this time in the service (Leaders Edition, pp. 639–642):

- The Solemn Reproaches ("O my people, O my church . . .") may be sung by a cantor to a simple tone. The assembly may respond with "Holy God, holy and mighty, holy and immortal, have mercy on us." The service music includes three settings of this response (#159–161). More elaborate settings of the reproaches text are available in other sources.
- We Glory in Your Cross. Settings of this text are provided in seasonal music resources from Augsburg Fortress.

The service concludes with the dialogue "We adore you, O Christ . . . ," sung to a simple melody echoed by the assembly, and a hymn of adoration. Two hymns especially appropriate are "Sing, My Tongue" (#355–356) or "There in God's Garden" (#342).

Worshipers depart in silence. The service continues the next day.

Vigil of Easter

Portions of the Vigil of Easter are very flexible and may shaped in many ways, depending on the size of the assembly, the architecture, whether there are baptisms or not, and so forth. The musical possibilities are endless. This at first can seem daunting to the worship planner and music leader. When planning this liturgy, start with what's most important and keep everything simple musically. The more complex the rite, the simpler the music should be. More straightforward services can benefit from more complex music.

Gathering

The assembly gathers at the fire in silence. If silence is not natural to the assembly, it might be better to gather with a quiet refrain (such as "Wait for the Lord," #262) and draw them into a time of silence.

Behold, the life-giving cross,
on which was hung the Savior of the whole world. **Oh, come, let us wor - ship him.**

As the procession of light moves from the fire to the place of the word, an assisting minister chants the dialogue (Leaders Edition, p. 645). Once all are gathered around the candle, the assisting ministers continue singing the Easter Proclamation. The text of this ancient chant is on pages 646–647 of the leaders edition. Musical settings are available in seasonal music resources from as well as on SundaysAndSeasons.com. This is one of the most beautiful, yet challenging, chants of the repertoire. A nonprofessional singer committed to doing his or her best might need several months to learn this proclamation. Other musical settings of this text are available from other publishers and may be used instead of the chant version.

Word

A significant part of the Easter Vigil is hearing stories from salvation history. Each of the appointed Old Testament readings has a psalm or other portion of scripture intended to be sung as a response. Twelve stories are appointed. At least four are considered essential. More can be added. Four are prescribed for use every year: Creation (Gen. 1:1—2:4a), Deliverance at the Red Sea (Exod. 14:10-31; 15:20-21), Salvation Freely Offered to All (Isa. 55:1-11), and Deliverance from the Fiery Furnace (Dan. 3:1-29). Although including a sung response after each reading adds a rhythm to the pattern of read-sing-pray, it is not necessary that all reading include a sung response, especially when the vigil is first introduced. Simple tones may be used for the responses, and some simple creativity can add life to these readings and responses.

The gospel acclamation on this night is very important, with abundant alleluias breaking our Lenten fast and announcing the resurrection gospel. Whatever instruments, bells, or percussion are available may be added to the assembly song. Choosing an alleluia refrain for this moment in the liturgy is a challenge—not because we're lacking repertoire but because there are so many from which to choose! They are included in each setting of Holy Communion, in the Service of the Word, in service music (#168–175), and many other hymns and songs include alleluia refrains. If a longer canticle is desired, a festive setting of "Glory to God," "This is the feast," or a hymn with alleluias may be sung.

Moving to the baptismal font may be a few steps in some churches and a major procession of the entire assembly in others. However short the route, music can help highlight the prominence of the shift from hearing God's word to the celebration of the sacrament or the affirmation of baptism by the assembly. The Litany of the Saints (#237) is a powerful reminder that as we gather at the font of God's grace we are not alone. Through baptism we are joined with a cloud of witnesses who have come before us and for whose lives and examples we give thanks. Like the Easter Proclamation, this litany requires a well-prepared singer to lead it. Notice that each assembly response echoes the melody immediately before it that was sung by the leader. Knowing this makes it much easier to imagine an assembly singing this litany. A choir or a few prepared, confident singers may lead the responses, especially as they change from section to section.

The baptism or affirmation of baptism continues as described on pages 13–14. On this night of all nights, alleluias should be sung in abundance whenever possible.

If movement is required to get the assembly from font to table, alleluias may be repeated or a canticle of praise (if not used earlier) or hymn sung. Again, leading an assembly to the first service of holy communion for Easter should be a jubilant time.

The service continues with a simple but joyful service of holy communion.

Life Passages

In *Evangelical Lutheran Worship* each of the life passages services—Healing, Funeral, Marriage—have opportunities for music within the rite.

Healing

During the healing service, as individuals come forward to receive the laying on of hands with or without anointing, the assembly may offer support by singing acclamations psalms, hymns, and other music. If the entire assembly may be coming forward, brief acclamations or refrains may be best. Several possibilities are included in the pew edition (see #218–221).

Funeral

Many of the suggestions for a regular service of holy communion can also be appropriate at a funeral. Depending on the assembly's level of familiarity with the liturgical music used in a congregation, careful decisions should be made so that as many member and nonmember Christians as possible are able to participate easily. For example, if chanting a psalm is common practice on a Sunday, but few congregational members will be present, it may be wise to sing a hymn paraphrase of a psalm. Holy Communion Setting Ten provides paraphrase versions of all the sung portions of the liturgy set to familiar, simple hymn tunes. Funerals may be a time to use Setting Ten.

Following the commendation, a farewell may be sung. "Now, Lord, you let your servant go in peace" is appropriate. *Evangelical Lutheran Worship* has settings or paraphrases of this canticle following communion in Holy Communion Settings One and Two, in Night Prayer, and at #200–203, 313, and 440. Other acclamations, such as #222 or 223, or another hymn or song may be sung.

Marriage

Music may be played and sung before the service begins. Music—hymn, song, psalm, instru-mental music—may accompany the entrance.

Many of the suggestions for a regular service of holy communion can also be appropriate at a wedding. Depending on the assembly's level of familiarity with the liturgical music used in a congregation, careful decisions should be made to ease and encourage participation. For example, if chanting a psalm is common practice on a Sunday, but few congregational members will be present, it may be wise to sing a hymn paraphrase of a psalm. Holy Communion Setting Ten provides paraphrase versions of all the sung portions of the liturgy set to familiar, simple hymn tunes. Weddings may be a time to use Setting Ten.

Even with an assembly that includes many who are not regular worshipers at this particular church, planners are encouraged to include at least one time for the assembly to sing its support to the couple. See #585 and 586 for two specific marriage hymns. Both are set to ecumenically familiar tunes. Other hymns and songs are possible.

Following the spoken acclamation with the response "Thanks be to God," the assembly may offer acclamation with applause. A sung acclamation, hymn, or other music may follow. This could be an alleluia sung by the assembly, or a choral, solo, or instrumental piece.

A hymn may be sung or instrumental music played as the wedding group and the ministers depart.

Daily Prayer

Morning Prayer

This service may begin in silence or with music as the assembly gathers. Silence may be the most appropriate, however, when the opening dialogue is "O Lord, open my lips . . ."

This service is led by a leader, lay or ordained. Although the service could be spoken, its inherent beauty is enhanced with the simple tones for chanting.

Two options are provided for the opening. Both end with an alleluia that may be omitted during Lent.

Psalms follow. Psalm 95:1-7a, sometimes called the Venite ("Oh, come"), has long been the traditional opening psalm and is printed in the service. It is divided into three stanzas, separated by the refrain. Notes in the service folder could allow for the entire assembly to sing the psalm or for portions of it to alternate between men and women, left and right sides, or some other division. Other settings of this psalm are at #224 and 225 in the service music section. An invitatory ("Give glory to God . . .") may be sung before and after the psalm, each time with the assembly response "Oh, come, let us worship and praise." The leaders edition (p. 694) includes invitatories for various seasons.

The assembly response remains the same.

Psalm 63:1-8, 67, 100 or others appropriate for morning, the season, or the day, may be sung instead of or in addition to Psalm 95.

Each psalm should be followed by a time of silence. In the leaders edition each psalm is accompanied by a psalm prayer. Although not necessary, the prayer appropriate to the psalm just sung may be chanted or spoken by the leader to conclude the silence. See page 7 about chanting prayers.

Following the scripture reading(s) are numerous options for reflection, including some musical possibilities. See the rubric about reflection on page 302 in the pew edition. The list includes "interpretation through music." This could include a choral cantata, an instrumental interpretation of the texts just read, or a simple bell rung occasionally throughout a time of extended silence. The creative possibilities are endless.

The reflection concludes with a sung dialogue (two options are provided) that leads into the gospel canticle "Blessed are you, Lord." This canticle from Luke's gospel has long been associated with morning prayer. The setting in the service includes a refrain sung by the assembly and verses sung by assembly, soloist, or choir. If possible, the verses should be sung in harmony. Other assembly settings of this canticle are at #226, 250, and 552. On occasion, especially during Easter, "We praise you, O God" may be sung. See #227 and 228 for two settings.

The prayer conclude with the Lord's Prayer, which may be sung to the traditional chant setting on page 305. After the blessing, a hymn may be sung.

Especially on Sundays, morning prayer may conclude with thanksgiving for baptism. Two forms are provided (pp. 307–308). The first includes a prayer of thanksgiving; the second includes the resurrection gospel. Both are set to music in the leaders edition. Both forms include singing "We praise you, O God" (#227 and 228). If sung here, "We praise you, O God" should not be used earlier in the liturgy.

Evening Prayer

The leader for this service may be either lay or ordained. Although the service could be spoken, its inherent beauty is enhanced with the simple tones for chanting.

Evening Prayer has numerous options for the opening dialogue, including seasonal texts. Only the first option appears with music. All the texts may be sung using that same tone, simply moving pitches at the point (ǀ). Since the assembly sings the same melody as the leader for their text, different melodies may be used (see pages 6–7). On occasion, these simple dialogues may be dressed up with bells, simply adding a cluster (such as C, D, E, G, A in the key of C) at the beginning of each phrase. Other creative musical treatments can be added, depending on the nature of the gathering.

A hymn of light may follow. *Evangelical Lutheran Worship* includes numerous options, including #229–231, 560–563. On occasion, a choral setting of a "light" hymn may be used. The ancient text *Phos hilaron* ("Joyous light") is especially appropriate. The thanksgiving for light is sung by the leader.

Psalms follow. Psalm 141, long connected with Evening Prayer, is printed in place in the service. Sections of this psalm are designated All, Group One or All, Group Two or All. This allows for the entire assembly to sing the psalm or for portions of it to alternate between men and women, left and right sides, or some other division. Other settings of Psalm 141 are at #232 and 233 in the service music section.

Psalm 121 or others appropriate for evening, the season, or the day may be sung instead of or in addition to Psalm 141.

Each psalm should be followed by a time of silence. In the leaders edition each psalm is accompanied by a psalm prayer. Although not necessary, the prayer appropriate to the psalm just sung may be chanted or said by the leader to conclude the silence. See page 7 about chanting prayers.

Following the scripture reading(s) are numerous options for reflection, including some musical possibilities. See the rubric on the bottom of page 313 in the pew edition. The list includes "interpretation through music." This could include a choral cantata, an instrumental interpretation of the texts just read, or a simple bell rung occasionally throughout a time of extended silence. This is an opportunity for creative approaches, always keeping in mind the character of the service.

The reflection concludes with a sung dialogue (two options are provided) that leads into the gospel canticle "My soul proclaims the greatness of the Lord." This canticle from the Luke's gospel has long been associated with evening prayer. The setting that appears in the service includes a refrain sung by the assembly and verses sung by assembly, soloist, or choir. The accompaniment edition includes a descant for the refrain, which could be sung by the choir or played on an instrument. Other assembly settings of this canticle are at #234–236. Hymn paraphrase versions are at 251, 573, 723, and 882. On occasion, a choral setting of "My soul proclaims the greatness of the Lord" could be sung.

Although other forms of prayer may be used, the litany appears in place (pp. 316–317). If at all possible, the assembly should be encouraged to sing their response in harmony. Each time after singing "Lord, have mercy," the assembly turns the F major into a hum that continues as the leader sings the next petition. Notice how the music is notated. The final word, "Lord," of the leader's part, overlaps with the "Lord" that begins the assembly response. This continues throughout the litany until "Help, save, comfort, and defend us, gracious Lord," when a time of silence is kept before continuing. The response, "To you, O Lord," although the same music as the previous response, should *not* be sung overlapping, because the text is different. The musical notation should help.

Several prayers are provided to conclude the litany. The leader may sing one, two, or all of these prayers, before continuing with the Lord's Prayer. (See page 7 for chanting prayers.) The leaders edition includes two options for introducing the Lord's Prayer.

After the blessing, a hymn may be sung.

Night Prayer

This ancient service also known as Compline, which brings the day to a quiet close, has significant parts that are sung by the leader and the assembly. Although it can be spoken, its true beauty is in the simplicity and calming effect of the chant. Since it can be led by either a lay or ordained person, someone in the congregation should be able to lead the song. This is a time to sing unaccompanied, though light accompaniment will be helpful as the assembly is first learning the chants. Having strong voices scattered through the assembly will encourage less confident singers.

After gathering in silence, an opening is sung. Two options for dialogue are provided.

A hymn follows. "All Praise to Thee, My God, This Night" (#565) is especially appropriate, but other night hymns (#560–572) may be used.

One or more psalms may be sung. Simplicity is important in this service. Each psalm is followed by silence. If desired, a psalm prayer (following each psalm in the leaders edition) can be chanted to conclude the silence.

Another hymn or song follows. This may be another night hymn, or one suited to the season or occasion. Consider, though, the quiet character of the service.

After the reading(s) and an extended silence (a minute or more may not be too much for this service), the responsory (p. 323) may be sung. The response is not difficult and is the same each time.

The gospel canticle for Night Prayer is "Now, Lord, you let your servant go in peace." The antiphon (refrain), "Guide us waking, O Lord, . . ." is traditional for night prayer. Again, this setting is not as difficult as it may first look, and experience has shown that it is easily learned by assemblies. However, another setting of the canticle, even without the antiphon, may be sung instead. Additional settings are at #200–203, 313, 440, or after communion in Holy Communion Settings One and Two.

The prayers follow. Any or all of the six options may be sung, adapting them to the tone given for the first prayer. The prayers conclude with the Lord's Prayer. Two optional introductions to the Lord's Prayer are provided in the leaders edition.

The service ends quietly with the blessing. No additional hymn should be sung.

Psalms

See page 33 in the chapter on chant for information about singing the psalms.

3

SKILLS FOR LEADING ASSEMBLY SONG

The musical repertoire of Christian song is grand and richly varied. Each locale and group of people within that world has its own vocabulary and syntax. As musicians in the church we need to lead the assembly in singing these various styles as best we (as leaders) and our assembly (as the primary musical ensemble of the church) are able and to respect the integrity of those particular styles as we do so. Exploring diverse music together is a never-ending quest. Yet all these styles of song are united in important ways. They help people to sing the faith. They are true to themselves and to the word. And because their language is that of music, they possess basic elements that don't change from one style to another. It is those common aspects of leading assembly song that are addressed in this chapter.

Tactus

Life is rhythm: the beat of the heart; the rising and setting of the sun; the turn of the seasons; the church year. Life is rhythm, and all God's creatures have it. It is rhythm that gives music its life.

Of all technical rhythmic considerations, none is more important to leaders of the assembly's song than that of *tactus*, more commonly called the beat. Tactus (pronounced TAHK-toos) is the larger pulse that propels melody and harmony in time. Depending on the style of music, the tactus may be experienced very differently, from the subtle shifting pulse of chant to the steady beat of a drum or careful attention to articulation on an organ—but it always governs the movement of a piece.

The key element regarding tactus is dependability. A dependable and steady beat sets the structure that allows the assembly the freedom

to participate. A dependable tactus fosters trust between singers and leader. The leader gains the assembly's trust by setting and maintaining the tactus appropriate to the particular stylistic and cultural considerations of a piece. An assembly that trusts its music leader(s) will sing.

Tactus is the life of assembly singing. From the book of Genesis to the present, life is breath. The assembly is made up of people who need to breathe. When the leader (especially a keyboard player) hasn't taken this into consideration, the person in the assembly is often left feeling either rushed or dragged. Breathing is natural process, and singing is (or should be) a natural process as well. Songs should virtually float out of people with their breath. Those leading the song need to learn how to breathe with the people in much the same way a good choral conductor breathes on his or her preparatory beat. For those who lead from instruments, this does not necessarily mean singing along with the assembly, which may impede the leader's listening and responding role. Rather, it highlights the necessity that the musician understands each piece's phrasing and knows the places where a subtle "give" in the tactus might facilitate corporate breath.

The suggestions in this book, for each hymn or song in *Evangelical Lutheran Worship*, generally preference the bigger beat as the fundamental tactus. That means that in a $\frac{4}{4}$ hymn, the tactus would usually be the half note; in a song with a $\frac{3}{4}$ meter, the tactus would be the dotted half (or one beat to the bar); in $\frac{6}{8}$, the tactus would be the dotted quarter (two beats to the bar); for chant and some rhythmic chorales, the tactus may shift between groupings of 2 and 3; in much African American music the tactus may be what otherwise would be the upbeats (beats 2 & 4 in a $\frac{4}{4}$ meter or beats 2 & 3 with a $\frac{3}{4}$ meter), and so forth. The song may have notes on all beats (and often more in between the beats), but the idea encouraged here is that the internal driving pulse (tactus) is the larger beat. This keeps many hymns from sounding choppy or plodding. Without a clear tactus, music may seem lifeless and dull. This doesn't mean that the other beats are unimportant. The smaller beat (perhaps the quarter or even the eighth) adds an internal drive providing energy between the bigger beats. The larger phrase provides an organizing arch under which these other layers of rhythm function.

Of course, there are exceptions. If a room has a very live acoustic or the assembly is very large, or lethargic, a quarter-note tactus (in $\frac{4}{4}$) or a half-quarter combination (in $\frac{3}{4}$) may be necessary to keep the rhythm alive. Certain songs (such as some early American revival tunes) may require a quarter-note tactus to provide the energetic drive appropriate to that style. Chant may have a barely perceptible tactus, but it still must be present and intentional, especially to the leader of the song.

There may be times when the tactus should be the slower pulse (such as a half note) but, because of a very slow tempo, it would be difficult to maintain. With hymns or song like this, it may be wise to treat the quarter note as the tactus, but always mindful of the larger pulse to keep the tune moving forward.

A leader, once having determined the tactus to be used in leading a particular song, must employ various articulation techniques (see below) to provide the accents that bring the tactus to life for the singing assembly. Once determined and carefully rehearsed, an excellent leader of singing will be prepared to adjust to the temperament of the assembly on that day.

Once the pulse is established, it is not inviolable. The most obvious "give" in the tactus is the relaxation that occurs naturally at the end of the final stanza. A judicious rallentando is nearly always in order at this point. Sometimes it should be grand, other times modest. This slowing down gives the hymn a sense of finality and completion. Most of us do this instinctively. Be aware that there are some musical styles that do not need a rallentando. The rhythm itself may draw the melody to a natural conclusion. Make no assumptions. Keep the assembly in mind, plan what you're going to do, and practice it.

A few hymns call for tempo fluctuations within a stanza, specifically where rhythmic intricacy and/or angular melodic lines require a bit more time and effort for the assembly to execute. This will be addressed below.

Tempo

Tempo is another factor to consider in leading the assembly's song. It is the responsibility of the leader not only to set a steady and dependable beat, but also to determine at what speed the beat will move. Choosing the tempo can be a challenge, because there is never one correct tempo for all situations. Generally, the terms fast and slow are unhelpful and often misleading. Somewhat more descriptive and accurate terms include "less fast," "not too slow," or "moderate." Remembering that the goal is the full and authentic participation of everyone present, establishing and maintaining a reasonable and intelligent tempo is a top priority for all leaders of assembly singing.

Factors calling for a "less slow" hymn tempo—that is, on the spectrum of possible tempos, moving away from the slow end—include: dry acoustics, small- or medium-size rooms, smaller organs, small gatherings in small or large rooms, and a lethargic assembly. In a vast oversimplification, we can say that hymns from Germanic traditions are generally sung "less slow." Naturally, the opposite conditions would suggest tempos that are "not fast." The longer a room's reverberation, the more time it takes for musical phrases to unfold, particularly when a large crowd is involved. Hymns simply cannot be taken quickly in a room with five-second reverberation. In another oversimplification it is possible to say that hymns from the English tradition are generally sung "less fast."

Factors that need to be considered are:
- the character of the music and text;
- the size of the assembly;
- the time of day;
- the acoustics; and
- the instruments being used to lead.

The tempo of a joyous hymn of praise sung by a group of ten worshipers in a chapel with little reverberation and no instrumental accompaniment may be very different from the same hymn sung by hundreds in a large, reverberant cathedral, supported by organ and brass. It's most likely that the group in the chapel will be able to progress at a much brisker tempo than the assembly in the cathedral. The reverberant acoustics of a large space would advise against swiftly moving group song. In this book, the tempo suggestions provided with each hymn and song in *Evangelical Lutheran Worship* represent this range of possibilities.

The leader must be aware of the general musical ability of those making up the gathering:

- Are these people gathered here used to singing at all? (Weddings, for instance, often present a very different challenge from Sunday morning.)
- What is the level of musical literacy?
- Is the hymn familiar or new?
- How can I, as one called here to facilitate them in this endeavor, help them find their voice?

Musical literacy does not necessarily equal ability to sing just anything at any given tempo. A group that has done much singing together, although individually not strong music readers, may rise to surprising challenges. Get to know the people in your assemblies. Discern what to expect and make appropriate decisions.

The tempo is set during the introduction. Whatever the content and form of the introduction, the tactus must be clear and unwavering by the end of the introduction so that the assembly begins the hymn at the speed the leader has determined. The player who introduces a hymn at lightning speed, only to play stanza one at a decidedly slower pace, has defeated both hymn and assembly. The organist who spins out a beautiful, subdued, improvisatory reverie as an introduction, only to throw on a big sound and play the hymn faster at the outset of the first stanza also has missed the mark. (There are, of course, exceptions, such as a Bach chorale prelude that must be taken at a tempo different from the sung hymn. In such cases, the leader can either play an additional, brief tempo-setting introduction, or at least be very clear about the tempo in the first few notes of the first stanza.)

Familiarity with liturgical texts and tunes sometimes gives way to "liturgical time" in which the leader and assembly make mad dashes through the responses and canticles, all sung at the same pace. The liturgy is not something to rush through simply for the sake of accomplishing it. As in hymnody, the text is the governing factor. Does the singing of the "Holy, holy, holy" conjure up Isaiah's great vision of God's majesty (Isaiah 6)? Is the plea for mercy in the Kyrie sung at the same speed as the canticle of praise, "Glory to God"? They differ greatly in both function and content. Does the opening dialogue of the Great Thanksgiving ("The Lord be with you. / And also with you.") actually embrace the characteristics and rhythm of a spoken dialogue? Is the natural rhythm (spoken or sung) of the presiding minister's part consistent with the assembly response?

As stated earlier, more often than not the tactus (fundamental pulse) of a hymn is the half note (in a $\frac{4}{4}$) or the dotted half note (in $\frac{3}{4}$). (See page 21 for more discussion about tactus.) With a larger tactus, hymns often become livelier, more forward-moving, and even easier to sing, without necessarily going *faster* to achieve a new level of energy.

Certain hymn tunes, such as TRURO (#389), present a special challenge in finding the right speed. A sprightly tempo that works for the first phrase, in which the half-note pulse is strong, clear, and predominant, seems hurried when faced with the quarter notes in the second phrase. By the last phrase, with its large leaps and quarter-note energy, the original tempo is positively frantic. How can these conflicting concerns be reconciled? Consider the hymn as a whole, taking into account the contrasting requirements of the first and last phrases, then strike a compromise. The right tempo will accommodate both.

The tune CWM RHONDDA (#618 or 705) is a good test case for hymn tempos.

CASE A

CWM RHONDDA is scheduled for a summer Sunday service with a small congregation (20–30) in a modestly-sized church with dry acoustics, a low ceiling, and a four-rank unified organ. In this instance, a speed of ♩ = 60 would not be unreasonably fast. A radically slower tempo would be a mistake. Why? The few singers present would be overtaxed physically and musically and would not be able to sustain their energy beyond the first two stanzas or so. The third and fourth stanzas then become a chore and endurance test rather than a joyful, life-giving event. The last thing a hymn leader wants is a congregation thinking "Can we just get this hymn over with, please?"

CASE B

The same hymn is slated for the dedication service of a new church—a cavernous building with ample reverberation and a large, commanding organ. A crowd of a thousand is expected for the service on this grand occasion. Practicality necessitates a more relaxed pace of perhaps ♩ = 42. (Note that in this particular case, with such a large assembly and lively acoustics, it may be necessary to work with a quarter-note tactus.) This broader pulse allows phrases to unfold naturally and musically with crescendo and diminuendo emerging effortlessly as the congregation unites in song. It also leaves plenty of room for everyone to breathe between phrases. A significantly faster tempo would soon deteriorate into a jumble or, worse, a contest between organist and assembly to see whose notion of speed will prevail.

Considering all the variables, there is no ideal tempo for any hymn or song. Whatever the selected tempo, stick with it. The assembly needs to be able to rely on a steady tactus. When you come to the end of a stanza (except for the final one), don't slow down. If necessary, add a pulse to the final chord of the stanza, add some breathing room (see "The Space between Stanzas" on page 42), but maintain the pulse.

Finally, a rallentando lends a sense of dignity and finality at the very end of some hymns (but not at the end of every stanza). The same principles that determine the hymn's tempo also govern the amount of slowing down that is appropriate in the final cadence. As in previous stanzas, the final chord should be of determinate length. It is best to hold this chord the same number of beats as in earlier stanzas. Because the rallentando has just altered the tempo, however, the final chord will last somewhat longer in real time. In any event, a chord of indefinite length is not helpful anywhere in the hymn, including the last chord. If held too long the assembly inevitably runs out of breath long before the organist lets go. With consistency of leadership, an assembly can be conditioned to sing together with the leader; they just need to know what to expect.

Note: Any metronome indications suggested for hymns, including the suggestions in this book, are helpful—provided they are always viewed as negotiable. Each entry in this book gives a possible range of metronome markings. It is important to pay attention to the suggested tactus, as well, because the tempo marking listed corresponds to that pulse.

Articulation and Accent

If tactus and tempo together provide the heartbeat of music, it is articulation that brings the spark and rhythm of life to the rest of the body. Articulation is the key to movement, to helping a piece, individual or corporate, instrumental or vocal, take on life and color. Basically, articulation is the connective tissue between notes in a melody or chords in a harmonic progression. It is the contextual relationship of one note to another. Movement from one note to another may be accomplished in a smooth, even fashion without any break between the notes *(legato)*. It may be *marcato*, accented and stressed. It may be *staccato,* detached, with each note separated from the next by quick releases. Some notes may be more accented than others. Some may achieve greater stress (or weight) by being "leaned into." In general the overall articulation of a specific phrase may appear fairly uniform. The actual movement from note to note, however, may be comprised of a rich mixture of subtle nuances (some notes more detached, louder, softer, etc.) Again, but in another way, the text, rich in word accents, vowel colors, and natural flexes, serves as the best guide.

For those who lead from instruments (keyboard or ensembles), the task is somewhat different. They face a challenge: how can this type of leader, without the luxury of words or explanation, but simply by the way in which they play, communicate to the assembly the sense of the piece as a whole, particularly its spirit and flow? How can they actually take what the assembly is producing (singing) and simultaneously, by means of articulation, heighten their awareness of the magic that is happening in the production, the mystical union of text and tune, of composer and performer, of creator and creature, of art?

Articulation at the keyboard is a helpful tool to provide a clear tactus. The way in which a keyboard player articulates a phrase can do much to assist the assembly in the way they are singing. It is by means of articulation that the person at the keyboard can provide real leadership in subtle ways. Sometimes it becomes necessary for the leader to highlight a specific element of area of the music, such as tempo, ritards, or dynamic climaxes. On instruments that are dynamically touch-sensitive (piano and some synthesizers) this can be accomplished by means of employing accents, of playing some notes harder (hence louder) than others, or by placing more space between the notes. On keyboard instruments that are not dynamically touch-sensitive (organ, harpsichord, and other synthesizers), expression comes through an entirely different approach. Since on these instruments the way in which a note is struck, firmly or lightly, has no effect on the way it will sound, the secret of articulation lies in how the notes are *released*. This has bearing on the way the *following note* will sound. Playing a melody at the organ and making it come to life involves varying degrees of separation, with great attention to the notes' endings. Just how much space, if any, is placed between the notes gives a phrase character as well as clarity.

Keyboard players can learn much about articulation from observing bowing techniques on stringed instruments and tonguing techniques on woodwind instruments. An oboist or flutist achieves flavorful phrasing by tonguing (creating a "stop" by executing the syllable *doo*) on important notes while slurring (no tonguing) others that are less important. Bowing—the necessity of reversing bow directions—affects phrasing on stringed instruments. The way in which the hair of the bow grips the string, the sound it makes when changing directions, and the different quality between up and down bow aurally resemble the process of breathing. These techniques of tonguing or bowing essentially create a tactus. Keyboard players need to figure this out as well. If a hymn is played with the same degree of separation between each note the result can be monotonous. Again, music needs to breathe. Players, especially players who do not make use of their own breath (keyboard and string players), need to be aware of this. Articulation is breath.

"I don't know what you did today to help us sing like that, but thanks!" is the highest compliment a leader of assembly song can receive. The way in which we support and lead assembly singing through sensitive articulation can be our greatest gift to that community. Very often, when a well-meaning member of a worshiping community complains that a hymn or song was "too slow" or "boring," the culprit may be the lack of clear articulation and tactus, not necessarily a slow tempo. Subtle nuances in articulation are valuable tools by which we can help propel the assembly to new levels of musicality, textual awareness, and community. Then we can get out of the way and let them sing!

Instrumentation

Not all hymns or songs require instrumental support. Some are best sung with the one instrument we all possess: our voice. In this book, "instrumentation" includes the voice as an important possibility.

The type of instrumentation the leader employs to support assembly singing affects the way the people sing and influences their participation. The foremost question always should be, "Will this instrumentation serve to help support the assembly in their corporate song?" Of course, the words *help* and *support* are relative. The leader should always begin with the idea of unaccompanied singing as the model for all assembly song. When an assembly is asked to sing without the aid of instrumental forces, the individuals making up the assembly listen to themselves and to others. It is here that an assembly can best become aware of and find its true voice. Something happens when a group of people joins their voices in song, especially in unison song. Voices, each with its own character and timbre, come together. Barriers drop. The individual gives way to the corporate. The singing takes on a life of its own. The group gels. This is the goal of the leader of the people's song.

The leader's role is never to overpower or lead by means of force, dynamically or otherwise. The operative terms here, again, are *support* and *guidance*. In choosing the type of instrumentation best suited to a certain group singing a specific piece, several factors need to be taken into account:

- the size of the group, the spatial setting, and the acoustical environment
- an inventory of the instruments that are or could be used
- some exegesis of the piece, determining its "life setting," including original instrumentation

- deciding what kind instrumental or vocal leadership would best bring out the character of the tune, of the text
- the possibility and advisability of recasting the instrumentation for a fresh take on the hymn. A sixteenth-century chorale sung in unison with a jazz style accompaniment of a flute and string bass might simultaneously jar, enlighten, and uplift.

Using What You Have

Work with what you have. Just as in Jesus' parable of the talents, we have been given certain gifts. What we do with them is up to us. We may or may not have wonderful musical resources at our disposal. For each grand and glorious organ there are a dozen that are less than adequate. For each trained professional choir there are thousands of modest ones with fewer than a half-dozen voices. Yet within every limitation lurks opportunity. The challenge is to get the most out of what we have. Stretch yourself. Demand high standards from your choir. Challenge your congregation. Take them all as far as you think they can go without breaking them, remembering always to balance the new with the familiar, the difficult with the easy.

Some of the most wonderful hymn singing comes from small congregations in out-of-the-way places with only humble organs to lead them. Even with a dismal instrument there are ways to bring out a hymn's full potential. Perhaps there are at least a few stops that blend well together. If the pedal sounds are pale, consider more frequent "manuals only" hymn stanzas. Consider working with a good high school instrumentalist and write a simple obbligato for the last stanza. Encourage your choir to take its rightful leadership role in the hymn singing. Train your assembly to sing unaccompanied on a stanza or part of a stanza now and then. It can be thrilling when an assembly can hold its own without the aid of accompaniment. They will love it, and their singing will improve dramatically over time.

Bringing Out the Melody

Especially when teaching a new song, it is important for the melody to be clearly heard. On a piano, it is possible simply to play that line more loudly, or up an octave. Adding an instrument, when available, is also helpful. Prepared voices (solo or choir) are also valuable.

Organists have a special challenge. They need to develop the ability to solo out the tune. Aside from supporting the assembly with a clear melody, this practice can lend variety to your hymn treatments. It is also an opportunity to exploit the solo colors of the instrument. Bolder reeds, whether penetrating or noble, are highly suitable for this, as are mixture sounds. A cornet (typically 8', 4', 2⅔', 2', 1⅗') or diapason color works well for quieter hymns.

The technique of soloing out may seem clumsy at first but quickly improves with practice. Begin by learning to read and play the alto and tenor voices together in the left hand on more subdued stops, omitting the right hand and pedal for purposes of practice. Though it takes getting used to, your skill will improve so that you can do this at sight. The bass line remains in the pedal on a sound that is balanced with the left hand. The next step is to combine the left hand and pedal (alto, tenor, and bass voices). Then practice soprano and bass voices together (right hand on solo stop[s], and pedal). Finally, combine right hand, left hand, and pedal. The tune will soar out over the supporting voices. A solo treatment of the tune need not last for an entire stanza. It can come and go, phrase by phrase, as the text dictates. Always read the text first and use your imagination.

Vocal Leadership

Those who lead the assembly vocally (such as a cantor, song leader, or choir) most likely do so by example. Through vocal leadership an assembly can learn what it means to sing sensitively with an eye to the text. This type of leadership is usually simultaneous, occurring while the people are actually singing. As cited in the discussion concerning the setting of tempo, the first measures are vitally important. The solo leader or choir sets the stage, giving the assembly cues as to the spirit, tempo, dynamics, and flow of the piece.

Vocal leadership has nothing to do with singing out "over" the assembly or overpowering them. Vocal leadership should be conceived as coming from *within* the group. It's like the

elementary school teacher who speaks in a whisper in the midst of a noisy classroom so the children have to quiet down in order to hear. It's learning to be community. It involves learning to listen, both on the part of the leader and on the part of those in the congregation.

Your Best Ally: the Choir

Church choirs exist, fundamentally, to lead God's people in worship. Every church choir director should be clear on this and take every opportunity to remind their choirs that this is their primary calling and most important business. No matter how polished an anthem may be, if the hymns and liturgical music in a service do not have the choir's full attention and commitment, the music hasn't fulfilled its mission.

Before any service the music leader should decide how each hymn is to be rendered. Choices about which stanzas will be sung in unison, harmony, with descants and so forth, should be made by the director and communicated to the instrumentalists and choir. Then, a portion of every Sunday morning choir warm-up should include adequate rehearsal of the hymns, so that the choir can lead the assembly competently. Hymn rehearsals should cover phrasing, punctuation, treatment of tactus between stanzas, and anything else that will contribute to the assembly's ability to sing a hymn well. Remind the choir of any unaccompanied stanzas or phrases and that its leadership role then becomes doubly important. Too many choir directors neglect or ignore the hymns, assuming that they will take care of themselves or that they are not worth the same care and effort as the choral pieces. They may even think that the thoughtful rehearsal of hymns with the choir would be lost in the midst of assembly singing. This is a serious mistake. Corporate worship demands and deserves only our best efforts. Nothing in a service should ever be considered thrown away or unimportant, particularly the hymns. The choir is in a unique position to support the instrumentalists in bringing the hymns to life.

Insisting on a conscientious approach to the hymns also brings fringe benefits. The musical concepts that every director wants to impart to the choir—phrasing, intonation, word painting, rhythmic vitality, dynamic control, blend, and subtlety—are available in the pages of a hymnal. Hymns provide wonderful teaching tools for building the skills of choir members. This is particularly true with children or singers of limited experience.

The choir that is well rehearsed on the hymns enables a congregation to soar to new levels in their singing. Everyone is enriched, and God is praised.

Singing in Unison or Harmony?

The pew edition of *Evangelical Lutheran Worship* was designed primarily for the members of a communal worshiping assembly. Therefore, if a hymn or song is intended to be sung in unison, only the melody line appears. Keyboard, guitar, and other instrumental accompaniments are in other editions for leaders. When it is a melody that may (or sometimes should) be sung in harmony, it is provided with a singable harmony. For worshipers with limited music-reading ability, this makes it much simpler to manage the music on the page and participate more fully. For those worshipers who are able and prefer to sing in harmony, it is clear which arrangements work for singing in harmony. In a strophic (multi-stanza) piece that is sufficiently familiar, alternative harmonies can refresh, surprise, and enlighten successive stanzas, if agreement is made about which stanzas can be sung in harmony and which need to be in unison.

Remember, the primary concern when leading assembly singing is to encourage all worshipers to participate. If singing in harmony causes confusion or frustration for those around you, it is always better to opt for singing in unison. As Christians worshiping in community, we should be willing to yield our individual desires for the sake of the body.

There is, of course, a great deal of subjectivity in these decisions. Many tunes that appear in harmony work perfectly well in unison, with or without a keyboard supporting the unison singing with the harmony. Many tunes that appear in unison only may be harmonized effectively. The pew edition provides a common starting point. Local composers and future published resources may provide additional variety. Although the editors of *Evangelical*

Lutheran Worship made initial decisions on this matter, there are numerous items for local consideration:

- What is the character of the tune? Long, floating lines? Rhythmically energetic phrases?
- Does harmony potentially slow down or add weight to a lighter melody?
- Is it better sung in unison or is sung harmony a necessary element? Does it come from a genre that prefers one or the other?
- Might the group prefer to sing in harmony? Are they able to do it well?
- Might singing in harmony intimidate some and hinder the song?
- What kind of accompaniments might be possible if the group sings in harmony?
- Might an accompaniment be different if they are singing in unison?
- Could I do something in my accompaniment that might help the group's endeavor to sing in harmony?
- Might the assembly even be able to "go it alone," sing without any instrumental leadership?

Acoustic or Amplification

Assembly song is, by nature, participatory—a group of individuals singing together. Since the dawn of civilization communities, especially those drawn together for the purpose of ritual, have joined their voices in some type of chant or song. Sometimes chanting served communication in settings too expansive for spoken word. Chanting—speaking on pitch—is more easily projected and heard than the spoken word. Children know this instinctively when they make themselves heard by voicing a descending minor third (often set early on to "Mommy"). Unison chant helped propel the sound of both voice and text in the cavernous, reverberant architecture of great medieval cathedrals and churches.

The advent of electronic amplification and and other technology revolutionized communication. With relatively little effort an amplified singer or speaker could be heard even in extremely large spaces. Electronics have played a major part in the evolution of music in general. The wind chests of pipe organs are filled and sustained by means of motors. The tones of some instruments are produced totally by electronic means. Electronic organs, electric guitars, and synthesizers all offer new sounds with which we can experiment. By means of sequencers and MIDI, the church musician's palette of colors has broadened enormously. New sounds blend with old, old songs take on new sonorities. Even a congregation that doesn't own congas or a marimba or have in its membership anyone available to play the guitar or string bass can experience these sounds by means of electronics. A melody from Japan might be accompanied by organ and synthesized koto; a South American refrain could be orchestrated for piano, guitars, trumpet, and synthesized marimba; computer-sequenced loops of multi-layered African drum patterns might underlie a Tanzanian hymn. We are bound only by the limits of our own creativity.

Great care must be taken, however, lest electronic synthesis or amplification in any form interfere with or, worse, supplant the voice of the people. Synthesizers can be useful tools, or they can become gadgets that divert the leaders and people from their fundamental song. Sequenced, electronically copied music, whether percussion or organ, is lifelike but not alive. Such technology has its place in church but calls for careful discernment from those who facilitate the people's song.

Similarly, in both corporate speech and musical vocal leadership, amplification has the power to make the role of the people superfluous. In situations in which an assembly reading or prayer is "led" using a microphone, members of the assembly often do not participate with the enthusiasm they may have had they been left to their own capabilities. Rather than participating, they find themselves listening: the leader's voice has become primary, usurping the role of the people. This does nothing to nurture the community to respond on its own, with its own voice.

Knowing What You Lead

Musicians in the church who are entrusted with the people's song are interpreters of song, and interpretation calls for research. This can be helpful especially in determining things like tempo. We can begin by asking questions concerning a tune's origin and character:

- Who is the composer?
- When was it written?
- Was it written specifically for this text?
- How does this tune relate to other music written by this composer?
- Is there anywhere I can go to hear other music by this composer? (See, for example, the indexes in *Evangelical Lutheran Worship*, its Hymnal Companion, and resources available through the Hymn Society of the United States and Canada.)
- What type of musical instruments or ensemble may have been used to lead the tune at the time of its first appearance?
- How does the melody move—mostly in a stepwise fashion (which tends, for the most part, to be easier to sing) or by leaps?
- Is it memorable? (That is, will it be easy for the people to remember its contours after the introduction and maybe one stanza?)
- Was it conceived as a vocal piece (for one singer), or a choral piece (a part song for many singers)?
- Was it most likely sung in harmony or unison? What works best for this assembly at this time?
- Does the melody relate to any other type of music popular at the time (e.g., dance tunes, ballads)?
- Are there any repeated motives that deserve attention?

Delving into such research might even change your opinion about how a piece might be led, regarding tempo or otherwise. The position of the piece within the context of the service also may play a role in determining the tempo at which it will be sung. Does it serve as a reflection on something that just happened liturgically? What was the spirit of that action? Worship is alive and fluid, never static. In the course of a service the assembly experiences and participates in many different functions, each with its own mood or flavor. These might include praise, prayer, reflection, or proclamation. Tempos should reflect these accordingly. Because it is the function of the introduction to set the spirit, the place of a piece in the service will undoubtedly have some influence on the way it is introduced.

Many techniques that lie at the heart of effective hymn playing defy written description. They can only be learned by doing them with a living and breathing assembly. We also learn from hearing others who lead assembly singing. It is easy for church musicians to become isolated and absorbed in our corner of the church. We should make opportunities to break out of routines and participate in the worship of neighboring churches or go to church music conferences where we are sure to hear a variety of hymn playing. It is extremely helpful to our musical growth to attend a live concert of chamber or symphonic music, or a solo recital. Our musical horizons can never be too broad. Such enrichment is sure to enhance our hymn playing. God's people gathered at worship depend on us. They deserve our finest efforts.

Tactus, tempo, articulation and accent, vocal and instrumental leadership, unison and harmony singing, the role of electronic amplification—these are the sorts of issues that need to be addressed for any type of church song. Clearly, some questions will be more urgent for some styles than for others. But even when the answer seems obvious it can be beneficial to ask the question. For example, "At what tempo should I play this hymn?" A fresh look at it, a slower or faster tempo, might be just the thing to give it new life. This sort of continual reexamination takes energy, but in approaching church song of all forms, we would do well to heed the advice of the apostle Paul, "Do not lag in zeal, be ardent in spirit, serve the Lord" (Rom. 12:11).

CHAPTER FOUR

CHANT

Chant takes us back to a fundamental aspect of worship: people reaching out to God and to one another with the instrument God gave us, our singing voices. The mysterious and profound beauty of its pure melody, at once distant and detached but also intense and personal, has for centuries drawn people closer to their divine creator. The melody style of chant can range from a simple recitation of a prayer on a single note to a long melodic line sung on a single syllable.

Rhythm

The beautiful and gentle wave of movement in chant is not entirely arbitrary. Chant does have rhythm—that is, "ordered movement." On the basis of this concept, most chants or chant-like music can be grouped into two- or three-note units. Keep in mind that the first note of a unit is not necessarily accented or stressed. (Let's not call it beat one, if only for that reason.) It is simply a touchpoint, a place in time to keep singers together while singing the text naturally.

When leading DIVINUM MYSTERIUM (#295), for example, one would count the first two phrases as follows:

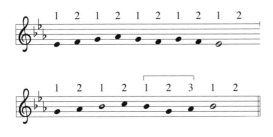

VENI CREATOR SPIRITUS (#577) might be felt like this (notice that it begins with an "upbeat"):

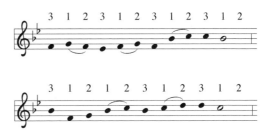

When singing from chant notation (no stems), it is helpful to remember not to over-value the longer notes. Black notes generally receive one count and the open notes two, but flexibility is needed to chant the text naturally.

Many settings of the liturgy, even those composed in recent years, are also based on patterns of twos and threes. For instance, look at the beginning of Richard Hillert's setting of "Glory to God" (Holy Communion Setting Three, p. 139). Notice how in the intonation triple and duple patterns are established to create a steady pulse that becomes the quarter note when the assembly begins to sing.

Some pieces shift between a metered tactus and chant. In the service of Evening Prayer, consider the gospel canticle "My soul proclaims the greatness of the Lord" (pp. 314–315). The refrain is in a simple meter (feeling the half-note tactus). The verses are written as chant to be sung freely as the text dictates. Notice that the final measure of the verses (and compare in the accompaniment edition) has stems again, indicating the return of refrain's rhythm.

Sections that are sung on a reciting tone (notated ▶) should have a speech-like rhythm, roughly equal to a black-note pattern, but with a natural variability.

Longer litanies, such as #237 and 238, are a special rhythmic case, relating to the dialogue between leader and assembly. The natural inclination of most people is to reach the white note at the end of a phrase, hold it for two pulses, take a quick break, then launch into the next phrase. That approach works fine, but other assemblies have found that a manner in which the next phrase begins immediately after the last syllable preceding it both moves the litany along and creates a sense of unending prayer.

Accompaniment

Gregorian chant (or plainsong) was originally sung by unaccompanied voices. That is still the best way to capture its beauty. An instrumental introduction may be helpful, even before unaccompanied singing, but a good cantor can also sing the first phrase on a neutral syllable before directing the assembly into the singing. Prepared choirs can be a valuable help. What is most important is that chant is led in a way that embodies one key element—prayerfulness.

However, especially when using chant as assembly song, circumstances will often call for supporting accompaniment, most often from organ or other keyboard. This is particularly true of modern compositions built on chant style, such as David Hurd's "Glory to God" from *New Plainsong Mass* (#162) or hymn tunes like Richard Dirksen's INNISFREE FARM (#560).

Generally speaking, accompaniment for chant is best kept as unobtrusive as possible. With assembly chant you may at first need to solo out the melody (see pages 26–27). As soon

as feasible, though, move into the background, accompanying almost imperceptibly.

Just as the performance of a $\frac{4}{4}$ hymn is often improved by thinking in two pulses to the measure rather than four, the movement of chant benefits by thinking in groups of notes rather than in single notes. In most cases the placement of chords should coincide with your groupings or vice versa. If your rhythmic instinct differs from a published accompaniment, it is possible to shift certain chords to a rhythmic position that is one pulse earlier or later than notated. However, changing the chord too often can establish a restless harmonic rhythm. Consider at times changing the underlying chord only once or twice in a phrase.

When leading chant from a keyboard:

- Introduce the chant as you expect it to be sung.
- Vary the texture by adding or reducing the number of voices in the accompaniment, usually keeping accompaniment to a minimum. Pay attention to the touch or articulation, being sensitive both to the acoustic and to the text and structure of the piece. If they are singing well together, less articulation may be best. If they need to sense the natural rhythm to sing better, articulation that is a bit more distinct may be needed.
- Finally, remember that in chant accompaniment less is more. It is better to err on the side of simplicity. Chant singing can be memorable without turning it into a grand production. Whenever possible, encourage the assembly to chant without instrumental support.

Psalm Singing in *Evangelical Lutheran Worship*

From their origin, the psalms were intended to be sung. Certainly the meaning of the text can be communicated when spoken, but the quality of this ancient poetry is inherently musical. *Lutheran Book of Worship* (*LBW*) first provided us with a system simple enough for singing by a cantor, choir, or assembly. *Evangelical Lutheran Worship* continues this, but with a few differences.

The system for singing remains the same as *LBW*: a singer stays on one pitch, singing the text naturally until the "point" (in *Evangelical Lutheran Worship* this is a superscript vertical bar— $^|$) then the singer moves on to the next pitches. The singer should always reach an accented syllable on the last note. The goal is for a clear and natural proclamation of the text.

To get the accents right, the singer must not automatically slow down at the point. The syllable at which you change pitches is not necessarily an accented syllable. For good proclamation, always sing through the change of pitches to the end of the phrase. Singers may feel the natural accents in different places. However they are placed, it is important that the text is proclaimed naturally.

In *Evangelical Lutheran Worship*, all 150 psalms are included. They are the first 150 numbers in the Assembly Song section of the book. This is a reminder that the version of the psalms included in *Evangelical Lutheran Worship* is intended for singing.

The introductory material to singing the psalms is on pages 335–336. That information will help explain this further. On pages 337–338 are eleven single tones and five double tones. While any psalm can be sung to any tone, care should be taken to match the text with a tone of appropriate mood.

These tones may also be helpful when singing the verses of a gospel acclamation. They are especially useful during Lent and the services of the Three Days.

The Music of Taizé

Chants such as those from the Ecumenical Community of Taizé in France (see p. 1193 of the source index of *Evangelical Lutheran Worship* to identify these) have become well-known to many worshiping assemblies. Because of their freely improvisatory and repetitive character, they often accompany other actions, such as holy communion, footwashing, anointing, and so forth. However, these simple refrains are at their best when time is not an issue and the assembly has no distractions. The multiple repetitions result in the analytical brain becoming bored and ceasing to dominate. This allows the intuitive brain to become active. If this is true, we may then notice that the singer's spirit is open to transcendence, to prayerful reception. In the worship of Taizé, such chanting is seen not as an aid to prayer but as prayer itself.

Taizé chants and others composed in a similar style come in several forms. Those included in *Evangelical Lutheran Worship* include the following:

- Ostinatos are musical units sung in continuous repetition by all the people. Often a cantor sings other texts over the top of a repeated refrain (see #262, 348, 388, 406, 472, 528, 616, 642, 751).
- Litanies have a pause between repetitions while a cantor sings a verse (see #175, 472).
- Canons can be sung in unison throughout, but are designed so they can effectively be sung in two- or more part canon (see #236).

When a Taizé chant has verses for a cantor, they are optional. For *Evangelical Lutheran Worship*, they may be found in both the standard and simplified keyboard accompaniment volumes.

Leading such chants requires the art of getting out of the way. If an assembly can sing in harmony with no support from instruments doubling their part, let them do it. If support is needed, a keyboard (or four wind or string instruments) could provide the harmonic support. Again, less is best, and if they get singing well, drop the instruments out. Obbligatos may be added by melody instruments but should never overshadow the vocalists. An instrumentalist skilled at improvisation can simply create these other lines as they go. Others may refer to the instrumental parts from GIA Publications, Inc., the U.S. publisher of music from Taizé (see bibliography, page 347).

Communities unfamiliar with this kind of prayerful chant may at first be hesitant to keep it going. Prepare a few leaders to keep singing, and it will come with time. If the chant is being sung when nothing else is going on, there is usually an unspoken communal decision about when to bring it to a close. If the chant is accompanying an action and needs to end, a leader with a strong voice can crescendo her own voice and slow the assembly down with a large ritardando and fermata.

There are, of course, different systems of chant than those addressed here. For example, the setting of "We praise you, O God" (#228) is Anglican chant. It's essentially the same as discussed here, but with harmony. Whatever the system of chant, the text should dictate the movement. Do not automatically slow down upon reaching pitches that change or put accents on moving notes unless they are the natural accents in the text.

To many people, chant can be daunting—enjoyable to listen to, perhaps, but challenging for assembly song. An exception, of course, is "O Come, O Come, Emmanuel" (#257), plus a few others that have entered the mainstream repertoire (and are usually later examples with more of a metered feel). There are times, though, when chant can add just the right tone of reflection, a reference to things timeless. It is also particularly well suited to carrying the text without overshadowing it. The music leader who includes it in an assembly's repertoire may be surprised at how positively they respond.

CHAPTER FIVE

5

NORTHERN EUROPEAN HYMNODY

Many Christian hymns that are well known to North Americans come from the northern European tradition. Others may have originated in other parts of the globe, but their musical language—and thus how leaders interpret them—is grounded in northern Europe. The vast genre discussed in this chapter encompasses the mainstream of northern European and American Christian hymnody from the Reformation to the present, drawn from many cultures. Much of the practical material discussed here can be applied to the leadership of hymns and songs in other styles.

The examples discussed in this chapter cover both metrical and rhythmic hymns. Some definitions are in order.

A *metrical hymn* (such as most English and some German hymns) is one that has a regular meter and a recurring pulse. Such hymns may exist in a four-part singable harmony, as a unison line with organ or other instrumental accompaniment, or sung by voice alone. An example is WIE SOLL ICH DICH EMPFANGEN (#241). Many of these German hymns evolved from early rhythmic forms, and you will sometimes find both metrical (or *isometric*) and rhythmic versions of the same tune, such as EIN FESTE BURG (#504, 505, 509 [isometric]; 503 [rhythmic]) or HERZLICH TUT MICH VERLANGEN (#351, 606, 703 [isometric]; 352 [rhythmic]).

A *rhythmic hymn* (such as earlier German chorales and Genevan Psalter tunes) is also characterized by a steady pulse (tactus), but does not necessarily have a constant number of beats in a measure, if there are measures at all. In some cases, a rhythmic hymn may have a *shifting* tactus, as in chant. In either case, the tactus usually underlies a rugged, often syncopated,

melody. These hymns were generally sung in unison, often without organ accompaniment. An example is MIT FRIED UND FREUD (#440).

With the Reformation's encouragement of active assembly participation in worship, there arose an urgent need for music that the average worshiper could manage. On the European continent, the German chorale and the Genevan Psalter tunes, with their straightforward lines and appealing, earthy rhythms, soon took hold. In England this new congregational music took the form of the metrical psalm tune. At the same time, influenced by this more formally composed hymnody, communities were nurturing their own folk hymns that, in time, would be brought into wider use. Within a short time, strophic hymnody had taken root within the hearts and musical minds of worshiping Christians, forming the backbone of congregational music as many know it. Every century since the sixteenth has had its metrical hymns, and they are still being composed.

Why is this form of assembly song so firmly entrenched in the fabric of Christian worship? The reasons are as simple as its elements:

- it repeats itself (stanzas, as well as phrases)
- it has a recurring pulse
- its movement is predictable
- it is easily remembered
- a large gathering is able to sing it together as a unified voice

When we think of hymns like "O God, Our Help in Ages Past" (#632), we probably imagine it sung by an organ-led assembly. This is not to say, of course, that other instruments cannot be used. Pianos and synthesizers are possible, and unaccompanied song is an option we should use more often for metrical hymnody. Since the organ is the standard support for this type of hymnody, though, we will focus on it. However, many of the suggestions are equally applicable for those leading with piano, other instruments, or voice.

Tactus

The notes, of course, must be learned well. Once the notes are learned, then focus on the pulse—the tactus—of the hymn. A strong, clear, and steady rhythm is critical to lead an assembly in song. It needs to be consistent, and the congregation has to be able to recognize it.

German chorales (c.1517–1650) and hymns from the Genevan Psalter (after 1536) were written in a period when bar lines and time signatures were largely nonexistent. The natural pulse of the music, the tactus, was *felt* rather than discovered through music notation. In fact, modern notation is often misleading. For example, hymns that appear to be in $\frac{4}{4}$ time usually have a half-note tactus; hymns that appear in $\frac{3}{4}$ often have a dotted half-note tactus. Two examples with stress marks indicating where the tactus would fall are shown:

This broader feel of the tactus has a profound effect on how the hymn is played and sung, propelling the melody along. The English tune KINGSFOLD (see #251) is an example. Though it appears to be in a $\frac{4}{4}$ meter, it has a half-note tactus.

The Welsh tune THE ASH GROVE (see #547), with its triple meter, has a tactus of one pulse per bar:

The same technique works for more conventionally composed hymns. The popular EASTER HYMN (see #365), for example, can march along with a quarter-note tactus,

but apply a half-note tactus and it soars:

Evangelical Lutheran Worship (along with many other hymnals) follows the practice of not including time signatures in the pew edition. The tactus must be discovered naturally by playing the melody and rhythm and *sensing* where the strong and weak beats of the music occur. (See the section on tactus, pages 21–22 above.)

Consider the tune ES IST DAS HEIL if it appeared in $\frac{4}{4}$ time. When played with each quarter note getting a strong pulse, the result is laborious:

Now look at how it appears in rhythmic form in *Evangelical Lutheran Worship* (#590). Even without understanding the concept of tactus, one could easily feel that this would be laborious in $\frac{4}{4}$ time. But apply a strong accent to the larger beat, allow the in-between pulse to feel lighter, and a rhythmic, dance-like quality results:

The rhythms of some early hymns can be quite energetic, as is the case with ES IST DAS HEIL. Others, especially from the Genevan Psalter and some folk traditions, are quite rhythmic but in a more dance-like way.

Both rhythmic chorales and Genevan Psalter hymns originally were sung in unison without accompaniment. We should encourage our assemblies to sing them in this way today, at least occasionally. When accompanying them on the organ, be certain that the registration is gentle and does not dominate the voices. At the same time, keep the tactus clear and strong. This can be a bit more challenging with non-metered tunes than it is with a regular number of beats in a measure and clearly delineated bar lines.

As is true with most of the suggestions in this book, there is never just one way to do something. One possibility for FREU DICH SEHR (see #256) is to keep a perfectly steady half-note pulse. This means that some accented syllables will fall between pulses (e.g., "com-" in the second "comfort"), creating a very syncopated feel.

Alternatively, the same melody can be thought of more along the lines of chant with a combination of twos and threes. In this case the second "comfort" falls on a strong beat, and the melody's interest lies in the alternation of triple and duple meter.

Similarly, the concept of tactus can be applied in a number of ways to the original rhythmic version of EIN FESTE BURG (see #503). One way to interpret this is as a regular pattern with a half-note tactus. This will provide a sense of the lively syncopation inherent in the tune:

Or, alternately, number the melody with twos and threes as in chant (beginning on the upbeat 2) to sense the alternating pattern of duple and triple meter:

Without sensing the underlying pulse of a tune, especially when holding a longer note or encountering a dotted rhythm, it is too easy to cheat the rhythm and rush through it. Leaders of assembly singing who learn to internalize the tactus will rarely fall into the trap of robbing notes of their full value. *A dependable tactus is the single most important factor in confident assembly singing.*

However, it is important to remember that there is no one absolutely correct way to articulate a particular hymn in every situation. An organist must learn all the possibilities, then listen carefully to instrument, space, situation, and assembly, applying all the techniques in the process. In every instance, attention to tactus and articulation will give more life to a hymn.

Articulation

When playing a harmony written primarily for voices, an organist needs to make adjustments from the printed page for playing. The organist is, in effect, creating a transcription of the vocal score for keyboard. The careful handling of repeated notes is essential to keeping the tactus strong and evident in effective hymn playing. Think of the hymn tune HANOVER (#842). The tactus is the dotted-half note (one pulse per bar), with the first note treated as a pick-up. This gives that note a sense of lift as well as adding weight to the following downbeat.

The soprano line (the melody in most cases) should be articulated clearly, including every repeated note, with a slightly larger articulation before the strong beats. Repeated notes in the bass line might be tied together from strong to weak beat but articulated when leading into a strong beat. The bass line can help reinforce the tactus. Repeated notes in the inner voices (alto and tenor) can either be tied together or detached to reinforce the tactus, depending on the circumstances. Consider the following possibilities:

When a stronger tactus is needed (perhaps due to a livelier acoustic or lethargic assembly) the articulation should be adapted. In this example, in addition to the articulations marked above, repeated notes in the inner voices as well as arrivals to the tactus in the bass line are now articulated. Occasionally, in $\frac{3}{4}$ time a 2 + 1 articulation can be very strong. That means consistent articulations before the tactus (beat 1) but also separating the upbeat (beat 3).

Again, these are only possibilities, and they will need to be adapted to fit individual circumstances. When you think of all the possibilities of articulation, the levels of gradation between these examples are many. As a new concept to an organist, this kind of thinking can seem overwhelming; suddenly, a simple hymn becomes complex. Once mastered, however, careful management of every articulation can help a hymn come alive and will result in better assembly singing.

Accent and Articulation on the Organ

On instruments such as a piano, accents (which create the tactus) can be heard by striking the desired downbeats more loudly than others. On instruments such as an organ, striking one note harder than others does not result in an accent; rather, the same effect is achieved by careful use of articulation, the slight separation before and subtle elongation of the stressed pulse (agogic accent). Articulation is one of the principal components in determining how the listener will perceive tactus, phrasing, and texture.

On the organ, try playing a simple C major scale completely legato using the fingering 1,2,3,1,2,3,4,5. Next, try to achieve the same legato, but playing the entire scale with the same finger (such as 1, 1, 1, 1, 1, 1). Now, using that technique again, try to slightly lengthen every other note (**1**, 1, **1**, 1, **1**, 1), thinking down-up-down-up as you do this. Note, however, that the finger shouldn't pop up, even after the shorter notes, but be drawn inward toward the palm. After practicing this skill, a crisp (but not choppy) duple rhythm will be heard. Experiment with the size of the articulation preceding the lengthened beat to create stronger or more gentle accents. Shift the larger articulation and elongated notes to create a triple rhythm (**1**, 1, 1, **1**, 1, 1, **1**, 1, 1). With all these techniques, remember to strive for clear, connected playing, with subtle articulations providing the rhythm. It takes a lot of patient practice to do this.

This is the kind of legato that is very effective in hymn playing on the organ. Of course, you won't be playing hymns with one finger. But once you have a sense for how the notes flow together using this type of legato, you will more easily achieve a clear sounding of the tactus, which in turn will result in confident, rhythmic assembly singing.

The Space between Phrases

Organs or pianos don't need to breathe, but singers do. The organist can help the assembly breathe and sing together by giving attention to the transition between phrases and especially between stanzas.

Consider HANOVER (#842). The first phrase and a half are written:

written:

To provide time for a breath, however, an organist may need to borrow some time from the last chord of the phrase, allowing the next phrase to begin exactly in time. In an average acoustic, an organist may play:

played:

It is important for the organist to remember that the releases of notes, as well as the attacks, are part of the rhythm. Be certain to lift the chord precisely on the pulse that you intend. The assembly will hear that lift as part of the rhythm. If, in the example above, a stronger tactus is needed, a quarter rest would be better (rather than the eighth, as shown). Such as:

played:

. . . could be *played*

A phrase that ends with a whole note may requires a quarter-note breath on the final beat. A phrase that is *written*

Another example is BEREDEN VÄG FÖR HER-RAN (#264), where three phrases end with a dotted half note tied to a half note. A phrase *written* as

. . . could be *played*

. . . or *played*

Many hymn tunes require some variation of this approach. Always be attentive to the assembly's breathing.

The Space between Stanzas

Hymns are, by their very nature, a cyclical musical form. The melody keeps repeating for as many stanzas as there are. Handling the transition from the bottom of the page to the top is equally as important as the internal rhythms. Once a song, hymn, or liturgical piece is begun, the tactus must be maintained, even *between* stanzas. When you reach the end of a stanza:

- Keep the tactus going internally. You may need to elongate a bit, but the fundamental pulse should remain.
- You may need to add a pulse or two to what is printed. (Carefully determine this in advance.)
- Then you must borrow a bit of time from that final chord to allow for a clear and adequate breath before beginning the next stanza.

Again using HANOVER (#842) as an example, the end of stanza one and beginning of stanza two are printed like this:

written:

gird-ed with praise. The earth with its

If the organist is feeling a tactus of a dotted half note (one beat to the bar), one full pulse may be added, then borrow two quarter notes to allow for a generous breath. Stanza two then can proceed with a confident upbeat. Written out it would look like this:

played:

gird-ed with praise. The earth with its

This sounds far more complicated than it is. As with any issue regarding tactus, *predictability* is the key.

Sometimes the printed note values provide enough time between stanzas (see, for example, "Praise and Thanksgiving," #689). But for other hymns the leader may need to borrow some time from the final note of a stanza to allow the assembly to breathe before moving to the next stanza.

Consider SONNE DER GERECHTIGKEIT (#362). This sturdy tune has a strong half-note tactus. In most acoustical settings, the final whole note (two pulses) is adequate. However, the organist may need to borrow some time from the last note for a breath. The phrase *written* as

. . . might be *played*

. . . or, in a livelier acoustic, *played*

Remember that many factors effect exactly how you adapt this technique to your unique situation. These are general suggestions; hymn playing is an art, not a science. For example, some might feel that with the above example, it is better to add a half rest after the closing whole note. If you are uncertain about the best approach for a particular hymn, try out different solutions with your choir. You will know from their musical and verbal response what feels natural and works well.

Musical Phrasing

When to articulate for the assembly to breathe within a hymn stanza is another important issue to consider. As with other decisions, many factors determine the choices you make, including tempo, acoustics, musical ability of the assembly, and so forth. There are three ways to approach this issue:

1. Adhere to the phrasing of the text, articulating only at punctuation, regardless of the musical line:

Or:

2. Follow the musical phrase with both singers and organ breaking at the end of the musical line, no matter what the text:

3. Strike a compromise, such as:

As the leader of the song, determine how you intend to treat each phrase, and adjust your articulation to make it clear to the singing assembly. If you have a choir available to prepare in advance, they can be a great help in leading the singing.

Playing the Text

Hymns, songs, liturgical responses, psalm settings, the musical portions in which the assembly participates through singing—all are bound to texts. The music to which a text is set is intended to reflect the character of that text. Some texts are more inward and contemplative in nature; others are merry and joyful. Reflection on the text is the starting point for all who are prepare to lead assembly song:

- What is the text saying? An analysis of the content of a text's message, imagery, character, position, and use within the context of the service is always in order.
- How does the text make you feel? How does it sing?
- Are there words or phrases that do not roll easily off the tongue? (The word *baptism*, for example, is always hard to sing.)
- Are there any mood changes in the hymn as a whole?
- What is the meter and poetic structure?
- Does the text involve dialogue?
- Is there an emotional climax in any stanza?
- Is the text doctrinal, devotional, didactic?
- Is it a hymn of praise or a prayer?
- Who is being addressed in the text?

Which of these facets do I want to emphasize for the assembly in this time and place? How might I do that? Try to capture the character of the text in your own rendition. Think about the speed at which you're singing. Are you using legato (connected) or more bouncy, detached phrases? See how you can make the text come alive just by means of the tune.

There are many ways to enhance the meaning of the text through creative hymn playing. One simple idea is to revert to unison accompaniment, playing the melody in octaves in the manual and the pedal, when accompanying text that articulates messages of unity or oneness. "Sent Forth by God's Blessing" (#547) is one such example. The middle of the second stanza reads:

> *. . . unite us as one in this life that we share.*
> *Then may all the living with praise and*
> *thanksgiving give honor to Christ and his*
> *name that we bear.*

When leading this hymn, it might be appropriate to play the phrase "unite us as one in the life that we share" in unison, followed by four-part playing during the subsequent phrases. In a similar manner, whole stanzas can be played and sung in unison (better yet, sung unaccompanied), building on the melodic power embodied in these tunes. Returning to harmonized accompaniment for later stanzas lends new energy to the singing.

Alternation

Where texts employ a dialogue or refrain, consider some form of alternation between soloist and/or choir and the assembly as a means of heightening the dramatic character of the hymn. This technique of alternation was common with German hymns that often had ten to twenty or more stanzas. Singing that many stanzas in a row can challenge the heartiest of congregations. Today, even though most of those long hymns have been shortened, this practice is still useful and appreciated by many congregations. Using this technique, one simply divides stanzas between different forces. For example, in "The Angel Gabriel from Heaven Came" (#265), the first three stanzas could be divided between a narrator, the angel Gabriel, and Mary. The assembly itself would sing the fourth stanza, summing up the message of the hymn.

Take advantage of the story being told in Luther's Christmas hymn "From Heaven Above" (#268) by adding some alternation and turning it into an engaging proclamation of the word. When sung lightly like a Renaissance dance, with percussion, this can even be fun!

1. solo	8. women
2. choir	9. men
3. solo	10. women
4. choir	11. all
5. solo	12. choir
6. all	13. all
7. men	14. all

A pattern such as this is particularly helpful when learning a new hymn:

1. cantor
2. choir
3–4. all

Another example:

1. all
2. higher voices (women and children)
3. lower voices (men)
4. all

To make it clear that children have a part to sing, it is helpful to use "higher voices" or "treble voices"—rather than "women"—to differentiate that range from that of "men" or "lower voices."

Of course, it is critical that you communicate clearly to the assembly which stanzas they are to sing. And don't let your creativity stop with gender. Look at your worship space; it will probably suggest some logical divisions between sides or areas. It is also possible on occasion to employ a purely instrumental stanza to interpret the text. If this is new to your congregation, you might encourage them to meditate on the words of the stanza at that time.

Registration

Successful hymn playing requires variety of all kinds, including color—and part of the fun of being an organist is playing with the colors, or timbres, of the instrument. Depending on the nature of the hymn text and tune, the skill and confidence of the player, the instrument, and assembly itself, changing registrations may add welcome variety. Some organists will change registrations every stanza and often within each stanza. Others prefer more consistency within a hymn, although not to the point of boredom. The most important question is: "How can I best carry this text for this congregation at this time?" That may mean getting out of the way, or it may mean doing some tone painting, if that is within your abilities.

The possibilities for hymn registrations are unlimited. Some of the basic sounds (depending, of course, on the instrument available) include:

- Principal chorus (Principal or Diapason 8', 4', [2⅔',] 2') with or without mixtures
- Chorus reeds (those that add color rather than dominate)
- 16' manual sounds for thickness and grandeur
- Pedal reeds for emphasis

When soloing out a melody (see pages 26–27), colors such as reeds, gapped registrations such as 8' and 2' and mutations may be effective. Some classic solo combinations using mutations are 8', 4', 1⅓' and the cornet of 8', 4', 2⅔' and 1⅗'. There are many others, and the organist is limited only by his or her imagination.

Introducing the Hymn

The minimum requirements for a hymn introduction are to inform the assembly of the tune and to set the key and tempo. Through the kind of articulation applied it can also identify the spirit of the hymn—whether joyous or contemplative, for instance. Unless a hymn is new, unfamiliar, difficult, or all the above, it is unnecessary (through not wrong) to play the entire hymn as an introduction. Some would say that playing all the way through a well-known hymn serves only to disengage a congregation. On the other hand, an imaginative introduction (not necessarily difficult), well-suited to the hymn, can help make even the most reluctant churchgoer want to stand and sing.

Some points to keep in mind for any introduction, whether improvised or written out:

- Play the introduction with the same tempo and rhythmic feeling you will be using when the assembly sings.
- In general, keep the tactus going between intro and first stanza, just as you would between stanzas (see "The Space between Stanzas" on page 42).
- If a hymn is familiar, you might play just enough to make the melody, pitch, and rhythm clear (e.g., the first and last lines).

Introductions to familiar hymns are an excellent place to begin composing or improvising. In devising hymn introductions, write them out, particularly if you are uncomfortable with improvisation. Putting them on manuscript paper or computer will improve your compositional skills, force you to think about voice leading and harmonic progressions, and provide you with a written record of your hymn treatments. To stimulate your creativity, take time to study some of the excellent published collections of hymn introductions and harmonizations. Writing your own hymn settings, whether simple or elaborate, will bring you satisfaction and growth. However, always be aware of the assembly. Do not overwhelm them with constantly changing, dramatic introductions. The goal is to inspire them to sing confidently.

Chorale Preludes as Introductions

A simple, straightforward hymn introduction will give an assembly the necessary information: key, tempo, and style of the hymn. But an honored tradition, especially in the Germanic churches, is the chorale prelude—generally a longer, more elaborate form of hymn introduction. The genre includes everything from the small-scale masterpieces of J. S. Bach's *Orgelbüchlein* to a tonally challenging contemporary piece. What is the place of such works within today's worship?

The answer will depend in large part on the history and character of each worshiping community. One assembly may value chorale preludes, even insist on them, as hymn introductions, particularly for the hymn of the day, when Lutherans understand the assembly to be participating in the proclamation of God's word through their song. That assembly is willing to allow the extra time required so that they may consider the commentary provided by the composer. But another assembly may feel that the regular use of chorale preludes is an imposition, with the organist grabbing the spotlight. Some assemblies want to have the hymn tune identified simply and then start singing.

Matters such as this require sensitivity. If chorale preludes within the service are undesirable, they may still add much as pre- or post-service music. If they are used to introduce hymns, the organist needs to balance artistic considerations with the liturgical character of that part of the service. What sort of piece would work well here? Does this prelude work with this text? Are the keys the same? If not, how will I deal with that, or should it be used at all? Perhaps the most important consideration is whether the tune is clearly presented in the prelude so that at its conclusion the hymn can simply begin, or does it need to be extended in some way to provide a clear tempo and pitch for the assembly to sing?

Variety

When an organist becomes confident in basic hymn playing with clean articulation and a clear tactus, variety in hymn playing can be achieved through the use of passing tones, neighboring notes, and other decorations, primarily in the supporting voices. Such devices help the singing by propelling a line forward, by suggesting a crescendo, by setting up a rallentando, and the like. They should never get in the way, however. A walking bass line can give a hymn wonderful new energy on the last stanza. But if such a pedal line is clumsy or ill-conceived it will call undue attention to itself and hinder the flow of the hymn.

Singing a hymn is a pilgrimage complete with preparation and anticipation, the first step, the journey itself, the final stretch, and the arrival. The organist serves as tour guide—coaxing, encouraging, inspiring, giving directions, and pointing toward the goal. The last stanza, being the final stretch, may call for something different. In most cases, depending as always on the text, people want to move with renewed vigor, for the end is in sight. A varied harmonization, descant, or decorated version may be just what is needed and will serve to bring the assembly into a strong unison.

All hymns in *Evangelical Lutheran Worship* that are printed with harmonies can be *sung* in harmony. In the service music and hymns accompaniment edition, a small [U] or [H] next to a hymn number indicates whether the pew edition presents that hymn in unison or harmony. While looking for varied hymn accompaniments, keep in mind that the harmonizations in the book should not be abandoned altogether. Many people enjoy singing hymns in harmony and will appreciate it—and sing more enthusiastically—if you frequently stick to the printed harmony. A common practice is to agree that everyone will sing in unison on the first stanza (allowing the melody to be presented for the less confident singers) and the last stanza (allowing the organist to use an alternate accompaniment), and the inner stanzas sung in harmony.

Some organists improvise or compose a brief interlude before the final stanza, during which time a modulation sometimes occurs, usually up a half step. Judicious use of this practice is critical. As is true with many good ideas, used too often it weakens the hymn and destroys its integrity.

CHAPTER SIX

FOLK SONGS AND HYMNS

A folk hymn, whether from Europe, America, or another part of the world, might share similar characteristics with the metrical hymn. What sets the folk hymn apart is its origin outside the culture's art traditions. These hymns have evolved, and many continue to do so, because they are often a product of oral tradition. Folk hymns are also on a journey. They wander from one cultural and geographic setting to another, finding new homes in diverse communities far removed from the traditions that created and nurtured them. Along the way, new cultural expectations affect the performance of these hymns. Folk hymns are slowly altered to fit the requirements of the present-day communities in which they are sung. These alterations ordinarily occur within individual motives or phrases of a tune; therefore, many variations of these melodies exist. Be careful when using resources other than *Evangelical Lutheran Worship* that the melodic shape and rhythms are compatible. (See #251 and 723 to see two versions of a tune with common roots.)

Because folk songs begin with the people and gradually move into print resources, their tunes tend to be melodically and harmonically simple. Folk melodies are often based on a pentatonic scale or other tonalities with little chromaticism. The tune PROSPECT (#684) is an example. You'll notice that there are no B♭s or Es in the melody. It only uses the five notes of a pentatonic scale:

This simple quality of folk music often calls for a light and gentle accompaniment. Let the voices be primary.

Many newer tunes that have not gone through the evolutionary process described above still have a folk-like quality, such as John Ylvisaker's WATERLIFE (#732). For the purposes of leading the assembly in singing these tunes, they may fall in the folk category as well.

Leading Folk Songs and Hymns

Much of the information in the Northern European chapter is helpful here as well. Folk hymns are a diverse body of music that calls for an equally diverse approach to musical leadership. In the process of making decisions regarding the accompaniment, one important element to consider is instrumentation, or lack of it. With the help of a good cantor or choir, one of the most effective ways to sing folk hymns is unaccompanied. It is almost certainly the most historically accurate approach to much of this literature.

When leading unaccompanied singing, remember that visual cues are very important. Without the presence of an accompanying instrument the assembly relies on sight more that it would otherwise. Yet the assembly as a singing body does not require a conductor in the same manner as a choir. It is capable of sustaining its own song with the occasional use of subtle hand gestures to unify the beginnings and ends of stanzas.

Tempo is also a critical consideration in an a cappella performance. Help the assembly find a natural, communal tempo that provides ample space for the text and supports the melodic properties of the tune. In general, unaccompanied singing works better with tunes that are stately or lyrical such as IN BABILONE (#522).

Of all the accompanying instruments used with folk repertoire in church, the organ remains the most common. Many standard approaches to hymn playing on the organ work well for folk hymns. In addition to the organ, a number of other instruments possess unique properties that enable them to function effectively with folk repertoire. The piano is particularly important in this regard. The combination of its inherent lyricism and percussive qualities makes it a wonderful option for leading folk music. When playing folk melodies that have a slow harmonic rhythm on the piano, consider adapting the printed accompaniment to a simple arpeggiated figure. See the alternate accompaniment for BUNESSAN (#456) as an example.

In more intimate settings, instruments that strum, arpeggiate, or improvise counterpoint, including harpsichords and guitars, can be effective either in a solo capacity or in combination with wind or string instruments. While harpsichord is most commonly associated with music from Renaissance and Baroque periods, it is also effective to accompany much nineteenth and twentieth century folk music.

Types of Folk Hymns

Folk hymns can be organized into several general categories based on the melodic and rhythmic characteristics of the tune.

Dance Hymns. Tunes of dance origin or character probably constitute the largest single category in folk hymnody. Indeed, dance and movement itself are often connected with the origins of folk song. The word *ballad* comes from *ballare,* which means "to dance" and is related to *ballet.*

The most prominent characteristic of dance tunes is their rhythmic vitality. Meters range from simple duple ($\frac{2}{4}$) to compound triple ($\frac{9}{8}$), although the bulk of these tunes are in triple meter of some sort. Texts generally speak of animation, activity, travel, rejoicing, or singing, such as GELOBT SEI GOTT ("Good Christian Friends, Rejoice and Sing!" #385) or THE ASH GROVE ("Let All Things Now Living," #881). As one might expect given the positive nature of these texts, dance hymns are usually written in major keys.

Since rhythm and tempo are such important features of dance hymns, these elements have a strong impact on the performance of this literature in the context of the assembly. The first step in deciding how to sing and play dance

hymns is to arrive at an appropriate tactus or pulse for the music. It is important to understand that feeling tunes in one beat per measure does not necessarily imply a fast pulse, but does allow for a natural ebb and flow necessary for anyone who dances this music. Playing these hymns in a manner that provides a strong, consistent tactus, coupled with a buoyant, open touch throughout, will enable members of the assembly to "sing lighter on their feet."

When playing these tunes on the organ, it is best not to over-register. Transparent combinations, such as 8' flute, 4' principal, 2' principal, with or without a light mixture, work well. Solo out lines with a clear, bright trumpet that is not too heavy in character (see page 26 on soloing out a melody). Marcato pedaling, either on strong beats or harmonic changes, may further stress the dance-like character of these tunes. This idea may be extended to include chords played by the left hand. With good choral leadership it is even possible to abandon the tune altogether, playing marcato chords in vital, enlivening rhythmic patterns intended to energize the assembly's singing. Along these same lines, consider playing a drone or percussive ostinato figure in the left-hand pedal while the right hand plays the melody.

Hymns of Lament. These hymns often couple tunes possessing a strong character of longing with reflective texts. KAS DZIEDĀJA ("Once We Sang and Danced," #701) is an example. They usually lean toward step-wise motion and are often in minor keys. Yiddish and other Jewish tunes such as TIF IN VELDELE ("Light One Candle to Watch for Messiah," #240), based on plaintive Eastern European scales, are excellent examples of lament.

With hymns of lament, unaccompanied singing can be an excellent option. Lovely tunes known by the assembly, such as LAND OF REST ("How Long, O God," #698) work well with no instrumental accompaniment. If organ or other instruments are used, the registrations should be warm and simple.

Pastorales and Lullabies. Another prominent style in the genre of folk hymns is the pastorale or lullaby. Though not identical in affect, lullabies such as W ŻŁOBIE LEŻY ("Infant Holy, Infant Lowly," #276) and pastorales such as CRADLE SONG ("Away in a Manger" #278) share a characteristic gentleness and calm. These folk hymns are often in triple or compound meter. Again, gentle organ registrations (perhaps only 8' and 4'), depending on your assembly, are appropriate for leading these hymns. Consider introducing them using a single voice, such as an 8' or 4' flute (resembling the speaking range of a soprano recorder) or solo oboe stop. If available, treble instruments can lead these tunes beautifully. Keep organ registrations for the pedal very light, perhaps only an 8' stop.

Ballads. These are narrative folk songs, and the repertoire of folk-song hymns includes several fine examples, including THE FIRST NOWELL (#300), DEO GRACIAS ("Oh, Love, How Deep," #322), and THE SINGER AND THE SONG ("When Long before Time," #861). While these hymns are beloved, their nature as stories or folklore mean they are lengthy, presenting a special challenge to the leader of the assembly's song.

To capitalize on the narrative nature of these hymns, try dividing the stanzas so that each is taken by a different part of the assembly. If there is a refrain, invite the entire assembly to sing it. When leading the assembly in these ballads, the organ accompaniment should support the drama of the text. Reserve full organ for those occasions when the entire assembly is singing together. See page 45 for more on alternation.

Hymns of Procession or Proclamation. While folk hymns of this type often have texts similar to those of the dance genre of folk hymnody— rejoicing, moving forward with purpose— they are more often in duple meter and more conducive to performance in a stately, walking tempo. The strong half-note tactus for HAF TRONES LAMPA FÄRDIG (#244) and the similarly powerful, angular melody of KING'S LYNN (#305) suggest the need for sturdy, rhythmic leadership. A marcato touch and strong plenum registrations, perhaps incorporating solo and chorus reeds, provide the powerful image of grandeur associated with these tunes.

7

NORTH AMERICAN HYMNODY

Note: Much of the information in the Northern European and Folk Hymnody chapters also applies here, as well as to the following chapter on African American song.

North American indigenous hymnody includes a wonderful variety of music that can add energy and joy to our praise in worship. Increasingly, mainline denominational hymnals include tunes from the many truly American traditions, including shape-note tunes, North American folk tunes, white spirituals, camp meeting tunes, revivals, Sunday School movement, Gospel, and others. This is true for *Evangelical Lutheran Worship* as well, which contains more songs from this era than any previous Lutheran hymnal.

Tempo

Rhythm is vital in performing much music from this genre. The downbeat is usually very strong and once the tempo is set, it doesn't vary, except perhaps for a slight ritardando and lengthening of the final chord. The strength of these tunes needs to be evidenced in their tempos without sacrificing their energetic nature; so don't drag, but move the tempo confidently.

Even with a strong tune, tempo decisions are determined by reflection on both the text and an understanding of how it will function in worship. For example, CORONATION (#634) may take a confident, energetic tempo, while a reflection on the saving death of Jesus Christ, such as NEAR THE CROSS (#335) may require a much slower tempo so that each note has its own sounding, as does each word. Many of these songs depend on a combination of quarter and eighth notes. Be sure not to rush the tempo, so each word can be clearly articulated by the singers. Many of these tunes are well served by feeling a quarter pulse as the tactus, rather than the usual bigger beat in other genres.

Melody, Harmony, and Vocal Quality

Especially for tunes from the shape-note tradition, melody is the most important element. An example is WONDROUS LOVE (#666). Even when sung in harmony, the melody should remain prominent.

Hymn tunes from the revival and Sunday school movements in the late 1800s, such as JESUS LOVES ME (#595) and ASSURANCE (#638), depend much more on their harmonies. If the melody is unfamiliar, the introduction might include the melody soloed out on the organ or with an instrument (see pages 26–27 for help with bringing out the melody), ending with full harmony on the last phrase. During the singing of these tunes, the melody will be equal with the harmony parts. Encourage singing in harmony when possible.

Songs in these genres generally have a rugged character. Encourage robust, hearty singing. Even those sung at a slower tempo have an internal energy that continually propels the hymn forward.

Accompaniment

Early North American tunes call for confident unaccompanied singing, piano leadership or, if leading from the organ, a straightforward registration of principals, occasionally adding other stops for color and volume as the text, assembly and occasion demand. Other instruments may be added, as available. With gentler tunes, in a quiet worship setting, guitar, dulcimer, or autoharp would be appropriate for introduction and perhaps an introductory solo stanza (it would be lost under assembly singing). Adding an instrument playing the melody would assist the assembly in their singing.

In those hymns where harmony changes are slow (once per measure, or even two measures), those accompanying on organ may find it more effective to articulate in order to reinforce the primary beats, rather than lifting between every repeated note which in this case will produce a choppy accompaniment:

Revival, Camp Meeting, and Sunday School Movement

Hymns from the revival, camp meeting, and Sunday school traditions form a large body of repertoire, and it is difficult to generalize about their performance. All these hymns lend

Shape Note

Early American tunes from the shape-note tradition are well known by many North American worshipers and have melodies that are generally easy to sing, yet memorable. Because of this, many newer hymn texts have been paired with these melodies. Read the text carefully and note its place in worship for clues to the appropriate tempo, whether stately, somber, or joyful.

The tunes were often set in four-part harmony (often with the melody in the tenor) and sung unaccompanied, with gusto. Even the tunes carrying sweeter texts kept a vitality about them. Examples of this phenomenon include WONDROUS LOVE (#666), and FOUNDATION (#796). However, some of these tunes, such as BEACH SPRING (#445), are also appropriately sung in unison with gentle accompaniment. (See chapter 6 on folk hymns.)

themselves to piano accompaniment, perhaps even organ and piano playing together. With small assemblies or choir, a simple guitar accompaniment could work well.

These tunes tend to be energetic; even the more reflective of them, such as PILOT ("Jesus, Savior, Pilot Me," #755) should not be dragged out sentimentally but rather sung as faithful expressions of earlier generations.

Many of these songs were originally sung as call and response, echoing the call of God and humanity's response. Soloists or quartets would sing the stanzas while the congregation responded with the refrains. Examples are "Blessed Assurance" (#638), "Great Is Thy Faithfulness" (#733), and "Come, We That Love the Lord" (#625). Texts such as "Shall We Gather at the River" (#423) ask a question in stanza one, followed by a corporate response in the refrain. Consider using a soloist on stanza one, with the entire assembly joining on the refrain. If accompaniment is used in leading any of these hymns, be sure to vary the texture and volume to accommodate the singing voices. Another common practice is to alternate singers on the verses, while everyone joins on the refrain. There are many possibilities: men/women, girls/boys, children/adults, right side/left side, back/front, either with notation in the bulletin, by a song leader's direction, or with projected instructions. (See pages 45–46 for more on alternation in other styles.)

Many of these tunes were meant to be sung in four-part harmony. Examples include CONVERSE (#742) and SHOWALTER (#774). If your congregation generally sings in unison, teach the choir to sing the harmony, then place the choir throughout the assembly to encourage singing in parts. Keyboard accompaniment can support the harmony. These tunes lend themselves particularly well to piano accompaniment. Pianists may delight in adding pianistic elements without losing sight of the primary goal of enabling congregational singing. Adding chords on the piano during long held notes in the voices may be helpful to keep the pulse clear and strong to fill in any long notes on the piano. Consider, for example, this excerpt from CONVERSE:

Hymns from this repertoire are generally based on scripture, presenting a simple, straightforward message. Because of the refrains, these hymns are a good way to involve children and developmentally challenged persons. These hymns have helped bring many persons to faith, and they can still do it today.

CHAPTER EIGHT

AFRICAN AMERICAN SONG

In traditional African American worship neither the length of service nor the length of the songs is dictated by the clock. In assembly singing it is common for the final chorus to be repeated as directed by the song leader. Similarly, soloists frequently interject such textual phrases as "I believe I'll say that one more time" to signal repetition of a particular phrase or stanza. In neither of these instances is repetition viewed as boring or grandstanding; instead, repetition serves as an essential tool for generating and sustaining the spiritual fervor that has historically distinguished the worship of African Americans in the United States.

Singing in the traditional African American worship is an expression of jubilation, power, and praise. Even when the text of a spiritual communicates lament, the vocal quality of the singer remains strong. Vocalists are expected to convey their total sincerity and complete absorption in communicating both outward, to others present at the event, and upward to God. The vocal timbre in gospel solos may vary constantly, alternately utilizing moans, groans, shouts, wails, and growls. Similarly, in assembly singing the concluding verse or refrain may be hummed, allowing the assembly to experience the song's meaning through another timbral dimension. Whereas in the singing of spirituals the vocal timbre is more closely aligned with that of Western music, maximizing the use of the head voice, in gospel music the commanding power of the chest voice is highly valued in women's singing, and male soloists frequently utilize falsetto.

Most spirituals and many gospel songs have very short texts, a feature that was helpful in committing them to memory. These brief texts are, however, repeated many times with improvised variations, the repetition helping to convey their message. Another way these texts are extended is through the interjection of "wandering"—independent couplets and quatrains. Sometimes these are closely related to the text of the song, sometimes not. So influential is this variation on the oral tradition that at times the standard text will be replaced entirely by the wandering couplet or quatrain. The same situation may be found in gospel music where at times only the refrain text will remain, the rest having been displaced by the "oral" text.

Much assembly song takes the African-influenced form of call/response. The soloist, a strong and experienced singer, will issue the call in a firm manner that elicits an equally bold, full-voiced response from the congregation. It may take time and consistent use to develop the trust necessary for this assured back-and-forth song, but it is integral to the African American style of worship.

A highly valued dimension of timbre, representing a continuing African tradition, is percussive delivery both in vocal and instrumental performance. Particularly in highly syncopated songs with faster tempos, short phrases are strongly punctuated to accent the rhythm. For example, in the opening line of "What a Fellowship, What a Joy Divine" (#774), breaks will commonly occur after *what* and *a*. The line is not sung as a single continuing legato melodic phrase, but is instead chopped up into short, percussive fragments. The phrase is deliberately broken after the first word, adding rhythmic and timbral (percussive) interest.

Principles that govern African American religious music performance must not be viewed as inflexible rules that must be applied in the same way in every performance, for the underlying premise of African American music is fluidity, constant change.

Improvisation

Clearly, in orally based music like African American sacred song, improvisation plays an important role. At least some basic filling in beyond the written notation is essential to accompanying or leading this music. In singing the solo part, the leader will freely add runs, riffs, or motives to make the line more expressive. The melody line itself may be altered; rubato or rhythmic alteration may be employed. The best way to learn such techniques is to listen to an experienced singer, either on recording or live, and then gradually, as you feel comfortable, add to your performance style. The freer you can be with the music (within the parameters of the style), the closer you will come to the spirit of the song.

In gospel music, it is common for a soloist to sing the verses, with the assembly singing the refrains. The soloist must feel free to alter rhythms when so moved. Notes may be held longer than written, they may be shorter than written, and notes may be anticipated—coming slightly earlier than indicated in the score. The same is true for congregational singing in both spirituals and gospel. Each member of the assembly is free to personalize the singing experience, to make it one's own. Of course, all of these practices fall under the rubric of improvisation—a skill that can be learned, but only through diligent and regular practice. Improvisation is a dimension of performance, without which African American music loses its defining character.

A basic principle for accompanists, especially of gospel music, is that open spaces are always filled in by the keyboard. At the very least this would require repeating chords during longer, held notes. Even more effective would be adding an arpeggiated figure leading from one phrase to the next. It requires listening and practice, but such fills, even simple ones, can add immeasurably to the song. See the alternate accompaniment for CONVERSE (#742) as an example.

A next step could be to add a moving bass line such as these examples for JESUS LIFTED ME "I'm So Glad Jesus Lifted Me" (#860):

Or:

Few "upper limits" exist for the amount of improvising open to the keyboard player. Once the assembly is familiar with the hymn, even the melody is optional for the pianist. Arpeggios, scale passages, passing tones, upper and lower neighbor tones, even the occasional glissando are all possibilities within the style. Harmonic alterations that support the singing are also welcome. The player must sense when to let loose and when—especially when the vocalists are more active—to back off.

Instrumentation

Spirituals are often sung unaccompanied or with an acoustic piano; Gospel music often relies on the Hammond organ. The pipe organ simply does not produce the same effect; it can be used, but preferably in conjunction with other, more percussive instruments such as piano. The significance of the drum in African tradition continues in African American music by singing or playing nonpercussive instruments percussively. As Bernice Johnson Reagon has said, "You can take away the drums, but you can't stop the drumming." Instruments of all kinds may be combined to provide accompaniment for gospel songs—piano, organ, drums (trap set, congas, African drums), tambourine, trumpets, vibraphone, saxophone—the possibilities are unlimited. In all of these, though, pay close attention to attacks and releases. Notes may be shortened for added percussive effect and placed on the offbeat to enhance the underlying rhythm. For example, see "Soon and Very Soon" (#439):

written:

1 Soon and ver - y soon
2 No more cry - in' there
3 No more dy - in' there   we are
4 Soon and ver - y soon

goin' to see the King.

played:

In virtually all forms of African American music, instrumental accompaniment functions to complement the voice; its role is not a secondary one, but rather one of equal importance with the voice. At the same time, instruments such as horns playing riffs or obbligatos should be careful to play on the response section, not on the calls that are reserved for the leader.

Rhythm

More than by any other factor, African American music is driven by its rhythm. Rhythm is preeminent in both vocal lines and instrumental accompaniment; rhythm establishes the character of the piece. Each beat must be clearly sensed and heard. The principal pulse, of course, is given a strong accent. However, frequently the weak beats are given an even stronger accent. To illustrate, look at the spiritual "I'm So Glad Jesus Lifted Me" (#860). It has four quarter note beats per measure, and it is played with the accents not only on beats 2 and 4 but also on the eighth-note offbeats (1 *and* 2 *and* 3 *and* 4 *and*):

In a triple meter, beats 2 and 3 are often emphasized. An example is ASSURANCE (#638):

This sort of syncopation pervades all forms of African American religious music. It should never be rushed, always a temptation when you are anticipating the accent. Keep a firm sense of the tactus so that the syncopation can play off it. As singers become more experienced in this style of music, they will often add layers of symmetrical and asymmetrical beat divisions over the basic pulse, contributing to the characteristic rhythmic complexity. Those less accustomed to the style, however, will be better off maintaining the basic rhythm. Above all, avoid smoothing out the rhythms; to do so will rob the music of its vitality and energy.

While rhythmic precision is critical to the performance of spirituals and gospel music, rhythm must never be mechanical. Precision is one thing, rigidity another. Although rhythm is unquestionably preeminent in African American religious music performance, text—the message—must not be minimized.

Spirituals and gospel songs are filled with rich biblical imagery and intense devotion. The text, regardless of its relative simplicity or profundity, must be given its due.

Pitch

The concepts of pitch that characterize African American religious music are distinguished in some marked ways. First of all, melodic lines in both spirituals and gospel music include a preponderance of blue notes—lowered third, sixth, and seventh degrees in the major scale. Just as rhythms should not be smoothed out, neither should pitches. Even if a flatted seventh in the melody conflicts with a diatonic seventh in the accompaniment, this is considered an acceptable dissonance. Slides, scoops, and bends are all so fundamental to gospel music performance that soloists and congregations alike employ these vocal techniques intuitively. They have learned to value how pitch is conceived in the African American tradition through years of exposure and practice.

Pitch is also one of those key variables used to generate change in the midst of repetition. In repeating choruses at the close of a hymn or gospel song, raising the pitch by increments of a half step serves to sustain the musical and spiritual spark.

Harmony

Two styles of harmonization coexist with standard Western harmony in unaccompanied singing. The first uses parallel thirds or sixths throughout the song, a constant parallel motion. In the second style, used especially with very slow-moving pieces, a parallel interval of a fourth or fifth predominates, creating an effect similar to organum. Whatever style is used, both spirituals and gospel songs are almost always sung in harmony, whether from the printed page, learned by rote, or improvised.

Meter

Meter is another area in which oral tradition frequently takes precedence over what is written. Especially in the case of hymns borrowed from white sources, a piece written in $\frac{4}{4}$ routinely will be sung in $\frac{12}{8}$, with a swing. For instance, "What a Fellowship, What a Joy Divine" (#774) is often written in $\frac{4}{4}$ but played in $\frac{12}{8}$:

Style of Delivery

Perhaps the dimension of African American religious music that poses the greatest challenge for cross-cultural sharing is its style of delivery, or physical mode of presentation. This dimension of performance includes variables that, in the European American tradition, may be considered extraneous. In the African American tradition, however, the visual dimension—the expressive behavior that characterized performance—is of equal significance to the sonic dimension. It's not just *what* is sung but *how* it's sung that counts.

The most striking aspect of delivery in African American music is the incorporation of dance. While singing, particularly during moderato or spirited, up-tempo selections, singers move side to side together on beats 1 and 3 and clap on beats 2 and 4, following the cues of the leader. Although clapping and dancing are important parts of the African American worship experience, they should never assume dominance over the singing itself.

Facial expression is equally significant in communicating the message of both spirituals and gospel songs. Whether the eyes are open or closed, facial expression is a powerful tool in helping to convey the spiritual message of the song. Neither soloist, choir, director, not instrumentalist should hesitate to openly express the personal meaning the song holds. The face, hands, and feet are all tools that musicians must fully use to convey meaning.

9

CONTEMPORARY SONG

The term *contemporary music* has been used to describe a host of diverse worship music styles developed within the last forty years. Among others, contemporary music embraces folk, country, rock 'n' roll, praise, alternative, and the eclectic music of the post-Vatican II Roman Catholic tradition. While each of these styles stands as a musical genre in its own right—and some have numerous subgenres—all hold enough in common to come under the same umbrella of "contemporary" music. In particular, these genres share:

- a common emphasis on strong accented rhythm
- orally conceived melodies
- roots reaching back to African American spiritual and Appalachian folk traditions
- accompaniment styles based on the unique technical possibilities and limitations of the guitar

Contemporary music is also set apart from traditional music in that it is usually performed by an ensemble combination of keyboards, guitars, bass, drums, melody instruments, and vocalists.

In most cases, contemporary music for assembly singing is led by a praise band or worship team. These come in all sizes and shapes. The most typical configuration for a worship team consists of one or two keyboards, a rhythm and a lead guitar, a bass, a drum set, and several vocalists. Sometimes there may be one or two obbligato instruments as well. Below are the functions of each instrument and their relationship to the typical worship team as a whole.

Working with a Smaller Ensemble

Many congregations may find it difficult to find all the musicians that make up a typical worship team. This does not mean that you cannot make use of contemporary music; it just means that you need to be a little creative! The minimum ensemble necessary to lead contemporary music is one keyboardist or guitarist and one moderately-skilled singer. In many cases where there is a second keyboard player on hand (or a guitarist and a keyboard player), one person might play the piano (or guitar), while the other would play the synthesizer, where the left hand functions as the bass player and the right hand plays the melody. Since almost all synthesizers have the ability to divide their keyboards into two or more different types of sound, such as strategy can easily be accomplished. Add one or more people to play some simple hand percussion such as bongos and tambourine and your congregation has almost all the components of a typical praise team, just in a simplified form.

Keyboards and Pianos

There are three basic ways electronic keyboards (synthesizers) and pianos function within a typical worship team. The first is as a solo instrument reinforcing the melody along with the vocalists. In small ensembles with weak vocalists this is essential for effective leadership in congregational singing. When using a synthesizer, the most important thing to remember when choosing solo sounds is to make sure they fit with the character of the song as well as blend acoustically with the rest of the ensemble.

The second way keyboards and pianos function within a typical worship team is by providing a harmonic "pad" that serves as a foundation for the rest of the worship team.

A pad is usually a middle-range (centered around middle C) accompaniment of sustained or repeated chords, or a repeated pattern of arpeggios. This rounds out the team's sound and provides support for the vocalists and other solo instruments, such as lead guitar. The following example is intended for "Lord, I Lift Your Name on High" (#857):

The third way keyboards and pianos function within the team is by serving as a bass or rhythm instrument, alone or by doubling the lines of other bass and percussion instruments. In most worship teams keyboards and pianos serve in at least two of these capacities. In larger ensembles their role becomes simplified and more confined to avoid a cluttered and confusing sound.

The ideal keyboard player for a worship team is able not only to read music but to improvise as well, because most music scores for contemporary music consist of only melodies, words, and chords. If your keyboard players do not know how to improvise, it will be important that they be provided with opportunities to develop this skill.

Rhythm and Lead Guitars

Guitars have two primary functions within a worship team: providing harmonic foundation through strumming chords or picking (playing repeated arpeggiated patterns) and providing embellishment and ornamentation through different kinds of melodic lines.

When a guitar provides a harmonic foundation it is playing the role of rhythm guitar. This role is primarily one of undergirding and supporting the rest of the ensemble. When a guitar is filling the lead role, playing a melodic line, it may be:

- soloing out the melody to support the vocalist and assembly
- playing descants and counter melodies (fills) to increase musical interest
- playing improvised solos between verses or refrains

Again the function is support, no matter how predominant the instrument may be at any given time.

There are also two basic types of guitars; acoustic and electric. Acoustic guitars are more often found in bands that play more folk, country, and "unplugged" alternative styles, or music from contemporary Roman Catholic traditions. Electric guitars are found in ensembles that play more mainstream praise, rock 'n' roll, aggressive alternative, and pure jazz and blues. Guitarists with a high level of proficiency often have both at their side to increase their worship team's flexibility in presenting diverse musical styles. Both can fulfill the roles of lead and rhythm.

Guitarists must be able to play in tune and should also be able to perform the chords found in most contemporary music or be able to learn new chords quickly. When working with guitarists of lesser skill, more complex chords like $Amin^7$ and $Cmaj^7$ can be simplified to chords such as Amin and C.

Bass Guitar

The bass guitar comes in four-, five-, and six-string models. The four-string bass is most common in congregations. Four-string basses are tuned just like the bottom four strings of the guitar (E, A, D, G), except they sound one octave lower. Likewise, the bass sounds its notes one octave lower than the music written for it. Although a bass player may encounter written-out parts from time to time in more sophisticated music, he or she typically reads from the same lead sheet (melody and chord score) as the guitarist. Sometimes on such scores there will be chords with nonroot inversions as well as polychords. When this happens the bass player always plays the lowest note implied. For example, if the score reads CM^7/F, the guitarist and keyboard player may play the CM^7, but the bass player always plays the F. If playing from a keyboard score without such bass inversions, a bass player who can read music may follow the bass keyboard line.

Beyond this principal function, the bass commonly takes on two other roles: to work in consort with the drums in proving a rhythmic foundation for the worship team—often the bass will play the same rhythm as the kick (bass) drum; and to increase musical interest by improvising ostinato patterns throughout any given song. Occasionally the bass will be called on to play an extended melodic phrase. When that happens one of the keyboards will need to provide the foundation normally assigned to the bass.

Percussion

One of the most significant components of any worship team is the percussion section. The primary role of percussion is to provide rhythmic stability to music. At times this means holding the rest of the worship team back from rushing. At other times the team will need to be pushed so not to drag the tempo. Well-executed and reliable percussion also allows other members of the worship team to be rhythmically creative and flexible without risking instability or loss of momentum. This helps the assembly feel more confident in its singing, because the tempo remains comfortable and predictable. Within worship teams, the most common percussion section is a drum or trap set. Most drum sets consist of:

- *Bass (or kick) drum.* This acts as the cornerstone of the rhythmic ostinato patterns so common to contemporary music percussion. Usually it is played on beats one and three.
- *Snare drum.* This works in tandem with the bass drum to complete the rhythmic ostinato pattern. Usually it is played on beats two and four in $\frac{4}{4}$ time and on beats two and three in $\frac{3}{4}$ time. Metal wires under the bottom drum head cause the characteristic sharp white-noise sound associated with snare drums.
- *Mounted and floor toms.* These drums provide various kinds of rhythmic augmentation (fills) between phrases, periods, and other major sections. Often toms help signal the beginning or end of an introduction, verse, or refrain.
- *Cymbals.* Usually there are three kinds of cymbals used in a drum set: crash cymbal, ride cymbal, and hi-hat. The main job of the crash cymbal is to accent phrase

beginnings as well as underscore the major divisions within a given piece. Usually some kind of fill provided by the toms precedes such accents. On the other hand, both ride and hi-hat cymbals almost always play a constant ostinato pattern of quarter, eighth, or sixteenth notes. Whereas the crash cymbal and the bass and snare drums emphasize certain beats within a measure, the job of the ride and hi-hat cymbals is to bring out the rhythmic flow of a measure. This gives the listener a sense that the music is dynamic and moving beyond itself.

This example shows how bass drum, snare drum and cymbals would commonly combine in rhythmic patterns for $\frac{4}{4}$ and $\frac{3}{4}$ time:

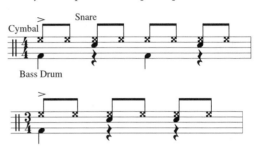

Other percussion instruments found in worship teams are those used in Latin and Afro-Caribbean music. These include:

- congas, timbales, bongos (drums of various sizes)
- claves (two wooden bars struck against each other)
- tambourines of various types
- guiros (hollowed-out gourds, notched on the sides and scraped by a stick)
- cowbells of various sizes
- maracas and other shakers
- finger cymbals

These can be used in combination with a drum set or alone. Often when a drum set is unavailable, one or more of these instruments can provide the rhythmic pulse and stability so necessary for confident assembly singing.

Vocalists

The primary role of vocalists is to guide and support the assembly in its singing. This may be done by simple hand gestures or short instructions at the beginning of a song. But the most common way they accomplish this is by unison singing. Even in very large congregations where worship-team vocalists are at a professional level in their technique, almost seventy percent of what they do is unison singing. Now and then, when the congregation is confident with a particular song, the vocalists will add some simple harmonies to the melody. In some cases one of the sopranos or tenors may embellish a final refrain with an improvised descant.

Solo Instruments

Within a worship team, instruments such as trumpet, sax, violin, or flute perform much the same function as lead guitar. That is, they reinforce the melody, play descants and counter melodies, and improvise embellishments between verses and refrains. Many congregations have several moderately skilled musicians who play solo instruments. One of the best ways to introduce them to worship leadership—and to motivate them to improve their skill level—is to have them play simple, slow moving descants or counter melodies during one or two songs per service. This allows them a front door into your worship team while not sacrificing the overall quality of your team's sound.

Leading the Assembly

In traditional European worship music, the organist or pianist leads the assembly by main-taining a steady beat (tactus) throughout the hymn, as well as employing slight rhythmic articulations or lifts at the beginning of each verse or refrain. Much of this is present within contemporary music as well. That the entire ensemble keeps a steady beat is essential to the proper execution of all contemporary music styles. But the primary task of leading falls to the vocalists. Typically, vocalists on a worship team guide the assembly in three ways. The most obvious is by singing the melody. This is especially crucial in contemporary music where instruments such as piano and synthesizer are unable to articulate all the vocal embellishments so common to this genre. Vocalists also lead contemporary music by physically conducting the assembly through the use of small but clear hand gestures at the beginning of a song or after an extended interlude. Finally, vocalists lead with their breathing. An obvious breath right before an entrance makes it clear when the assembly should begin to sing.

Although not as central as the vocalists' role, the drummer also helps the congregation know where to sing. Usually the drummer will play fills (rhythmic augmentation) on the toms and/or cymbal crashes of various sorts right before the assembly needs to start singing. Together with the vocalists' leadership, these cues make it easy for the congregation to know when to begin singing.

INTRODUCTION TO GLOBAL MUSIC

Crossing into another's culture reminds us that we are all neighbors and that our church is truly a global church. Evangelical Lutheran Worship includes hymns and songs from many cultures and languages. But what does it take to truly sing another's song? How much do I need to understand about the performance practice of the original culture before I attempt it in my local context? What can I know of the cultural and theological background from which a song comes? When is it time to step into the waters and try to make music from another culture?

The chapters in this book that deal specifically with global music step into the waters of various cultures and describe how they might be applied in a North American context. The cultures represented here are not exhaustive; for example, no attention is given to music from the Middle East or to American Indian musical traditions. This is not because there is not a dynamic tradition of church music in those places. It merely reflects that music from those cultures is still making its way into our worship books and hymnals. We still have much to learn from many places, at home and around the globe. These chapters are a humble beginning to encourage our efforts to meet our neighbor, near and far, in the church's music.

When learning another's culture's music, we are not attempting to replicate a hymn's original context. In each local context, any hymn takes on its own life through its contextual presentation. That is as it should be. In order for any new hymn to become meaningful, it must become an expression of the community that sings it. But by learning what we can about another cultural context and by drawing connections between that context and our own, we can find entry points into a culture different from our own. The three chapters that follow point us to signs we can look for when we first approach a Latino, African, or Asian tune or text. They give us a glimpse of what to look for, and what we might want to know in order to sing it. These are some of the clues that can equip willing musicians for trying music that may be new to them.

In sharing one another's music, we share more than music. Music of various cultures brings us a glimpse of one another's experience of God. As any culture connects its experience of the holy to its music, a unique context for God's presence is created—we experience together the way God weaves a varied, diverse tapestry of revelation among us. The church's song is a great place to experience this sharing. Step in. The water's fine.

10

LATINO/HISPANIC SONG

Because the designation Hispanic or Latino includes such a broad spectrum of peoples, traditions, cultures, and cross influences, it is difficult to speak of Latino music as a generic whole. Latino music is, in fact, extraordinarily diverse: the mariachi tradition of Mexico, the Tejano of southern Texas, the Afro-Cuban tradition with its multi-layered rhythms, the Dominican merengue, the Caribbean calypso, the ethereal sound of Andean pipes from Peru and Ecuador, the influence of dances like the tango in the music of Argentina, the flamenco of Spain, the fado of Portugal, and the cross-pollination of it all that takes place in geographically central places like Costa Rica.

This resource is not exhaustive for all these different styles. Rather, it offers a place to begin. For many, simply playing the *Evangelical Lutheran Worship* accompaniment on the piano, as printed, with the addition of one or two percussion instruments, may be plenty. Using the guitar edition of *Evangelical Lutheran Worship* for chords, guitarists can use the patterns suggested here as their place to begin. As skills develop, some may get more daring and try some of the more complex ideas, including many beyond the scope of this resource. Whatever is used, always remember that leading music for worship is primarily about enabling the assembly to sing. Make sure any accompaniment used is confident, consistent, and clear.

Note: In most cases, the standard keyboard edition can be used with the guitar chords in the guitar edition. However, the chords in the guitar edition will always match the keyboard parts in the simplified keyboard edition.

Rhythm

Rhythm is of primary importance when leading Latino music. However, it does not serve or show respect for people or their music when instruments are simply thrust into peoples' hands and they are asked to play. If this music is new to us, we may not get it all perfect right away, but it is important that the rhythms and styles be studied and rehearsed.

Begin simply. Start perhaps with only one percussion instrument, then two, three, and more. Not all percussion instruments need to play all the time. Faster tempos do not always require more percussion.

Some gentle layered rhythmic patterns may require more instruments (egg shakers and hand drum on a delicate waltz, for example) to accompany melodies cast in slower tempos.

A table of rhythmic possibilities appears on pages 66–67. It contains suggested rhythms and bass lines that can be adapted for use in leading many of the songs in *Evangelical Lutheran Worship* from these genres. Some of these rhythmic notations are written for guitar, some for piano, some for both. In cases where percussion suggestions are not given, the rhythms of the piano or guitar can be translated to various percussion instruments as well.

Certain songs are readily identified with specific rhythmic or dance forms. Other songs lend themselves to a variety of rhythms. In this resource, many individual pieces from these genres have one or two of these rhythmic possibilities suggested. However, a common practice among Latino musicians is to change the rhythmic pattern, hence the very character of the piece, perhaps even in the course of singing the song. Therefore, the suggestions in this resource are starting points; they are not the only way to lead a particular song.

This is a concept of freedom that many musicians find both surprising and challenging. It is not common for most non-Latino church musicians to take a piece written in $\frac{4}{4}$ meter and adapt it to another rhythmic structure. Latino musicians do this all the time, often employing various rhythmic structures in the course of several stanzas. Another example of this, mentioned in the African American chapter, is playing hymns that are printed in $\frac{4}{4}$ (especially those from the white spiritual and revival traditions) in a $\frac{12}{8}$ meter with a swing.

For songs that have no rhythmic suggestions, it may be best to simply use the printed accompaniment with little or no percussion added.

For many styles, it is critical to understand a basic three-against-two pattern. For any musician who has never attempted this it may be a struggle at first. Once mastered, however, it becomes a natural part of interpreting much of this music.

Imagine a melody written in $\frac{6}{8}$, which usually moves ahead in two groupings of three notes in each measure:

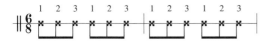

Now divide those six beats into three groups of two:

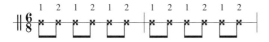

Now try these two rhythms *at the same time*, sounding the accents clearly. It may be easier to begin this with two different people or groups. Eventually, an individual will want to be able to do them both at the same time:

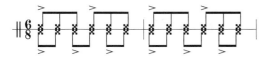

The example below shows a simple application of this two-against-three rhythm applied to CANTAD AL SEÑOR (#822). Notice that the melody moves with three beats to the bar (in this case in a $\frac{3}{4}$ meter), with the bass line moving in steady dotted quarters (two in a bar). This example also shows how percussion (in this example, claves) can be used to reinforce the "two" pattern while the cowbell plays on the downbeat of every other measure, accenting

the primary rhythm and phrases. The suggested guitar pattern (steady up-down) on eighth-note pulses supports the "three" pattern. Notice the small x in the guitar pattern on beat three. This symbol indicates a percussive string hit. Adding it on beat three of each bar adds yet another layer of rhythmic interest. Remember, you don't need to add all of this at once!

*↓ downward strum

↑ upward strum

↓̆ downward percussive string hit

In several of the examples below you will see this layering shown by the presence of both $\frac{6}{8}$ and $\frac{3}{4}$ meter signatures in the same example, often on the same system. Sometimes the rhythms shift between the two patterns; sometimes the melody is in one meter (which you won't see in these examples) while accompanying instruments (piano, guitar, or percussion) may be playing in the other (or both!).

A SAMPLING OF RHYTHMIC PATTERNS

Note: A bombo legüero is a type of drum originating in South America, fashioned from a hollowed section of tree trunk, with heads made from skins with the fur left on. It is played with sticks, alternating between striking the head and the wooden rim. A large muffled field drum would be a fair substitute.

1 Balada

2 Bolero

3 Bolero/ranchero

4 Calypso

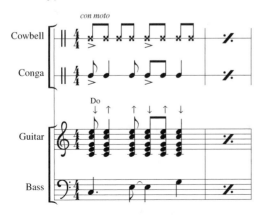

5 Carnavalito

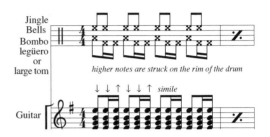

6 Corrido/polka

7 Cueca

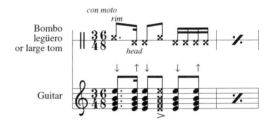

8 Danza

9 Danzón

10 Guaracha

Guitar

Bass
(opt.)

11 Huapango

12 Vals

13 Zamba

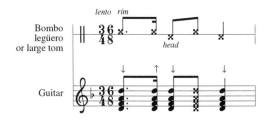

Bombo
legüero
or large tom

Guitar

14 Son centro americano

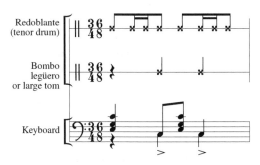

Redoblante
(tenor drum)

Bombo
legüero
or large tom

Keyboard

See *Libro de Liturgia y Cántico,* pages 627–639, for more examples.

Melody and Harmony

You'll notice that most of these tunes are presented in the pew edition with melody only. That tells us the importance of the melody. However, that doesn't mean that sung harmony is inappropriate. Some have singable harmonies that are integral to the song, such as "Glory to God, Glory in the Highest" (#164). It is also common for simple harmonies to be added (improvised) freely. As the assembly becomes more familiar with the melody, there may be some improvisation or enrichment of the melodic line, usually with parallel harmony moving along below or above the melody in thirds. For example, see TOMA MI VOLUNTAD (#583).

Many of these tunes include a refrain (*estribillo*). For assemblies just beginning to sing in these styles, it is a helpful practice to teach only the refrain at first, leaving the verses to soloist, choir, or band.

Keyboard

Most Latin American pianists think of their instrument as a percussion instrument. When accompanying a song or hymn the pianist generally does not play the melody line, leaving it to another instrument (flute, violin, trumpet, accordion) or strong vocalists. By doing this the pianist is able to achieve a strong rhythmic effect, the left hand playing the bass line (sometimes doubling it in octaves), the right hand playing chords on nonaccented beats, perhaps using patterns derived from the rhythm charts on the preceding pages transposed to the appropriate key. In this way the keyboard player becomes a part of the percussion section and drives the beat, thereby providing rhythmic leadership.

It is common for the pianist or other keyboard player to employ the concept of rhythmic "theme and variations" in the course of the execution of a song. This adds spice and interest to repeated sung stanzas and estribillos (refrains). The ability to adapt the printed accompaniment (when one is provided) by substituting rhythmic patterns depends on the keyboard player's ability to learn standard accompanying styles, such as those just listed, and transpose them to the specific key and chord structure of a given piece. This is much like following a chord chart comprised of melody line and chord names above to indicate where chord changes occur. The keyboard player becomes familiar with the desired rhythmic pattern and adapts it to each of the chord changes as the song progresses. This is, in fact, the way virtually all Latin American keyboardists play these tunes. Keyboard players who learn to do this confidently may find it helpful to play from the guitar edition rather than the keyboard accompaniment edition.

Guitar

Perhaps the greatest musical contribution of Spain to Latin America is the classical-style flamenco guitar. Impassioned flamenco technique includes strumming in a fan pattern (using all fingers across the strings, which may be employed in both directions), tapping the bottom of the instrument, and striking the fingerboard to produce percussive sounds. While this is most appropriate for solo performances, the style, combined with rhythmic forms like the cha cha, the polka, and other dances, has had a profound effect on the music of Latino culture in general.

The guitarist usually employs a mixture of different types of strumming (either up or down) as well as picking (a single note), striking the strings, and striking then holding for a percussive muting effect. Also, Latino musicians take advantage of various possibilities arising from the material with which their guitars are strung, whether nylon or steel. An upward strum on a steel-string guitar has a far different (brighter, crisper, more percussive) sound than the same movement on a guitar with nylon strings.

Other Instruments

There is no one authentic instrumentation to perform Latino music as a whole. The availability of instruments and musicians who can play them is certainly a place to begin. The creativity of a single musician or a group of instrumentalists working together can lead to a variety of possibilities as is often the case with Latino groups themselves. A solo guitar or piano can prove quite adequate in many cases. Percussion and solo instruments add variety and color. Common bands in the polka tradition consist of keyboards, trap set, brass, woodwinds, bass, and accordion. Other instrumental groups might consist of guitar, fiddle, mandolin, and various percussion instruments. The possibilities are endless. Group singing may be facilitated by a group of individual singers or soloist singing various stanzas. But in the end it's always the people's song.

Language

The use of the original Spanish certainly lends authenticity to these pieces. However, many worshiping communities may be unable to join in singing Spanish for the entire song. They may, however, find it possible and enriching to sing a short refrain in Spanish. It's important for them to know what they are singing, so be certain to point out the English translations in *Evangelical Lutheran Worship*. This works particularly well with many Latino songs, since refrains are a common element. Some interesting bilingual combinations might prove satisfying and even fun. The assembly might sing the refrain in Spanish and the stanzas in English. Songs like "When the Poor Ones/*Cuando el pobre*" (#725), and "Oh, Sing to God Above/*Cantemos al Señor*" (#555), are often done in this way. Another possibility is to have a soloist or choir sing the stanzas in Spanish and the assembly the refrain also in Spanish, or some other combination.

Why should primarily English-speaking congregations sing Latino music, or, for that matter, any music in another language or from a different culture? Music reflects culture. Language reflects culture and the thought processes that have given birth to that culture. The experience of singing another's song, of letting images, by means of words, pass though both mind and body, is a unifying experience for the whole people of God. The sensation of forming the words of another's language binds us together as a people of God. In singing together, in sharing our songs and our insights, we broaden who we ourselves are. We broaden our understanding of one another and our understanding of God.

Applying the Rhythmic Patterns

To get an idea of some performance possibilities, begin with an easy pattern. When a guitarist is accompanying a polka (see Corrido, pattern 6) or a waltz (see Vals, pattern 12), the downbeat (bass, root of the chord) is played with either the thumb (on a nylon-string classical guitar) or a pick (on a steel-string guitar). The two weaker after-beats are comprised of descending strummed chords—which might also be recognized as a basic bluegrass accompaniment.

The same effect can also be achieved on a keyboard. The strong downbeat might be played in a low octave, with the after-beats in right hand treble clef chords (in root position or first/second inversion). See the printed accompaniment for VAMOS TODOS AL BANQUETE (#523) for an example. With an electronic keyboard, it might by possible to use a string bass sound in the left hand while experimenting with different sounds for the right.

See how this would work with CANTAD AL SEÑOR (#822), played as a waltz (vals):

This song may also be led as a *bolero ranchero* by simply changing the rhythmic pattern in the accompaniment edition to the one shown below. Latino musicians often make use of a simple duple rhythm (*corrido* or polka) on the stanzas, and a brighter structure (*bolero ranchero*) on the refrain. Note that this is an example of a song being transformed from a triple to duple meter; such transformations are common in this genre:

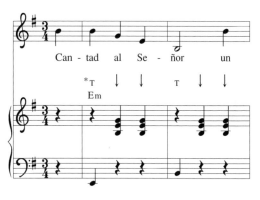

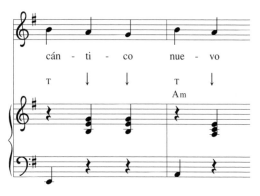

* Thumb (or pick) bass note
↓ - downward strum

Still using CANTAD AL SEÑOR as an example, consider some further possibilities. In the accompaniment edition there is a simple, bare-bones accompaniment that includes none of the rhythmic possibilities beyond the basic "three" in the melody. The example on page 65 showed a basic application of the two-against-three layered rhythms. This song could also be played as a modified zamba (notated in $\frac{6}{8}$):

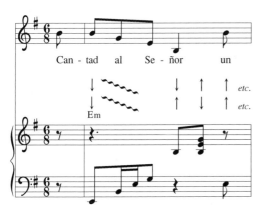

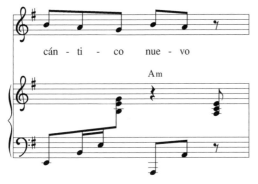

*↓ downward strum

⌇ downward finger fan from beat 2 through beat 3.

. . . or even casting it into a $\frac{4}{4}$ rhythm as a modified guaracha simplificada:

*↓ downward strum

↑ downward strum

⌇ downward finger fan from beat 2 through beat 3.

As you can see, the possibilities go on and on, and a lot of creative adaptation can and needs to happen to apply a particular stylistic pattern to a specific piece of music. Begin simply, but be bold. Just try it! In this type of music, virtuosity is experienced not in the fluency of the keyboard player but rather in the instrumentation and layering of it, the improvisation of bass lines, guitar runs, little keyboard or accordion flourishes (such as trilling the notes of a chord), and two- and three-part simple vocal harmonization. But these elements are frosting on a cake that suffices without additional toppings.

11

AFRICAN SONG

Performance Practice

Three steps might be helpful for North American congregations to best enter into the wealth of African sacred music: know the text, know the music, and join the heartbeat.

Know the Text. To know the text usually means to memorize it, especially the refrains. Such memorization frees one from books for clapping and other movements. But to know the text also means to know something about it. Despite our warnings about generalizations, some are here offered. Commonly across Africa, songs intended for group singing are arranged in what is known as the call/response form. There are four variations of this process:

- A solo or small group singing through an entire strophe of a song, and then the whole group repeats it. See, for example, "Hallelujah! We Sing Your Praises/*Haleluya! Pelo tsa rona*" (#535). Notice the repeat signs. This hymn was likely meant to be sung in this way.

- A single phrase is sung first by a leader, then repeated by all, as in "Come, Let Us Eat" (#491), similar to the "lining out" technique sometimes used to teach an unfamiliar song.

- A lead singer begins a phrase, and after a few notes the others join in. For an example see "Listen, God Is Calling/*Neno lake Mungu*" (#513).

- A lead singer, or singers, sings simultaneously with the others, though with different text and/or music, creating a kind of descant (a form that is rare in hymns but prevalent in choral music).

When African hymns are sung using the call/response form, the leader or leaders might sing without vocal or instrumental accompaniment, so that the responsive character of the hymn (unison/harmony) is made clear. One rhythm instrument might play to keep

Typically, Western, classically trained musicians read the page of written music and turn it into a musical event. There is, of course, another way: the way by which most Africans still learn and pass on their music, and that is the aural-oral method by which one sings or plays back what one first hears. This method assumes freedom in delivery and invites improvisation, two key characteristics of African song.

Because of this aural-oral tradition, it is impossible both to create "definitive" editions or make stringent pronouncements about performance practice. For example, a hymn such as "Gracious Spirit, Heed Our Pleading/*Njoo kwetu, Roho mwema*" (#401) likely began its life as a unison song, but may have been given improvised harmony soon after its inception. Nowadays it may be presented with complex parts for rattles, bell, and drums.

Sometimes the printed harmonization of these songs is more complex than what one would hear in African parish settings. The complexity and sophistication of church music from the African continent often comes in layered rhythms, in both voices and percussion instruments. While local characteristics and differentiations are noticeable to the expert, the repertoire of sub-Saharan African hymns available to the average Western assembly, when taken as a whole, comprise a body of music that is quite homogenous. Texts, especially in translation, are poetically simple and display a theological clarity that is biblically rooted, compelling, anchored in experience—and in many ways strikingly similar to early Lutheran chorales.

the motion going. Note that the call/response form permits easy memorization of the song by most people. It also further brings to life the pattern of dialogue inherent in all liturgy, indeed to the nature of the church.

For a case study in knowing the text, let's look at "Christ Has Arisen, Alleluia/*Mfurahini, haleluya*" (#364). The original text was written by Bernard Kyamanywa from Tanzania and translated by Howard S. Olson, a missionary from the United States. This text selects scriptural commentary on the resurrection and puts it into the mouth of an Easter angel (stanzas 3 and 4). To surround that message the poet offers a general Easter pronouncement and an exhortation to praise. Each stanza then ends with an outburst of praise. With that the hymn takes its rightful place alongside the texts of Luther and Watts, for a pattern common to all these hymns is the simple but bold proclamation of the gospel, which prompts expressions of praise. To praise God means first of all to know and rehearse what God does.

Each stanza of the hymn ends with the refrain. The form suggests that the first page (the stanza) be sung by a soloist or by a female-male duet in octaves. In either case this should happen without accompaniment other than perhaps light percussion. By having leaders sing the verses, only they need the text. The goal is that all others then would sing the refrain from memory. Strong, convincing, bold voices are needed to deliver the leader part.

Know the Music. Melodies for African hymns come from a variety of sources. Some are newly composed in a Western style. Others are newly composed in an African style, and still others are versions of folk melodies that have been transmitted via aural-oral tradition. Most harmonizations have been added to please Western ears or to honor the European harmonic tradition.

Again using "Christ Has Arisen, Alleluia/ *Mfurahini, haleluya*" (#364) as an example, we see that the form of the melody is AABA. Half of the refrain is sung two times by the leader before the people sing. Repetition is at the heart of African people's music.

While keyboards are also used in Africa to help the people sing and are useful here to teach

both melody and harmony, hymns like this are meant to be sung without melodic or harmonic accompaniment. Note how the structure makes such a task quite easy if a leader alone sings the stanza. For the refrain the people can sing the tune or add the harmony as indicated.

Join the Heartbeat. It is said that rhythm in Africa is closely linked to speech, language, signaling, and dance. Since Africans dance their identity as it relates to all of life, rhythm is therefore at the heart of existence. This brings the discussion to a core understanding about African music: *it takes at least two rhythms to bring a piece of music to life.* Traditionally, the layering of rhythms was accomplished by the addition of more people. Hence, rhythm by definition includes at least two people. You need community to make music.

The density or complexity of layered rhythms is sometimes constructed or recognized by differentiating among those rhythms that are slow, moderately fast, and fast. Inside these three groups is an underlying pulse, usually signified or implied by the moderately fast rhythmic layer. This would be a good rhythm to bring out by hand clapping.

To illustrate how the layering of rhythms works and functions as the heartbeat of the music, we again look at "*Mfurahini, haleluya*" (#364). Rhythm is at the heart of this music. The Haya people, from whom this hymn comes, live life rhythmically and understand the drum to be the voice of ancestral and royal wisdom. The music cries out for rhythm instruments, all the more so since these instruments will keep the music going in the absence of keyboard.

When this kind of music is performed in Africa, rhythm instruments usually begin first, the lowest drum (if more than one) setting the pace. In the same way, these instruments sometimes go beyond the vocal conclusion to add a kind of coda.

Pulse for hymns of this kind is related to normal heartbeat (here, ♩. = 56–62) and comprises an entire measure. Quarter notes should be felt as subdivisions of the pulse.

Though at least two rhythms are needed to bring a piece to life, in theory there is no upward limit. The example below shows a minimal approach, with the large drum playing the fundamental pulse and the smaller drum playing the smaller pulse:

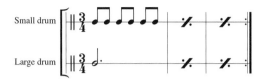

With the large drum keeping the downbeat strong, a slightly more complex rhythmic combination could be:

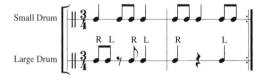

Additional instruments can be layered, adding various rhythmic textures, with the downbeat of each bar still prominent (notice the added hand clapping on the downbeat). In this example the cowbell is playing a duple rhythm (two steady pulses in a bar) against the triple meter:

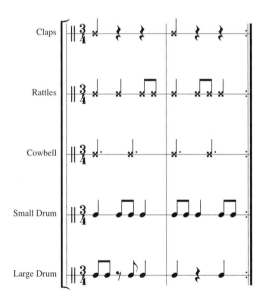

You'll notice that this is a pattern that repeats every two bars. As players become more skilled, the patterns may become four or even six bars long. Here is an example of a four-bar pattern:

In this example, notice that the large drum, in addition to always playing on the downbeat, is adding an accent on the second beat of measures 1 and 3, adding yet another layer of rhythm.

Slow patterns, such as that for the bell above, are almost like a drone and generally introduce a contrary rhythm of some sort (here, two against three). The fast patterns are subject to improvisation, which partly obliterates the sameness of repetition, making the entire rhythmic presentation an evolving experience.

Theoretically, just as the community always makes room for another individual, any piece of music with layered rhythms can always make room for another rhythm. Sometimes this is achieved, in more complex situations, by the introduction of "apart playing." That is, another drummer might take the rhythm assigned to the large drum and play it beginning one pulse later. This is not suggested for beginners.

The use of drum sets and drum machines contradict the foundation of African rhythmic purpose, for they ignore the importance of the individual in rhythmic compilation and make no room for a "community of heartbeats."

In one sense rhythms are understood to exist from eternity, that is, they are thought to be always sounding somewhere. Their incarnation at any given time or place means simply that this group is joining the rhythm for awhile, only to disengage until another opportunity for its incarnation comes around. There are deep connections to the wider community of ancestors (or communion of saints) in this approach to rhythm.

There are also implications for performance. Typically the rhythm instruments begin a piece, usually one by one, before the voices commence. Once everyone is engaged in the ensemble's praise, the rhythms and tempo continue onward without alteration, that is, without ritards or fermatas. At the conclusion, rhythm instruments trail off one by one after the voices have concluded their participation, or some "tag" formula fills the last measure of the piece, leading to a single strong pulse on the first beat of the next measure—a kind of farewell to the rhythm.

Instruments

While stringed and wind instruments are common in most parts of Africa, their use in African church music is rare, though theoretically welcomed. Should someone with expertise on these instruments (or perhaps even Western equivalents) be available, the melodies of the African songs could be reinforced or embellished with one of these instruments.

Instruments such as gourd rattles, other shakers, bells, or xylophones are common in all parts of Africa and are used in African church music. Many varieties of drums are used all over Africa, through their relative importance in local music varies from one ethnic group to another.

African inventiveness shows up in the variety of designs for drums: slit drums made from hollowed-out logs, drums with a single head, drums with double heads, hourglass-shaped drums that change pitch as the head is stretched tight, and sets of drums that parallel family structure. Symbolism of drums is profound among certain peoples.

Issues abound here as Western church musicians in the European American tradition seek to bring African church music off the page into actual praise. If you want to try for a more authentic sound, you can purchase shakers and rattles in African specialty shops scattered across North America. You should know, though, that their origin may be uncertain. What difference does it make whether one uses drums and rattles made by professional drum makers from Africa, instruments from a local supplier, or equivalents? Probably very little. Congas of various sizes work well, as do some of the deeper "toms" of drum sets. In any case it is useful to remember that African drummers play with and without sticks. Rattles from a specialty shop serve well, as do maracas—a Latin American version of rattles. African double bells are plentiful in well-equipped percussion shops, and a set of claves can be substituted for the bells.

The use of genuine African instruments brings the experience of African church music a little closer to its origins. But such concerns are ultimately peripheral. Of more importance to the spirit of African church music is the distribution of the rhythmic parts among several people, for the layering of individual parts is a deliberate manifestation of relationship within the community and a sign of the bonds rhythm creates even across cultures.

Leadership

It is worth stressing again that African church music is vocal and essentially unrelated to the keyboard. Therefore leadership from the keyboard is uncharacteristic and tends to rob the music of its charm.

How then does this music come into being? First, at least one percussion instrument makes it possible to maintain tempo and to offer a rhythm complementary to, but different from, the rhythm of the song. Like a master drummer, the church musician would be the obvious person to play and lead the percussion. Second, a rehearsed group of singers should be placed close enough to the people to provide leadership as well as harmony. Beyond these suggestions, let it be known that the hands are to be understood as a primary percussion instrument, and people should be invited to enter the clap patterns of the songs.

Not all songs require percussion. Some, in a more Western lyrical style, can be sung like conventional hymnody. But even these songs fare best when they are supported by a choral group alert to keeping the tempo moving.

If necessary, the keyboard (preferably piano, because of its percussive qualities) could be used to support and encourage the singing of the people. The goal in such cases would be to wean the people away from such dependence as quickly as possible.

Entering into African church music provides an opportunity for church musicians, choral groups, and the Christian assembly to discover for the first time, or again, the way musical presentation can be a manifestation of the baptismal community. Africans offer the rest of the church challenge: *Christian community means that everyone participates; no one can just sit and listen.*

12

ASIAN SONG

melody and text alone may constitute a hymn's delivery.

It is important to understand that the written notation is often a transcription from an oral tradition. In some cases, Asian hymn tunes are adapted from folk and traditional songs of a country or region. While these melodies are presented in Western written notation, the original tunes are not always based on a twelve-note chromatic scale. Pentatonic scales and equidistant five- and seven-notes scales are only some of the varieties of scales found in various Asian regions. Traditional Asian melodies use intervals of various sizes, including some larger and some smaller than major or minor seconds or thirds of Western music. Such variations cannot be represented in standard Western notation. In capturing a melody in a written form and presenting it in Western notation, some of the rhythmic and melodic subtleties are lost. It is important to see the score as a reflection, not a perfect representation, of an Asian song.

Being certain that the melody is clear is critical for most Asian music. Singing the melody alone focuses on its beauty. It also signals the importance of the relationship between text and tune. Even though the connection with tonal language is lost when sung in English, a single-line melody allows for focus on the text without other complicating musical factors.

"Lord, Your Hands Have Formed" (GAYOM NI HIGAMI, #554) exemplifies the cyclic nature of many Asian melodies and how text and tune are intimately wedded. The piece begins and ends with the melodic fragment A-B-D. From this low A, the melody rises to Fs, then A, then finally reaches the D, an octave and a fourth above the starting note. From this high midpoint the melody begins its decent, pausing briefly on A, then D, and finally repeating the opening A-B-D motive. This rising and falling motion of the melody also creates the tension

Asia is a group of regions and countries with greatly diverse musical cultures. The church music of Asia is as broad and diverse as the region. It includes the complex and simple; the traditional and newly composed; unaccompanied song and that incorporating the sound of flute, plucked strings, drums, cymbals, and more. From the complex raga of India to the simple beauty of Taiwanese pentatonic melody, there is wide melodic expression. From the multi-layered sound of a gamelan orchestra to the singular beauty of the bamboo flute, there is a wealth of timbre. While there are trends and values that tend to recur in music of many Asian countries, it is important not to overgeneralize or apply musical principles randomly from one region to another.

In looking at an Asian text with an Asian tune, it is important to consider the relationship between them. In many cases there is a particularly close connection between Asian speech and song, and it is a key to the performance of this music. One will frequently notice a deliberate holding back of musical language and resources, a spareness that helps to heighten attention to the present moment. This music is a fresh addition to many congregations' repertoires and can greatly enrich worship when presented with sensitivity.

Melody and Text

When approaching an Asian hymn, melody is of primary importance and demands first consideration. This emphasis comes through in timbre, melodic shapes, and subtle ornaments. Melody is the building block upon which other musical elements may be added. Sometimes

and release that the voice naturally follows. As the melody descends, the voice relaxes. The melody ends as it begins, in repose, in the lower register of the voice.

The images in the text convey a movement similar to the melody. "Water tumbling over rocks," "sprouting blossoms, crops and buds" seem to be musically depicted in the melody's rising and falling. This text shows a God who participates in the work of creation with human hands. The image of God rolling out the land like a mat would be a familiar one in traditional Asian homes where parents roll out mats each evening for their children. This loving human action is like God's divine action in creating the land for all humans. Describing this hymn, Francisco Feliciano likens this kind of musical phrase to a bird that comes to rest on a branch. The branch bends as the bird lights upon it, then comes to rest. Then the bird flies on to another branch.

Vocal Ornaments

Some Asian melodies require a vocal slide. Consider the third full bar of "Lord, Your Hands Have Formed" (GAYOM NI HIGAMI, #554) where there is what appears to be a grace note. It's actually an indication that the singer *slides* from the small note to the larger one during the duration of the quarter note. The syllable changes as the slide to the second note begins. These ornaments have the effect of softening the rhythmic pulse. Unlike music from other parts of the globe, here the pulse does not drive the melody. Rhythm rather becomes responsive to the slight changes in time that the ornaments naturally create.

Vocal Range

Many Asian hymns employ a vocal range of well over an octave. Such a large range may at first appear to be a block for a congregation accustomed to melodies that lie within the octave. However, if the piece is learned in melodic units, a phrase at a time, with the high points noted, assemblies may be surprised to find that the melodies are quite accessible. Led to the high point in a melody, a congregation can learn to build intensity and release into its singing style. In this process they will also learn about the construction and delivery of an Asian vocal line.

Harmony

When Western-trained musicians approach Asian music, there is a tendency to overlay Western harmonic patterns on an Asian melody. Harmony is not necessarily implied for an Asian tune, and functional Western harmony is even less frequently implied. By adding a chordal structure to an Asian melody, a Western musician may set up a harmonic form to the tune that was not originally intended. Unison, octave doubling, or open intervals more often characterize accompanying lines than does a chordal structure.

There are exceptions, however. Consider "Come Now, O Prince of Peace/*Ososŏ, ososŏ*" (ososŏ, #247). The printed harmony was original to the tune which, when possible, should be sung in harmony, ideally without keyboard accompaniment.

Instrumentation

Gongs, ching (small cymbals similar to finger cymbals), and larger cymbals are often used in Asian melodies for rhythmic color. Such sounds give the impression of rhythmic points of light, which punctuate the melodic line. Rather than adding a rhythmic accent on a downbeat, a gong or ching might be added at the end of a phrase or between two phrases, as a sort of interspersed timbre. For example, see "Golden Breaks the Dawn/*Qing zao qilai kan*" (LE P'ING, #852). A finger cymbal or triangle could be sounded after the half and whole notes; a larger gong could be sounded at the beginning and end of the melody. Such a technique is used in a gamelan orchestra, where the large gong signals a return to the beginning of the melody.

Other instruments may be added to an Asian melody. The bamboo flute is found in many forms throughout Asia. It is most commonly found as a transverse flute, with the blow-hole about one third of the way along its body. The bamboo flute has a distinct and beautiful tone color. The sound is reedier than the Western flute and less breathy than a recorder. However, either a recorder or flute would be an adequate substitute and an appropriate way to introduce or accompany many Asian melodies.

A Chinese instrument called the *erh-hu* is a two-string instrument played like a cello. Its range is similar to the viola, and its sound has a stronger presence than the viola. The erh-hu is often used to play the melody in the tenor range as an accompaniment to the melody. The viola or cello could be an acceptable substitute for the erh-hu. The advantage of a stringed instrument for Asian song is the possibility of showing the slides and lengthened grace notes that the vocal character often demands.

A guitar or—odd as it may seem—a banjo may sometimes function well as an accompanying instrument. A banjo comes reasonably close to the sound of the Japanese shamisen, among other instruments. A guitar can replicate the sound color of a plucked lute with a picking, rather than strumming, style. The Philippine hymn "When Twilight Comes" (#566), to the tune DAPIT HAPON, is an example of Asian song that could be accompanied well with guitar. It was originally composed for two guitars, one strummed while the other is plucked. The effect of that accompaniment is an undulating, undergirding support for the melody. Such an accompaniment does not obscure the melody but allows it to continue to take a leading place in the sound. For this hymn the addition of an instrument to double the melody would be helpful to reinforce assembly singing. A flute or stringed instrument could play the melodic line above the guitars. A song leader could also facilitate leading the melody for the congregation.

Piano and organ are not the best choice for leading Asian song. The keyboard is unable to render many of the subtleties of this song, especially the ornaments and slides. It also presents the temptation to add a Western harmonic structure as a left-hand accompaniment. When a keyboard is the only choice, use it sparingly as a melodic instrument, if needed,

adding a subtle pulse that will help keep an assembly together without becoming rhythmically driving. The accompaniment should always allow for the flexibility and dominance of the vocal line.

Some suggestions when using the piano or organ with an Asian melody:

- Use the right hand to lead the melody. Try the melody an octave higher on the piano for variety. On the organ, try various solo stops. Try a 4' flute only on the melody.
- Use the left hand (and pedal on the organ) sparingly. Less can be more here. Open fifths, repeated and varied slightly at a slow rhythmic pulse (even half note or whole note), may be enough to undergird the melody.
- Avoid harmonies that form a Western harmonic progression (for example, I–IV–V–I). Leave harmonies open. Use open fourths and fifths rather than complete triads.
- Let the piano be a strictly melodic instrument at times, doubling the melody. It isn't always necessary to add any harmony.

As North Americans begin encountering Asian hymnody, surprises await the guest. Here is the beauty of attention to the spareness heard in the beauty of the bamboo flute; there is the sound of the *ching* punctuating the end of the vocal phrase. Here is the notion of the human connection to all of creation; there is the plaintive call of the Kyrie. The landscape of Asian song offers to North Americans new sounds and new texts of peoples rooted in Jesus Christ, expressed through an Asian context. As we North Americans put on our Asian sandals we open ourselves to receive the hospitality of Christians from across the globe. We experience our unity in diversity as we find praises of the same God in others' cultural expressions. As we marvel at the diversity of God's creation we open ourselves to the variety of ways God works through all cultures and peoples. These diverse songs reflect a common theme: *praises of the God made known to us in Jesus Christ.*

AFTERWORD

So many ways of singing a new song to the Lord! We parish musicians read a book like this and become inspired to broaden the scope of song in our congregation. But then we remember what it's really like on Sunday morning. We remember the comments, the looks accompanying the smallest of changes. It takes so much work and can be so draining of the spirit to lead the song in new directions. And people are seemingly comfortable with the status quo, so why not take the easy way out?

But consider your calling. You are a leader of the church's song—in this particular place and time, to be sure, but are these parishioners well served by being limited to only a tiny fragment of the loaf that is the body of Christ in all times and places? Don't they deserve—even if they don't know what they are missing—to encounter the unfamiliar spices of "ethnic" song, the transcendence of chant, the immediacy of contemporary song? Is it not worthwhile to take a fresh look even at familiar hymnody?

Yes, it is worth the effort, the looks, the comments. But how do we put it into practice? Look again at the beginning of this book—many valuable ideas there can help you get started. And then, prepare . . . practice . . . present.

Prepare. If you just throw something new at an unprepared congregation, it will fail, and they will resent it and you. Instead, help them get ready to receive something new. Whatever the genre you are introducing, get it into their ears ahead of time. Use it as prelude, voluntary material, or during communion. You might play recordings during Sunday school and adult forums—maybe even do a presentation about music from that time or place. By all means, have the choir sing the music for the congregation before the congregation tries to do it. Then some people, at least, will be looking forward to trying out that new song for themselves.

Practice. Another formula for disaster is to lead the song—any song—when the leaders aren't ready. If they are fumbling around, the message that is communicated is "This music is too hard for them—it must be way beyond me!" So make sure that you and the choir, and any instrumentalists involved, are absolutely secure. And that means going over it as many times as necessary, making the rough places plain—you know the routine. Then when you stand up to lead the song, the congregation will sense your ease, and they will think, "This doesn't seem so hard!" And it isn't.

Present. Give careful thought to the manner in which the new song will be done. Give the people as much help as you can, in the form of words and music, support from the choir, and leadership. Many songs from around the world take the form of call and response—and there's a lesson there for us. Musically, ours is a largely illiterate society, so if the leaders can sing the music and have the people immediately repeat it, the chances of success are greatly enhanced. Where that is more difficult to do (e.g., chant), have the choir—so the congregation can hear a group of voices—sing a stanza or, better, two, and then help them find their own voice in the song. It will be halting at first. Remember that any new song needs to "pitch a tent" among the people for a few weeks between repetitions. Don't throw too much new music at the people at one time. All these are common-sense suggestions, but we need reminders from time to time.

Most of the decisions regarding how the church's song is led in your congregation are ones that you—and other members of the worship leadership—are best equipped to make. Must you segregate each genre into a separate service? In most cases, no. In fact, the people will gain a better sense of the inclusive household of God if they sing various styles within one service. Yet it is undeniable that some abrupt transition from one type of song to another can be jarring. Your judgment is called into play. With music from African, Asian, or Latino traditions, must the accompaniment be authentic, or is it more important that the song be heard, however it is presented? Within those boundaries, you must make the nuanced decision of how much effort to put into letting the song appear in its native garb.

Questions continue: How much weight do we give to lectionary relationships when we are trying to introduce a piece over time? Where in the worship will a given song best function? Those necessary questions are moot if we do not first decide that the church's song, from familiar to exotic, is worth doing and doing well.

In the end, one recommendation remains, and for us leaders this may be the hardest part: get out of the way. It is, finally, the church's song, the song of the people of God. In a sense, even to speak of leading it is too strong. We facilitate it. We enable the people to make it happen. We can prepare, enlighten, encourage, train, lead, and all the rest, but when the worship begins, it is the song of God's people of every time and every place, and we are privileged to be among them.

> *Lo, the apostolic train*
> *join your sacred name to hallow;*
> *prophets swell the glad refrain,*
> *and the white-robed martyrs follow;*
> *and from morn to set of sun*
> *through the church the song goes on. (#414)*

2

INTERPRETATIONS FOR THE MUSIC

IN EVANGELICAL LUTHERAN WORSHIP

A GUIDE TO USING THE INTERPRETATIONS

Each piece of notated music in Evangelical Lutheran Worship—music within the liturgies themselves, freestanding service music (#151–238), and hymns and songs (#239–893)—has an entry. Each entry includes:

Pulse

A suggestion for what the fundamental tactus of the piece may be. See pages 21–22 for a discussion of this topic.

Tempo

A range of suggestions for the tempo of the hymn/song. It is important to remember that all suggestions are not necessarily what is right for your specific context at a given time. Many factors must be considered. See pages 22–24 for a discussion of this topic.

In most cases, the metronome markings given for the tempo suggestions correspond to the suggested tactus. There are exceptions, however, which are noted, so pay attention to the note value.

Style

For most hymns, some descriptive words are provided about how this hymn or song may be led. As with all entries in this resource, they are suggestions, not prescriptions. Other appropriate ways of leading may be explored.

Chapter references

This note will direct you to the chapters in Part 1 that have the most bearing on this type of hymn or song.

Accompaniment

Here you will find suggestions for instruments that are best suited to the hymn or song, as well as rhythms and additional hints. If one instrument is preferred but another would also work, you will see something like: organ (piano).

Articulation

If a specific articulation or technique for creating accents is helpful for the style or a particular challenge, it will described. If nothing is mentioned, the general rule is that the hymn will be played legato.

INTERPRETATIONS FOR THE MUSICAL PIECES

Music within the Liturgies

Holy Communion, Service of the Word, and Daily Prayer

Music that is printed in place within a service is identified with an S before the page number.

HOLY COMMUNION: SETTING ONE

S 98   Kyrie

Pulse	Tempo	Style	Chpt Ref
The half note receives the pulse. The measures of free chant in the leader's parts flow according to the rhythms of speech. The metrical pulse begins in the second measure ("pray to the Lord").	♩ = 52–60	Legato, interceding, prayerful	2, 3, 4, and 5

Accompaniment
Organ (piano)

S 99   Glory to God

Pulse	Tempo	Style	Chpt Ref
The half note receives the pulse. Feeling the hymn in two beats per measure helps the melodic phrases move forward.	♩ = 60–76	Majestic, confident, proclamatory	2, 3, and 5

Accompaniment

Organ (piano). Brass and timpani parts for Setting One, as well as a vocal descant, are available in the festival setting available from Augsburg Fortress (978-0-8066-5385-3).

Additional Information

Leading hint: Notice the ascending melodic line of the opening figure ("Glory to God") and the inversion of that figure at "Lord Jesus Christ." In addition, the pitches of "have mercy upon us" match the intervals of the Kyrie (S98) and the Lenten Acclamation (S103). Paying attention to such details will help with teaching this music to an assembly.

S 101   This Is the Feast

Pulse	Tempo	Style	Chpt Ref
The half note receives the pulse. Be sure to keep a steady pulse during the transitions from the verse to the refrain. This keeps the momentum going.	♩ = 58–70	Festive, regal, victorious	2, 3, and 5

Accompaniment

Organ (piano)

Additional Information

Leading hint: The final four measures of the refrain (alleluias) serve well as an introduction to this canticle.

S 102　Gospel Acclamation

Pulse	Tempo	Style	Chpt Ref
The dotted half note receives the pulse.phrases move forward.	$\dot{\textstyle\frac{1}{2}}$. = 44–50	Solid, bold	2, 3, and 5

Accompaniment

Organ (piano) accompaniment is preferred.

Additional Information

Leading hint: The tempo and articulation should suggest a solid triple meter rather than a lilt or a waltz.

Leading hint: Notice that this melody begins the same as the Holy, Holy, Holy. Emphasizing this will help when teaching an assembly.

You will note that this gospel acclamation allows for two options: singing the text as printed or singing a proper verse that is assigned for each Sunday and festival. (For the list of proper verses, see page 217 of the liturgies accompaniment edition, or the Propers section, beginning on page 60, of the leaders edition.) Either can be sung by a cantor, choir, or full assembly. These verses should be sung freely, allowing the text to dictate the tempo and rhythm. Be sure to place the accents in the natural place, which is not always where the pitches move. The proper verse may be sung in harmony by the choir, using the harmonization from the liturgies accompaniment. See pages 9–10 in chapter 2.

S 103　Lenten Acclamation

Pulse	Tempo	Style	Chpt Ref
The half note receives the pulse.	$\frac{1}{2}$ = 50–60	Reflective, solemn	2, 3, and 5

Accompaniment

A very legato organ (piano) accompaniment is preferred.

Additional Information

Leading hint: Be careful not to shortchange the whole note in the fourth measure (Lord).

S 107　Preface Dialogue

Accompaniment	Chpt Ref
No accompaniment is provided for this dialogue, the melody of which is consistent through all sung settings in *ELW*.	4

Additional Information

The intent is that this will be sung without accompaniment; however, as assemblies are initially learning it, it will be helpful to play along lightly in octaves.

Some communities sing the first response with a slight tenuto on "al-" of "also."

S 108   Holy, Holy, Holy; *also* Christ Has Died; Amen

Pulse	Tempo	Style	Chpt Ref
The dotted half note receives the pulse.	♩.= 44–50	Solid, bold	2, 3, and 5

Accompaniment
Organ (piano)

Additional Information
Leading hint: The tempo and articulation should suggest a solid triple meter rather than a lilt or a waltz.

S 112   Lamb of God

Pulse	Tempo	Style	Chpt Ref
The quarter note receives the pulse.	♩= 76–92	Reflective, smoothly	2, 3, and 5

Accompaniment
Organ (piano/keyboard).

S 113   Now, Lord

Pulse	Tempo	Style	Chpt Ref
The quarter note receives the pulse.	♩= 76–92	Peaceful, smoothly	2, 3, and 5

Accompaniment
Organ (piano)

HOLY COMMUNION: SETTING TWO

S 120   Kyrie

Pulse	Tempo	Style	Chpt Ref
The half note receives the pulse. Note the chant-like quality of the leader's parts. Allow the pulse and tempo to follow the natural rhythms of speech. On "let us," set a steady half note pulse.	♩= 40–44	Relaxed	2, 3, 4, 5, 6, and 9

Accompaniment
Piano or organ accompaniment is preferred. Guitar support is optional.

Additional Information
This Kyrie has a moderate blues feel and should not be played too quickly.

S 121   Glory to God

Pulse	Tempo	Style	Chpt Ref
The half note receives the pulse.	$\half = 48–52$	Strong, marching	2, 3, 5, 6, and 9

Accompaniment
Piano or organ accompaniment is preferred. Guitar support is optional. Setting Two in a festival setting is available from Augsburg Fortress (978-0-8066-5386-0).

S 122   This Is the Feast

Pulse	Tempo	Style	Chpt Ref
The dotted half note receives the pulse.	$\half. = 48–56$	Joyful	2, 3, 5, 6, and 9

Accompaniment
Piano or a light organ accompaniment is preferred. Guitar support is optional.

S 124   Gospel Acclamation

Pulse	Tempo	Style	Chpt Ref
The half note receives the pulse.	$\half = 46–48$	Strong, marching	2, 3, 4, 5, 6, and 9

Accompaniment
Piano or organ accompaniment is preferred. Guitar support is optional..

Additional Information
You will note that this gospel acclamation allows for two options: singing the text as printed or singing a proper verse that is assigned for each Sunday and festival. (For the list of proper verses, see page 217 of the liturgies accompaniment edition, or the Propers section, beginning on page 60, of the leaders edition.) Either can be sung by a cantor, choir, or full assembly. These verses should be sung freely, allowing the text to dictate the tempo and rhythm. Be sure to place the accents in the natural place, which is not always where the pitches move. See pages 9–10 in chapter 2.

S 125   Lenten Acclamation

Pulse	Tempo	Style	Chpt Ref
The half note receives the pulse.	♩= 46–48	Strong	2, 3, 5, 6, and 9

Accompaniment
Piano or organ accompaniment is preferred. Guitar support is optional.

S 129   Preface Dialogue

Accompaniment	Chpt Ref
No accompaniment is provided for this dialogue, the melody of which is consistent through all sung settings in *ELW*.	4

The intent is that this will be sung without accompaniment; however, as assemblies are initially learning it, it will be helpful to play along lightly in octaves.

Additional Information
Some communities sing the first response with a slight tenuto on "al-" of "also."

S 130   Holy, Holy, Holy; *also* Christ Has Died; Amen

Pulse	Tempo	Style	Chpt Ref
The half note receives the pulse.	♩= 46–48	Strong, marching	2, 3, 5, 6, and 9

Accompaniment
Piano or organ accompaniment is preferred. Guitar support is optional.

S 135a   Lamb of God

Pulse	Tempo	Style	Chpt Ref
The half note or quarter note receives the pulse. A slow tempo allows one to feel the quarter-note pulse, but being mindful of the larger pulse helps keep the tune moving forward.	♩= 36–40	Reflective, contemplative	2, 3, 5, 6, and 9

Accompaniment
Piano or organ accompaniment is preferred. Guitar support is optional.

S 135b Now, Lord

Pulse	Tempo	Style	Chpt Ref
The half note or quarter note receives the pulse.	$\half = 40–44$	Reflective	2, 3, 5, 6, and 9

Accompaniment
Piano or organ accompaniment is preferred. Guitar support is optional.

HOLY COMMUNION: SETTING THREE

S 138 Kyrie

Pulse	Tempo	Style	Chpt Ref
As with all chant, this Kyrie flows according to the natural textual accents. In this case, the first syllable of "mercy" receives the accent. For chant, depending on the text, the beats will be grouped in twos or threes.	A fluid tempo that neither rushes nor moves too slowly works best. It should be free, yet moving forward.	Freely, flowing	2, 3, and 4

Accompaniment
While it is preferable to sing chant unaccompanied, you may need to use organ or piano for support. If keyboard is needed, keep textures thin, taking care that any accompaniment does not overshadow the melodic line.

Additional Information
Leading hint: One should remember that the purpose of chant is to highlight the text. The text should always govern the spirit of the music as well as the tempo. See chapter 4 for further guidance in leading chant.

S 139 Glory to God

Pulse	Tempo	Style	Chpt Ref
The half or quarter note receives the pulse, depending upon the acoustics and/or size of the gathering..	$\quarter = 72–88$. Keep the sixteenth notes in mind when setting the tempo.	Forward moving, bright	2, 3, 4, and 5

Accompaniment
Organ/piano

Additional Information
A festival arrangement of most of Setting Three is available from Concordia (97-5939).

S 140　This Is the Feast

Pulse	Tempo	Style	Chpt Ref
The half note receives the pulse.	$\half = 60{-}72$	Majestic, broad	2, 3, and 5

Accompaniment
Organ (piano) accompaniment is preferred. A trumpet can enhance the melody line.

S 142a　Gospel Acclamation

Pulse	Tempo	Style	Chpt Ref
The half note receives the pulse.	$\half = 60{-}72$	Majestic, broad, unhurried	2, 3, and 5

Accompaniment
Organ (piano) accompaniment is preferred. A trumpet can enhance the melody line.

S 142b　Lenten Acclamation

Pulse	Tempo	Style	Chpt Ref
The half note receives the pulse.	$\half = 72{-}84$	Smooth, reflective	2, 3, and 5

Accompaniment
Organ (piano)

S 144a　Preface Dialogue

Accompaniment	Chpt Ref
No accompaniment is provided for this dialogue, the melody of which is consistent through all sung settings in *ELW*.	4

Additional Information

The intent is that this will be sung without accompaniment; however, as assemblies are initially learning it, it will be helpful to play along lightly in octaves.

Some communities sing the first response with a slight tenuto on "al-" of "also."

S 144b   Holy, Holy, Holy; *also* Christ Has Died; Amen

Pulse	Tempo	Style	Chpt Ref
The quarter note receives the pulse.	♩ = 76–92	Majestic, full	2, 3, and 5

Accompaniment
Organ (piano)

S 146   Lamb of God

Pulse	Tempo	Style	Chpt Ref
The quarter note receives the pulse, yet choose a tempo that also allows for a comfortable half note.	♩ = 58–70	Legato, introspective	2, 3, and 5

Accompaniment
Organ (piano)

HOLY COMMUNION: SETTING FOUR

S 147   Kyrie

Pulse	Tempo	Style	Chpt Ref
As with all chant, this Kyrie flows according to the natural textual accents. In this case, the first syllable of "mercy" receives the accent. For chant, depending on the text, the beats will be grouped in twos or threes.	A fluid tempo that neither rushes nor moves too slowly works best. It should be free, yet moving forward.	Freely, flowing	2, 3, and 4

Accompaniment
While it is preferable to sing chant unaccompanied, you may need to use organ or piano for support. If keyboard is needed, keep textures thin, taking care that any accompaniment does not overshadow the melodic line.

Additional Information
Leading hint: One should remember that the purpose of chant is to highlight the text. The text should always govern the spirit of the music as well as the tempo. See chapter 4 for further guidance in leading chant.

S 148   Glory to God

Pulse	Tempo	Style	Chpt Ref
The half note receives the pulse.	$\half = 54–64$. Choose a tempo by speaking the phrase "Jesus Christ with the Holy Spirit."	Joyful, bright, forward-moving	2, 3, and 5

Accompaniment
Organ (piano) accompaniment is preferred. A festival arrangement of most of Setting Four is available from Concordia (97-6127).

S 149   This Is the Feast

Pulse	Tempo	Style	Chpt Ref
The half note receives the pulse.	$\half = 60–72$	Broad, majestic	2, 3, and 5

Accompaniment
Organ (piano) accompaniment is preferred. A trumpet can enhance the melody line.

S 151a   Gospel Acclamation

Pulse	Tempo	Style	Chpt Ref
The half note receives the pulse.	$\half = 64–72$	Majestic, joyful	2, 3, and 5

Accompaniment
Organ (piano) accompaniment is preferred. A trumpet can enhance the melody line.

S 151b   Lenten Acclamation

Pulse	Tempo	Style	Chpt Ref
The half note receives the pulse.	$\half = 44–52$	Legato, introspective	2, 3, and 5

Accompaniment
Organ (piano) accompaniment is preferred.

S 152 Preface Dialogue

Accompaniment	Chpt Ref
No accompaniment is provided for this dialogue, the melody of which is consistent through all sung settings in *ELW*.	4

Additional Information
The intent is that this will be sung without accompaniment; however, as assemblies are initially learning it, it will be helpful to play along lightly in octaves.

Some communities sing the first response with a slight tenuto on "al-" of "also." |

S 153 Holy, Holy, Holy; *also* Christ Has Died; Amen

Pulse	Tempo	Style	Chpt Ref
The half note receives the pulse.	♩= 60–72	Broad, majestic	2, 3, and 5

Accompaniment
Organ (piano) accompaniment is preferred. A trumpet can enhance the melody line. Follow the text, articulating clearly at the punctuation.

S 154 Lamb of God

Pulse	Tempo	Style	Chpt Ref
The half note receives the pulse.	♩= 48–56	Legato, peaceful, gentle	2, 3, and 5

Accompaniment
Organ (piano) accompaniment is preferred.

S 156 Kyrie

Pulse	Tempo	Style	Chpt Ref
As with all chant, this Kyrie flows according to the natural textual accents. In this case, the first syllable of "mercy" receives the accent. For chant, depending on the text, the beats will be grouped in twos or threes.	A fluid tempo that neither rushes nor moves too slowly works best. It should be free, yet moving forward.	Freely, flowing	2, 3, and 4

Accompaniment

While it is preferable to sing chant unaccompanied, you may need to use organ or piano for support. If keyboard is needed, keep textures thin, taking care that any accompaniment does not overshadow the melodic line.

Additional Information

Leading hint: One should remember that the purpose of chant is to highlight the text. The text should always govern the spirit of the music as well as the tempo. See chapter 4 for further guidance in leading chant.

S 158 Glory to God

Pulse	Chpt Ref
See notes for the Kyrie (S 157), above.	2, 3, and 4

Accompaniment

Unaccompanied singing is preferred for chant.

S 159 All Glory Be to God on High

Pulse	Tempo	Style	Chpt Ref
The dotted half note receives the pulse.	$\dot{\sjmath} = 50–60$. If taken too fast, this hymn can become breathless and difficult to sing.	Like a Renaissance dance, propelling, sparkling	2, 3, and 5

Accompaniment

Organ (piano). A clear, light sound serves this tune well. A flute playing an ornamented version of the melody up an octave could help convey the spirit.

Additional Information

A slightly detached articulation suits this dance-like tune.

S 160a Gospel Acclamation

Pulse	Chpt Ref
See notes for the Kyrie (S 157), above.	2, 3, and 4

Accompaniment
Unaccompanied singing is preferred for chant.

S 160b Lenten Acclamation

Pulse	Chpt Ref
See notes for the Kyrie (S 157), above.	2, 3, and 4

Accompaniment
Unaccompanied singing is preferred for chant.

Additional Information
Leading hint: The climax of this chant is **Je-** sus Christ. Even though it is the lowest note, it should receive the most stress

S 161 Preface Dialogue

Accompaniment	Chpt Ref
No accompaniment is provided for this dialogue, the melody of which is consistent through all sung settings in *ELW*.	4

Additional Information
The intent is that this will be sung without accompaniment; however, as assemblies are initially learning it, it will be helpful to play along lightly in octaves.
Some communities sing the first response with a slight tenuto on "al-" of "also."

S 162 Holy, Holy, Holy; *also* Christ Has Died; Amen

Pulse	Chpt Ref
See notes for the Kyrie (S 157), above	2, 3, and 4

Accompaniment
Unaccompanied singing is preferred for chant.

S 163   Lord's Prayer

Pulse	Tempo	Style	Chpt Ref
As with all chant, this setting flows according to the natural textual accents.	A fluid tempo that neither rushes nor moves too slowly works best. It should be free, yet moving forward.	Freely, flowing	2, 3, and 4

Accompaniment

While it is preferable to sing chant unaccompanied, you may need to use organ or piano for support. If keyboard is needed, keep textures thin, taking care that any accompaniment does not overshadow the melodic line.

Additional Information

Leading hint: One should remember that the purpose of chant is to highlight the text. The text should always govern the spirit of the music as well as the tempo. See chapter 4 for further guidance in leading chant.

S 164   Lamb of God

Pulse	Chpt Ref
See notes for the Kyrie (S 157), above.	2, 3, and 4

Accompaniment

Unaccompanied singing is preferred for chant.

HOLY COMMUNION: SETTING SIX

S 165   Kyrie

Tempo	Style	Chpt Ref
The tactus and tempo move freely with the text.	Freely, with energy	2, 3, 4, and 8

S 167   Glory to God

Pulse	Tempo	Style	Chpt Ref
The dotted quarter note receives the pulse.	♩. = 48–52	Lively, African American gospel	2, 3, and 8

Accompaniment

Keyboard such as piano, Hammond B3 organ, or synthesizer is preferred. Drums, bass, and improvisational guitar would also enhance this hymn of praise. Add clapping on beats two and three of each measure.

Additional Information

As with a waltz, emphasize the first beat of each measure.

S 169 This Is the Feast

Pulse	Tempo	Style	Chpt Ref
The half note receives the pulse.	♩ = 72–80	Lively, African American gospel	2, 3, and 8

Accompaniment

Keyboard such as piano, Hammond B3 organ, or synthesizer is preferred. Drums, bass, and improvisational guitar would also enhance this hymn of praise. Consider beating a tambourine on beats two and four of the refrain.

S 171a Gospel Acclamation

Pulse	Tempo	Style	Chpt Ref
The half note receives the pulse.	♩ = 48–50	Smooth, African American jazz	2, 3, and 8

Accompaniment

Piano or synthesizer accompaniment is preferred. Soprano saxophone could be added.

S 171b Lenten Acclamation

Pulse	Tempo	Style	Chpt Ref
For pulse and accompaniment, see S 171a.	♩ = 46–48	Smooth, deliberate, African American jazz	2, 3, and 8

Accompaniment

Piano and Hammond B3 organ would be stylistically appropriate. Drums played lightly with brushes would add a nice touch.

S 173 Holy, Holy, Holy

Pulse	Tempo	Style	Chpt Ref
The half note receives the pulse.	♩ = 50–54	Smooth, deliberate, African American jazz	2, 3, and 8

Accompaniment

Piano or synthesizer accompaniment is preferred. Drums, bass, and guitar could be added.

S 174   Lamb of God

Pulse	Tempo	Style	Chpt Ref
The quarter note receives the pulse. Feel an underlying triplet to each quarter note.	♩= 74–78. It is appropriate to relax the tempo slightly in the last four measures.	With a slow triplet feel, African American gospel	2, 3, and 8

Accompaniment
Keyboard such as piano, Hammond B3 organ, or synthesizer is preferred. Drums, improvisational guitar, or E♭ alto saxophone would enhance this gospel song.

HOLY COMMUNION: SETTING SEVEN

S 175   Señor, ten piedad (Kyrie)
Lord, have mercy

Pulse	Tempo	Style	Chpt Ref
The dotted quarter note receives the pulse.	♩.= 58–68	Inviting, hopeful	2, 3, and 10

Accompaniment
Piano, bass, and percussion accompaniment is preferred. Two melody instruments (flutes or violins playing an octave higher, or trumpets) can enhance the vocal lines. See the liturgies accompaniment edition for percussion rhythm suggestions.

Additional Information
Approximate pronunciation of Spanish: sen-YOR, ten pyuh-DAHD day noh-SOH-tros; KREE-stoh.

Leading hint: It is important to emphasize the two-against-three rhythmic pattern that appears in the left hand of the accompaniment. See measures one and five for two examples. |

S 176   Gloria, gloria, gloria
Glory to God

Pulse	Tempo	Style	Chpt Ref
The dotted quarter note receives the pulse.	♩.= 66–80	Praise-filled, joyful	2, 3, and 10

Accompaniment
Piano, bass, and percussion accompaniment is preferred. Two melody instruments (flutes or violins playing an octave higher, or trumpets) can enhance the vocal lines.

Additional Information
Keep the dotted quarter note quite accented throughout, without losing the underlying eighth-note beat.

Approximate pronunciation of Spanish: GLOR-ya en lahs ahl-TOO-rahs ah deeOHS; eeyen lah TYEH-rah pahz pah-rah-KAY-yohs KYAH-mael sen-YOR. |

S 177   Celebremos la victoria
Celebrate the feast of victory

Pulse	Tempo	Style	Chpt Ref
The dotted quarter note receives the pulse.	♩.= 66–72	Proclamatory, celebratory	2, 3, and 10

Accompaniment

Piano, bass, and percussion accompaniment is preferred. One or more melody instruments (flutes or violins playing an octave higher, or trumpets) can enhance the vocal lines.

Additional Information

To assure a constant "walking" feel necessary for the singing of this piece, consider this drumming pattern:

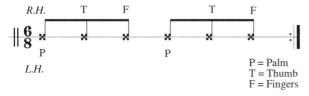

Leading hint: Although the overarching tactus should be felt in relation to the dotted quarter, the underlying eighth-note pulse is of utmost importance. Keep this eighth-note pulse in mind when setting the tempo. If too fast, assemblies may struggle with the text.

Even if the assembly isn't up to learning the Spanish verses, worshipers may well be able to learn the pronunciation for the refrain, which is more effective and natural when sung in Spanish. The verses could be sung in English.

Approximate pronunciation of Spanish for the refrain: sel-eh-BRAY-mos lah vik-TOH-ryah day nooES-troh deeOHS.

S 179a   Gospel Acclamation

Pulse	Tempo	Style	Chpt Ref
The dotted quarter note receives the pulse.	♩.= 80–96	Celebratory	2, 3, and 10

Accompaniment

Piano, bass, and percussion accompaniment is preferred.

Additional Information

To highlight the celebratory aspect of the acclamation, the assembly may clap this pattern throughout (with the final clap on the first beat in the final measure of the piece).

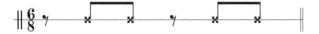

S 179b   Lenten Acclamation

Pulse	Tempo	Style	Chpt Ref
The quarter note gets the pulse.	♩ = 90–100	Reflective	2, 3, and 10

Accompaniment
Piano, bass, and percussion accompaniment is preferred.

Additional Information
Approximate pronunciation of Spanish: VWEL-vahl sen-YOR, too deeOHS, pwes es kohm-pah-SEE-voy kleh-MEN-teh, LEN-toh pah-rah lah EE-rah ee GRAHN-dayen soo mee-seh-ree-KOR-deeah.

S 181   Santo, santo, santo
Holy, holy, holy

Pulse	Tempo	Style	Chpt Ref
The half note receives the pulse.	♩ = 108–120. A quick yet not rushed tempo works best.	Mariachi feel	2, 3, and 10

Accompaniment
See S 175 for accompaniment suggestions. If other instruments lead the melody line, the piano might consider highlighting the rhythm (see attached). Consider adding hand claps on the second and fourth quarter notes.

Additional Information
Approximate Spanish pronunciation: SAHN-toh SAHN-towes el sen-YOR, deeOHS del oo-nee-VEHR-soh; hoh-SAH-nah en el seeYEH-loh, en lah teeEH-rah; ben-DEE-toh el kay veeEH-nayen el NOHM-bray del sen-YOR.

S 182   Cordero de Dios
Lamb of God

Pulse	Tempo	Style	Chpt Ref
The quarter note receives the pulse.	♩ = 104–118	Relaxed, yet with intensity	2, 3, and 10

Accompaniment
See S 175 for accompaniment suggestions. See S 177 for percussion rhythm.

Additional Information
It is important to emphasize the ♩. ♩. ♩ rhythm throughout. See the bass voice in the accompaniment.

Approximate Spanish pronunciation: kor-DEH-roh day deeOHS, too kay KEE-tahs el peh-KAH-doh del MOON-doh; ten pyeh-DADH day noh-SOH-trohs; dah-NOHS too PAHZ.

S 184   Kyrie

Pulse	Tempo	Style	Chpt Ref
The half note receives the pulse, but with a strong quarter-note subdivision.	♩ = 108–128	Confident	2, 3, and 9

Accompaniment

Piano/keyboard, guitar, bass, drums are preferred. Piano alone, perhaps with some hand percussion, could work.

Additional Information

The assembly sings the refrain. The verses should be sung by a soloist or band. The music is in the liturgies accompaniment edition, and the melodies for the verses are also on the liturgies CD-ROM and on Sundays and Seasons.com.

S 185   Glory to God

Pulse	Tempo	Style	Chpt Ref
The dotted half note receives the pulse. Feel the verses as one beat per measure rather than as a waltz.	♩. = 44–48. If too slow, this loses the feeling of one beat per measure.	Jubilant refrain, lyrical verses	2, 3, and 9

Accompaniment

Piano accompaniment is preferred. Allow the left hand bass line to be prominent and more detached in the verses than in the refrain. Guitar with bass (playing up an octave on verses) and an instrument supporting the melody could also be successful. If guitar is leading, strumming straight eighths in the refrain should alternate with a lighter, more sparse approach to the verses. If combined with piano, guitar arpeggiation in higher voicings would be appropriate for the verses. Hand percussion (egg shaker, claves, congas, and others) could be used on the refrain. Rhythms could include steady eighth notes and combinations of twos and threes:

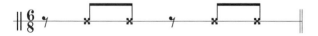

Additional Information

Be careful not to rush the syncopations. Though the piece can feel quite quick to the accompanist, the assembly should feel buoyant, never rushed. Allow the syncopations to be rhythmic, yet not choppy.

Leading hint: Consider having a choir/cantor sing the verses, with the assembly joining on the refrain. Once this is familiar, the assembly can join on the verses.

S 187   This Is the Feast

Pulse	Tempo	Style	Chpt Ref
The half note receives the pulse.	♩ = 50–60	Warm, flowing	2, 3, 6, and 9

Accompaniment
Piano, synthesizer (strings), guitar, and organ are possible accompaniments.

S 188   Gospel Acclamation

Pulse	Tempo	Style	Chpt Ref
The dotted half note receives the pulse.	♩. = 48–54	Joyful, flowing	2, 3, and 9

Accompaniment
Piano/keyboard, guitar, bass, drums are preferred. Piano alone, perhaps with some hand percussion, could work.

Additional Information
With the slow tactus it is important to still feel the quarter pulse in order to keep the rhythm alive. Taking the dynamic down a notch during the extended rests will help the assembly know when to enter.

S 189   Lenten Acclamation

Pulse	Tempo	Style	Chpt Ref
The half note receives the pulse.	♩ = 52–64	Trusting	2, 3, and 9

Accompaniment
Piano/keyboard, guitar, bass, drums are preferred. A solo woodwind such as alto sax on the melody could enhance the setting. Piano alone, perhaps with some hand percussion, could work.

S 190   Holy, Holy, Holy

Pulse	Tempo	Style	Chpt Ref
The quarter note receives the pulse.	♩ = 72–84	Legato, reverent	2, 3, and 9

Accompaniment
Piano accompaniment with acoustic guitar and flute is the preferred accompaniment. Organ is possible, as is oboe or violin

Additional Information
Leading hint: The $\frac{2}{4}$ measure may catch the assembly by surprise; strong leadership here will aid their singing.

S 191   Lamb of God

Pulse	Tempo	Style	Chpt Ref
The quarter note receives the pulse.	♩ = 64–72	With intensity, a rock ballad	2, 3, and 9

Accompaniment

Piano and guitar accompaniment is preferred. Organ is also possible. A rhythm section or hand drums could be added, perhaps using a rhythm like this:

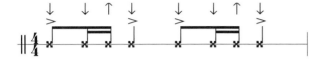

S 193   Kyrie

Pulse	Tempo	Style	Chpt Ref
The quarter note receives the pulse.	♩ = 68–76	Gently intense	2, 3, 4, and 5

Accompaniment

Organ (piano)

Additional Information

Leading hint: Note the chant-like quality of the leader parts; see S 138 for further guidance. The assembly parts, however, need to maintain a steady pulse. Holding the last note of the leader part ("Lord") exactly two beats helps the shift between the chant-like leader parts and the metered assembly responses..

S 195   Glory to God

Pulse	Tempo	Style	Chpt Ref
The half note receives the pulse.	♩ = 56–60	Joyful, majestic	2, 3, and 5

Accompaniment

Organ (piano)

Additional Information

Leading hint: Note the optional introduction in the liturgies accompaniment edition. Having a leader sing this phrase is especially helpful when introducing this to an assembly. It can also be played on the organ. The introduction is not printed in the pew edition; communicate clearly how it will begin.

Teaching hint: When learning this, consider having a cantor or choir sing the verses, with the assembly joining on the refrain and amens. Once learned, the full assembly can sing all parts.

S 196   This Is the Feast

Pulse	Tempo	Style	Chpt Ref
The dotted quarter note receives the pulse. A strongly articulated dotted quarter note helps keep this together, especially when the rhythm is tied over a bar line. Clearly lead the syncopations throughout.	♩.= 54–60	Robust, festive	2, 3, and 5

Accompaniment

Organ (piano)

Additional Information

Leading hint: Note the two possible introductions. The second is especially festive, but works best once this tune is well known. A well-prepared choir would be helpful in getting this started.

S 198a   Gospel Acclamation

Pulse	Tempo	Style	Chpt Ref
The quarter note or dotted half note receives the pulse. A slower tempo allows one to feel the quarter note pulse, but being mindful of the larger pulse helps keep the tune moving forward.	♩= 126–138	Grand, majestic	2, 3, and 5

Accompaniment

Organ (piano)

Additional Information

Leading hint: A clear downbeat on the bass note G is critical for a confident entrance by the assembly. Another option would be to have a choir/cantor sing the refrain and then have the assembly repeat it.

You will note that this gospel acclamation allows for two options: singing the text as printed or singing a proper verse that is assigned for each Sunday and festival. (For the list of proper verses, see page 217 of the liturgies accompaniment edition, or the Propers section, beginning on page 60, of the leaders edition.) Either can be sung by a cantor, choir, or full assembly. These verses should be sung freely, allowing the text to dictate the tempo and rhythm. Be sure to place the accents in the natural places, which are not always where the pitches move. The proper verse may be sung in harmony by the choir, using the harmonization from the liturgies accompaniment edition. See pages 9–10 in this guide.

S 198b Lenten Acclamation

Pulse	Tempo	Style	Chpt Ref
The quarter note receives the pulse.	♩ = 58–62	Smooth, intense, deliberate	2, 3, and 5

Accompaniment

Organ (piano)

Additional Information

Consider having a cantor or choir sing the verse once before the assembly sings.
Note the A-naturals in the melody—they give the setting a beautiful Lydian cast, but may catch people by surprise at first..

S 199 Preface Dialogue

Accompaniment	Chpt Ref
No accompaniment is provided for this dialogue, the melody of which is consistent through all sung settings in *ELW*.	4

Additional Information

The intent is that this will be sung without accompaniment; however, as assemblies are initially learning it, it will be helpful to play along lightly in octaves.

Some communities sing the first response with a slight tenuto on "al-" of "also."

S 200 Holy, Holy, Holy; *also* Christ Has Died; Amen

Pulse	Tempo	Style	Chpt Ref
The dotted half note receives the pulse. Feel the melody in one broad pulse per measure, but use the energy of the quarter note to propel it forward. This is especially important when the melody is tied over the bar.	♩. = 44–48	Expansive, grand, majestic	2, 3, and 5

Accompaniment

Organ (piano)

Additional Information

Leading hint: Prepare the assembly for the high E on "Hosanna" with a slight stretch and articulation. Clearly articulate the syncopations as well.

S 201 Lamb of God

Pulse	Tempo	Style	Chpt Ref
The quarter note receives the pulse	♩ = 58–62	Gently rhythmic	2, 3, and 5

Accompaniment
Organ (piano)

Additional Information
Be attentive to the syncopations in this tune. They may have to be more marked when being introduced to the assembly, but once familiar they can be more relaxed and gentle.

HOLY COMMUNION: SETTING TEN

S 203 Have Mercy on Us, Lord (Kyrie)
SOUTHWELL

Pulse	Tempo	Style	Chpt Ref
The half note receives the pulse.	♩ = 48–56	Introspective, confident	2, 3, and 5

Accompaniment
Organ (piano). Clearly articulate the repeated notes. See pages 38–39 for help with playing repeated notes on the organ.

S 204a Glory Be to God in Heaven
HYMN TO JOY

Pulse	Tempo	Style	Chpt Ref
The half note receives the pulse.	♩ = 56–66	Joyous	2, 3, and 5

Accompaniment
Organ (piano)

S 204b Come, Let Us Join Our Cheerful Songs
NUN DANKET ALL

Pulse	Tempo	Style	Chpt Ref
The half note receives the pulse.	♩ = 66–78	Spirited, strong	2, 3, and 5

Accompaniment
Organ (piano)

S 205a Alleluia! Lord and Savior (Gospel Acclamation)

UNSER HERRSCHER

Pulse	Tempo	Style	Chpt Ref
Either the half note or quarter note receives the pulse.	$\half = 56–62$; $\quarter = 100–116$	Lyrical, with breadth	2, 3, and 5

Accompaniment
Organ (piano)

S 205b We Are Turning, Lord, to Hear You (Lenten Acclamation)

KAS DZIEDĀJA

Pulse	Tempo	Style	Chpt Ref
The quarter note receives the pulse.	$\quarter = 72–84$	Mournful, longing	2, 3, 5, and 6

Accompaniment
Organ or piano accompaniment is preferred. A solo instrument such as oboe or violin could enhance the singing of this hymn.

S 207 Holy, Holy, Holy Lord; *also* Christ Has Died; Amen

LAND OF REST

Pulse	Tempo	Style	Chpt Ref
The dotted half note receives the pulse.	$\dottedhalf = 42–48$	Gentle, folk-like	2, 3, 5, and 6

Accompaniment
Unaccompanied singing, organ, or piano accompaniment is preferred. This tune also works well in canon, with the second voice entering one measure later.

S 208 O Lamb of God

TWENTY-FOURTH

Pulse	Tempo	Style	Chpt Ref
The half note receives the pulse, yet also keep a sense of the dotted whole note (the length of one measure).	$\half = 62–70$	Gentle, yet moving forward	2, 3, 5, and 6

Accompaniment
Organ (piano). Unaccompanied singing in unison works well.

Additional Information
Leading hint: When choosing a tempo, keep in mind the assembly's ability to sing through a phrase with adequate breath. This is especially important at the end of the second phrase, which ends on a high C.

S 213a   Kyrie

Pulse	Tempo	Style	Chpt Ref
The half note receives the pulse.	♩= 56–68	Imploring	2, 3, 5, 6, and 9

Accompaniment
Organ (piano). Guitar support is optional.

Additional Information
An assisting minister/cantor sings the first two bars of each system in either Greek or English.

S 213b   Glory to God

Pulse	Tempo	Style	Chpt Ref
The half note receives the pulse.	♩= 58–70	Joyful	2, 3, 5, 6, and 9

Accompaniment
Organ (piano). Guitar support is optional.

Additional Information
Teaching hint: When first teaching this to an assembly, have them only sing the refrains, leaving the verses for a soloist or choir. As the assembly becomes confident, teach them the verses.

S 216a   Gospel Acclamation

Pulse	Tempo	Style	Chpt Ref
The dotted quarter note receives the pulse.	♩.= 60–68	Joyful, rhythmic	2, 3, 5, 6, and 9

Accompaniment
Organ (piano). Guitar support is optional.

S 216b   Lenten Acclamation

Pulse	Tempo	Style	Chpt Ref
The dotted quarter note receives the pulse.	♩.= 70–80	Trusting, smoothly	2, 3, 5, 6, and 9

Accompaniment
Organ (piano). Guitar support is optional.

S 219   Canticle of Thanksgiving

Pulse	Tempo	Style	Chpt Ref
The dotted quarter note receives the pulse.	♪.= 64–84	Joyful	2, 3, 5, 6, and 9

Accompaniment
Organ (piano, keyboard, guitar, flute)

Additional Information
Leading hint: Watch the rhythm at "universe." It is different from the way it was in *With One Voice*. Teaching hint: When first teaching this to an assembly, have them only sing the refrains, leaving the verses for a soloist or choir. As the assembly becomes confident, teach them the verses.

MORNING PRAYER

S 298   Dialogue *and* Doxology
S 299   Dialogue *and* Doxology

Pulse	Chpt Ref
Sing to a natural speech rhythm.	2 and 4

Accompaniment
No accompaniment is provided for these chant sections.

Additional Information
The intent is that these will be sung without accompaniment; however, as assemblies are initially learning them, it will be helpful to play along lightly in octaves.

S 300   Come, Let Us Sing to the Lord (Psalm 95, Venite)

Pulse	Tempo	Style	Chpt Ref
The half note receives the pulse. Although the time signatures shift, keep a steady half-note pulse	♩= 72–84	Joyful, straightforward	2, 3, and 5

Accompaniment
Organ (piano)

Additional Information
Teaching hint: Consider teaching this with a choir/cantor singing the verses and the assembly joining on the refrain.

S 302a & b Scriptural Dialogue

See S 298 above.

S 303   Gospel Canticle (Song of Zechariah, Benedictus)

Pulse	Tempo	Style	Chpt Ref
The half note receives the pulse in the refrain.	$\half = 50\text{–}60$	Very legato, tender, assured	2, 3, 4, and 5

Accompaniment
Organ (piano) accompaniment is preferred for the refrain. The verses are best sung unaccompanied in four-part harmony, but may be supported with light keyboard.

Additional Information
This canticle is in two styles: a metrical refrain and verses in the style of Anglican chant. Sing the text set to the reciting tone (◖◗) as traditional chant, following the natural rhythm of speech. Treat the second half of the phrases more rhythmically. Leading hint: Be careful not to rush the triplet figure in the refrain; keep it relaxed and even.

S 305   Lord's Prayer
S 306a & b, S 307, S 308

Pulse	Tempo	Style	Chpt Ref
As with all chant, these settings flow according to the natural textual accents.	A fluid tempo that neither rushes nor moves too slowly works best. It should be free, yet moving forward.	Freely, flowing	2, 3, and 4

Accompaniment
While it is preferable to sing chant unaccompanied, you may need to use organ or piano for support. If keyboard is needed, keep textures thin, taking care that any accompaniment does not overshadow the melodic line.

Additional Information
Leading hint: One should remember that the purpose of chant is to highlight the text. The text should always govern the spirit of the music as well as the tempo. See chapter 4 for further guidance in leading chant.

S 309   Dialogue
S 310, S 311   Thanksgiving for Light

Pulse	Chpt Ref
Sing to a natural speech rhythm.	2 and 4

Accompaniment
No accompaniment is provided for these chant sections.

Additional Information
The intent is that these will be sung without accompaniment; however, as assemblies are initially learning them, it will be helpful to play along lightly in octaves.

S 312   Psalm 141

Pulse	Tempo	Style	Chpt Ref
The quarter note receives the pulse.	♩ = 60–72	Peaceful, flowing	2, 3, and 5

Accompaniment

S 314a & b Scriptural Dialogue

See S 309 above.

S 314c   Gospel Canticle (Song of Mary, Magnificat)

Pulse	Tempo	Style	Chpt Ref
The half note receives the pulse.	♩ = 60–68	Bright, lyrical	2, 3, 4, and 5

Accompaniment
Organ or piano accompaniment is preferred. A handbell cluster (C, D, E, and G, for example) could signal the beginning of each phrase of the verses. Consider having a flute or other solo instrument play the descant provided in the liturgies accompaniment edition.

Additional Information
Leading hint: This canticle is in two styles: a metrical refrain and chant-like verses. One should remember that the purpose of chant is to highlight the text. The text should always govern the spirit of the music as well as the tempo. See chapter 4 for further guidance in leading chant.

S 316   Litany

Pulse	Tempo	Chpt Ref
Sing the leader part to a natural speech rhythm. In the response, the quarter note gets the pulse.	♩ = 68–76	2 and 4

Accompaniment
Singing the response in harmony without accompaniment is encouraged. Traditionally, the last note of "mercy" is sustained, quietly, as the cantor chants the following petition.

S 318   Lord's Prayer
S 319a, b, c

Pulse	Tempo	Style	Chpt Ref
As with all chant, these settings flow according to the natural textual accents.	A fluid tempo that neither rushes nor moves too slowly works best. It should be free, yet moving forward.	Freely, flowing	2, 3, and 4

Accompaniment
While it is preferable to sing chant unaccompanied, you may need to use organ or piano for support. If keyboard is needed, keep textures thin, taking care that any accompaniment does not overshadow the melodic line.

Additional Information
Leading hint: One should remember that the purpose of chant is to highlight the text. The text should always govern the spirit of the music as well as the tempo. See chapter 4 for further guidance in leading chant.

NIGHT PRAYER

Pulse	Tempo	Style	Chpt Ref
As with all chant, these settings flow according to the natural textual accents.	A fluid tempo that neither rushes nor moves too slowly works best. It should be free, yet moving forward.	Calm, meditative, flowing	2, 3, and 4

Accompaniment
While it is preferable to sing chant unaccompanied, you may need to use organ or piano for support. If keyboard is needed, keep textures thin, taking care that any accompaniment does not overshadow the melodic line.

Additional Information
Leading hint: One should remember that the purpose of chant is to highlight the text. The text should always govern the spirit of the music as well as the tempo. See chapter 4 for further guidance in leading chant.

Psalms

See page 33 for a discussion of musical leadership of the singing version of the psalms in Evangelical Lutheran Worship *(#1–150).*

Service Music

151   Kyrie

Pulse	Tempo	Style	Chpt Ref
The half note receives the pulse.	♩= 44–50	Legato, penitential, blues-like style	2, 3, 6, and 11

Accompaniment

Unaccompanied singing is preferred.

Additional Information

The Greek text is better suited to the melody and is easily learned. Pronunciation: kee-ree-eh (krees-teh) eh-leh-ee-son.

152   Kyrie

Pulse	Tempo	Style	Chpt Ref
The quarter note receives the pulse.	♩= 80–100. A variety of tempos are appropriate, depending upon the worship context.	Sustained, reverent	2, 3, and 5

Accompaniment

Organ accompaniment is preferred. Consider singing unaccompanied in four-part harmony.

153   Kyrie
Nkosi, Nkosi

Pulse	Tempo	Style	Chpt Ref
The quarter note receives the pulse.	♩= 60–76	Legato, deliberate, penitential	2, 3, and 11

Accompaniment

Unaccompanied singing in four-part harmony is preferred. Piano can be added for vocal support if necessary. Drums would rarely be used with this South African song.

Additional Information

Note that despite its F-major feel, the B in the last measure of each line is natural.

Approximate pronunciation of Xhosa: nnKOH-sih (krays-too), yib-uh nen-kay-buh.

154   Kyrie

Pulse	Tempo	Style	Chpt Ref
The dotted quarter note receives the pulse.	♩.= 40–48	Prayerful, reflective	2, 3, and 8

Accompaniment

Keyboard such as piano, organ, or synthesizer with Hammond B3 sample is preferred.

Additional Information

In the gospel style, it would be normal to "fill in" the dotted quarters with arpeggios and passing tones.

Leading hint: This gospel song is played slowly with a deliberate triplet feel.

155   Kyrie

Pulse	Tempo	Style	Chpt Ref
The quarter note receives the pulse.	♩= 88–108. A slower tempo is more characteristic of Russian Orthodox song.	Legato, deliberate, bold	2, 3, and 4

Accompaniment

Unaccompanied singing in six-part harmony is preferred; addition of a basso profundo an octave down would be ideal! One possible harmonic arrangement has three-part men singing the first *Kyrie*, three-part women singing *Christe*, and six-part mixed voices singing the final *Kyrie*.

156   Kyrie

Pulse	Tempo	Style	Chpt Ref
As with all chant, this Kyrie flows according to the natural textual accents. In this case, the first syllable of "mer-cy" receives the accent. For chant, depending on the text, the beats will be grouped in twos or threes (counting an open note as equal to two black notes)	A fluid tempo that neither rushes nor moves too slowly works best. It should be free, yet moving forward.	Freely	2, 3, and 4

Accompaniment

Unaccompanied singing is preferred for chant.

Additional Information

Leading hint: One should remember that the purpose of chant is to highlight the text. The text should always govern the spirit of the music as well as the tempo.

See chapter 4 for further guidance in leading chant.

157 Kyrie

Pulse	Tempo	Style	Chpt Ref
The quarter note receives the pulse.	♩= 82–86	Deliberate, reflective	2, 3, 6, and 9

Accompaniment
Piano accompaniment is preferred. Guitar support is optional.

158 Kyrie

Pulse	Tempo	Style	Chpt Ref
The quarter note receives the pulse.	♩= 84–108	Legato, without accents	2, 3, and 12

Accompaniment
Piano accompaniment with a flute or violin to reinforce the melody is preferred. Adding a ching (finger cymbal) or gong on beat three after each "mercy" adds to the cyclical character of the piece.

Additional Information
Sing more than once.

159 Holy God

Pulse	Tempo	Style	Chpt Ref
The quarter note receives the pulse.	♩= 74–84	Plain, simple	3 and 8

Accompaniment
Piano is preferred. This gentle tune is similar in style to traditional African American spirituals. Simple, unadorned accompaniment works best.

Additional Information
Among other uses, the Holy God could be substituted for a Kyrie, or used as a response in the Solemn Reproaches in the Good Friday service.

160 Holy God

Pulse	Tempo	Style	Chpt Ref
The quarter note receives the pulse.	♩= 72–84. It is best to have the eighth notes in mind when determining tempo.	Reverent, dignified	3 and 4

Accompaniment
Unaccompanied singing is preferred.

Additional Information
Keep this chant legato, becoming slightly marked in the eighth-note passages. Among other uses, the Holy God could be substituted for a Kyrie, or used as a response in the Solemn Reproaches in the Good Friday service.

161   Holy God

Pulse	Tempo	Style	Chpt Ref
The quarter note receives the pulse. ♩ = 60–76		Declamatory, pleading, confident	3 and 5

Accompaniment

Singing unaccompanied in four-part harmony is preferred. Organ accompaniment would also be successful. If using piano, be certain to play this legato.

Additional Information

Among other uses, the Holy God could be substituted for a Kyrie, or used as a response in the Solemn Reproaches in the Good Friday service.

162   Glory to God

Pulse	Tempo	Style	Chpt Ref
As with all chant, this setting flows according to the natural textual accents. Depending on the text, the beats will be grouped in twos or threes (counting an open note as equal to two black notes).	A fluid tempo that neither rushes nor moves too slowly works best. It should be free, yet moving forward.	Freely	2, 3, and 4

Accompaniment

While it is preferable to sing chant unaccompanied, you may need to use organ or piano for support. If keyboard is needed, keep textures thin, taking care that any accompaniment does not overshadow the melodic line.

Additional Information

Leading hint: At the beginning, beware of feeling the black notes as triplets, three of them equal to one white note. If counting (a good way to approach a new piece of chant), it would begin 1-2-3-1-2-3-1-2-1-2.

See chapter 4 for further guidance in leading chant.

163   Glory to God

Pulse	Tempo	Style	Chpt Ref
The dotted half note receives the pulse.	♩. = 44–50	Spirited, bold	2, 3, and 5

Accompaniment

Organ (piano)

Additional Information

Leading hint: The tempo and articulation should suggest a solid triple meter rather than a lilt or a waltz.

164   Glory to God

Pulse	Tempo	Style	Chpt Ref
The quarter note receives the pulse. A strong quarter note keeps the eighth notes even. Feel the half note pulse at a faster tempo.	♩ = 104–132	Energetic, exuberant	2, 3, and 10

Accompaniment

Guitar accompaniment with conga drums, egg shakers, and guiro is preferred. See rhythms below. Panpipes would add an authentic Andean sound. Piano is possible. This also works well sung unaccompanied.

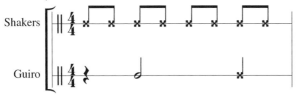

Additional Information

Leading hint: Allow the energy to build up to the final Amen. Consider repeating one or more times at a faster tempo.

165   This Is the Feast

Pulse	Tempo	Style	Chpt Ref
The quarter note receives the pulse.	♩ = 76–88	Regal, grand	2, 3, and 5

Accompaniment

Organ accompaniment is preferred.

Additional Information

A marked accompaniment works best.

166   This Is the Feast

Pulse	Tempo	Style	Chpt Ref
The half note receives the pulse.	𝅗𝅥 = 44–50	Joyful, but not too exuberant	2, 3, and 5

Accompaniment

Organ (piano/keyboard/guitar)

Additional Information

Smoothly, but not so much that the rhythms are lost.

Leading hint: A little ritardando at ". . . Lamb forever. Amen" would help to lead back into the refrain through the key change, and back to the original tempo at the refrain.

167   Now the Feast and Celebration

Pulse	Tempo	Style	Chpt Ref
The dotted quarter note receives the pulse.	♩.= 56–72	Buoyant, dancing	2, 3, 6, and 9

Accompaniment
Piano accompaniment is preferred. Guitar support is optional.

168   Gospel Acclamation

Pulse	Tempo	Style	Chpt Ref
Let the piece flow according to the natural textual accents. For chant, depending on the text, the beats will be grouped in twos or threes.	A fluid tempo that neither rushes nor moves too slowly works best. It should be free, yet moving forward.	Freely	2, 3, and 4

Accompaniment
While it is preferable to sing chant unaccompanied, you may need to use organ or piano for support. If keyboard is needed, keep textures thin, taking care that any accompaniment does not overshadow the melodic line.

Additional Information
Leading hint: You will note that this acclamation, which is sung prior to the gospel reading, allows for two options: singing the text as printed or singing a proper verse that is assigned for each Sunday and festival. Either can be sung by a cantor, choir, or full assembly. (For the list of proper verses, see page 217 of the liturgies accompaniment edition, or the Propers section, beginning on page 60, of the leaders edition.)

169   Gospel Acclamation

Pulse	Tempo	Style	Chpt Ref
The half note receives the pulse.	♩= 52–60. A slow tempo allows one to feel the quarter-note pulse, but being mindful of the larger pulse helps keep the tune moving forward.	Regal, grand; freely on the verse	2, 3, 4, and 5

Accompaniment
Organ accompaniment is preferred. Piano or unaccompanied singing would also be successful.

Additional Information
This has a chant quality. Allow the verse to flow according the rhythms of the text.

170   Gospel Acclamation

Pulse	Tempo	Style	Chpt Ref
The quarter note receives the pulse.	♩= 138–152	Marcato, driving rock style	2, 3, 5, and 9

Accompaniment
Piano or organ accompaniment is preferred. Guitar, band, and percussion are possible.

171   Hallelujah
Heleluyan

Pulse	Tempo	Style	Chpt Ref
The quarter note receives the pulse.	♩= 88–120	Marcato, earthy, rugged	2 and 3

Accompaniment
Unaccompanied singing in canon is preferred. Repeat several times. Drum can be added on beats one and three.

Additional Information
Leading hint: Native American chant is sung with an open-throated sound, not a classically-trained choir voice.

172   Halle, Halle, Hallelujah

Pulse	Tempo	Style	Chpt Ref
The half note receives the pulse.	♩= 92–104	Energetic, spirited	2, 3, and 10

Accompaniment
Piano accompaniment is preferred. Allow the left hand bass line to be prominent and more detached in the verses than in the refrain. Guitar with bass (playing up an octave on verses) and an instrument supporting the melody could also be successful. If guitar is leading, strumming straight eighths in the refrain should alternate with a lighter, more sparse approach to the verses. If combined with piano, guitar arpeggiation in higher voicings would be appropriate for the verses. Hand percussion (egg shaker, claves, congas, and others) could be used on the refrain. Rhythms could include steady eighth notes and combinations of twos and threes:

Additional Information
This Caribbean Hallelujah is best repeated at least twice. If this is done, the following could be substituted for the last two measures as a transition:

173   Gospel Acclamation

Pulse	Tempo	Style	Chpt Ref
The dotted half note receives the pulse.	𝅗𝅥.= 48–58. A relaxed but energetic tempo works best.	Strong, unhurried, joyful	2, 3, and 11

Accompaniment

Unaccompanied singing with drums and/or rattles is preferred. Support with piano only if necessary. A possible percussion pattern is:

Additional Information

Leading hint: Begin with the melody in the top line. Add lower voices (basses) on the bottom line, then high voices (sopranos and/or tenors) on the middle. Sing several times through with all voices.

174   Gospel Acclamation
Celtic Alleluia

Pulse	Tempo	Style	Chpt Ref
The dotted quarter receives the pulse.	♩.= 52–66	Swinging, joyful	2, 3, 5 and 6

Accompaniment

Piano or organ accompaniment is preferred.

Additional Information

Keep the dotted eighth-sixteenth rhythmic pattern crisp. The optional verses are in the accompaniment edition only.

175   Gospel Acclamation

Pulse	Tempo	Style	Chpt Ref
The dotted half note receives the pulse. While this makes for a very slow tactus, singers benefit by emphasizing the dotted half note with added weight on the first quarter note.	𝅗𝅥.= 34–42	Legato, urgent, joyful	2, 3, 4, and 5

Accompaniment

Unaccompanied singing in parts is preferred. Use organ or piano if necessary to support the singing and/or woodwinds on obbligato lines. See Taizé volumes in Bibliography, page 347.

176 Lenten Acclamation

Pulse	Tempo	Style	Chpt Ref
The half note receives the pulse.	$\half = 46–54$	Imploring	2, 3, and 5

Accompaniment
Organ (piano)

177 Lenten Acclamation

Pulse	Tempo	Style	Chpt Ref
The quarter note receives the pulse.	$\quarter = 96–98$	Dignified	2, 3, 4, and 5

Accompaniment
Organ (piano)

178 Hear Our Prayer

Pulse	Tempo	Style	Chpt Ref
The quarter note receives the pulse.	$\quarter = 88–104$	Meditative, smoothly	2, 3, and 9

Accompaniment
Piano and guitar (organ)

Additional Information
This refrain can be sung between petitions in the Prayers of Intercession instead of a spoken response by the assembly.

179 O Lord, Hear Our Prayer

Pulse	Tempo	Style	Chpt Ref
The quarter receives the pulse.	$\quarter = 72–88$	Meditative, smoothly	2, 3, and 9

Accompaniment
Piano and guitar (organ)

Additional Information
This refrain can be sung between petitions in the Prayers of Intercession instead of a spoken response by the assembly.

180   The Spirit Intercedes for Us

Pulse	Tempo	Style	Chpt Ref
The quarter receives the pulse.	♩ = 92–100	Trusting, gently rhythmic	2, 3, and 9

Accompaniment

Piano and guitar

Additional Information

This refrain can be sung between petitions in the Prayers of Intercession instead of a spoken response by the assembly.

181   Let the Vineyards Be Fruitful

Pulse	Tempo	Style	Chpt Ref
The quarter note receives the pulse.	♩ = 86–92	Lyrical, flowing	2, 3, and 5

Accompaniment

Piano accompaniment is preferred. Guitar support is optional.

Additional Information

This setting would mesh well with Holy Communion Setting Two.

182   Let the Vineyards Be Fruitful

Pulse	Tempo	Style	Chpt Ref
The half note receives the pulse.	♩ = 72–84	Legato, reflective	3 and 5

Accompaniment

Organ (piano)

Additional Information

This was originally composed for Holy Communion Setting Three.

183   Let the Vineyards Be Fruitful

Pulse	Tempo	Style	Chpt Ref
The dotted quarter note receives the pulse.	♩. = 52–78	Lively, gospel style	2, 3, and 8

Accompaniment

Piano or synthesizer with Hammond B3 organ accompaniment with drums is preferred. Bass and guitar could be added.

Additional Information

Leading hint: This gospel song with underlying eighth-note triplets can be accompanied with as much improvisation as possible within the ability of the musician. Use as many eighth notes as possible during the dotted quarter notes. See the introductory comments on African American song, chapter 8.

184   Let the Vineyards Be Fruitful

Pulse	Tempo	Style	Chpt Ref
The quarter note receives the pulse. The keyboard accompanist can sense the half note, but the complexity of the vocal line requires a quarter-note pulse as well.	♩ = 63–72. Speak the phrase "fill to the brim our cup of blessing" to find a relaxed tempo.	Relaxed, unhurried	2, 3, and 5

Accompaniment
Organ (piano)

Additional Information
This was originally composed for Holy Communion Setting Four.

185   Create in Me a Clean Heart

Pulse	Tempo	Style	Chpt Ref
The quarter note receives the pulse.	♩ = 84–88	Strong, crisp, rock feel	2, 3, and 8

Accompaniment
Piano, Hammond B3 organ, or synthesizer is preferred.

Additional Information
Maintain a crisp and forceful beat, always keeping the eighth notes short.

186   Create in Me a Clean Heart

Pulse	Tempo	Style	Chpt Ref
The quarter note receives the pulse.	♩ = 58–72	Flowing, dance-like	2, 3, and 5

Accompaniment
Organ (piano). Strive for a slightly detached articulation.

187   Create in Me a Clean Heart

Pulse	Tempo	Style	Chpt Ref
The quarter note receives the pulse.	♩ = 106–112	Energetic, jazz	2, 3, 8, and 9

Accompaniment
Piano or synthesizer is preferred.

188   Create in Me a Clean Heart

Pulse	Tempo	Style	Chpt Ref
The dotted half note receives the pulse.	$\dot{\half} = 38\text{–}46$	Forward moving, but not rushed	2, 3, and 5

Accompaniment

Organ (piano) accompaniment is preferred. Consider singing unaccompanied in four-part harmony.

Additional Information

Articulate the repeated notes clearly. See pages 38–39 for help with playing repeated notes on the organ.

Leading hint: There are several rhythmic versions of this tune. Be clear with the rhythm and meter.

189   Holy, Holy, Holy; Acclamation and Amen

Pulse	Tempo	Style	Chpt Ref
The half note receives the pulse.	$\half = 52\text{–}56$	Grand, with intensity	2, 3, and 5

Accompaniment

Organ accompaniment is preferred.

190   Holy, Holy, Holy; Acclamation and Amen

Pulse	Tempo	Style	Chpt Ref
The quarter note receives the pulse, yet also feel the broader dotted half note pulse. Take care that the dotted half note does not feel too waltz-like or the quarter note too slow.	$\quarter = 108\text{–}120$	Dignified, broad	2, 3, and 5

Accompaniment

Organ accompaniment is preferred. At a slower tempo, this can be very effective sung unaccompanied in four-part harmony.

191   Holy, Holy, Holy; Acclamation and Amen

Pulse	Tempo	Style	Chpt Ref
The dotted quarter note receives the pulse.	$\dot{\quarter} = 76\text{–}84$	Strong, rhythmic	2, 3, 6, and 9

Accompaniment

Organ (piano) accompaniment is preferred. Consider singing unaccompanied in four-part harmony.

Additional Information

Piano accompaniment is preferred. Guitar support is optional.

192   Holy, Holy, Holy; Acclamation and Amen

Pulse	Tempo	Style	Chpt Ref
The quarter note receives the pulse.	♩= 100–112. A broad, moderate tempo suits this cathedral tune.	Marked, regal, grand	2, 3, and 5

Accompaniment
Organ accompaniment is preferred.

193   Holy, Holy, Holy; Acclamation and Amen

Pulse	Tempo	Style	Chpt Ref
The dotted quarter note receives the pulse.	♩.= 46–58	Sturdy, joyful	2, 3, 5, and 6

Accompaniment
Organ or piano accompaniment is preferred.

194   Lamb of God
Agnus Dei

Pulse	Tempo	Style	Chpt Ref
As with all chant, this setting flows according to the natural textual accents. Depending on the text, the beats will be grouped in twos or threes (counting an open note as equal to two black notes).	A fluid tempo that neither rushes nor moves too slowly works best. It should be free, yet moving forward.	Freely	2, 3, and 4

Accompaniment
While it is preferable to sing chant unaccompanied, you may need to use organ or piano for support. If keyboard is needed, keep textures thin, taking care that any accompaniment does not overshadow the melodic line.

Additional Information
Pronunciation of the Latin: ah-nyoos deh-ee, kwee toh-lees peh-kah-tah moon-dee: mee-seh-reh-reh noh-bees; doh-nah noh-bees pah-chem.

See chapter 4 for further guidance in leading chant.

195 Lamb of God

Pulse	Tempo	Style	Chpt Ref
The quarter note receives the pulse.	♩= 92–106. A lilting, unhurried tempo works best.	Flowing, simple	2, 3, 6, and 9

Accompaniment
Piano or organ accompaniment is preferred. Guitar and cello is possible.

196 O Christ, Lamb of God

Pulse	Tempo	Style	Chpt Ref
The half note receives the pulse.	♩= 44–52. Choose a tempo by speaking "have mercy upon us."	Simple, majestic, quiet	2, 3, and 5

Accompaniment
Unaccompanied singing or organ accompaniment is preferred.

197 O Lamb of God
Oi, Jumalan Karitsa

Pulse	Tempo	Style	Chpt Ref
The quarter note receives the pulse.	♩= 88–100. This can be sung as slowly as the singers can sustain through the phrase.	Mournful, pleading	2, 3, 6, and 9

Accompaniment
Piano (organ)

198 O Lamb of God

Pulse	Tempo	Style	Chpt Ref
The quarter note receives the pulse. The quarter-note pulse helps the singers shift from the eighth-note pairs to the triplets.	♩= 46–48	Sustained, mournful, plaintive	2, 3, and 12

Accompaniment
Piano (organ). A simple accompaniment works best.

199　Jesus, Lamb of God

Pulse	Tempo	Style	Chpt Ref
The dotted quarter note receives the pulse.	♩.= 40–44	Legato, reverent, meditative	2, 3, and 5

Accompaniment
Organ accompaniment is preferred.

200　Now, Lord

Pulse	Tempo	Style	Chpt Ref
The quarter note or dotted half note receives the pulse, depending upon the tempo.	♩= 108–120. Either a very slow or an upbeat tempo is possible.	Lively, African American gospel	2, 3, and 8

Accompaniment
Piano (organ)

Additional Information
This is in gospel style, thus welcoming of a great deal of improvisation and fill-in on the part of the keyboard player. See page 55.

201　Now, Lord

Pulse	Tempo	Style	Chpt Ref
As with all chant, this setting flows according to the natural textual accents. Depending on the text, the beats will be grouped in twos or threes (counting an open note as equal to two black notes).	A fluid tempo that neither rushes nor moves too slowly works best. It should be free, yet moving forward.	Freely	2, 3, and 4

Accompaniment
While it is preferable to sing chant unaccompanied, you may need to use organ or piano for support. If keyboard is needed, keep textures thin, taking care that any accompaniment does not overshadow the melodic line.

Additional Information
See chapter 4 for further guidance in leading chant.

202   Now, Lord

Pulse	Tempo	Style	Chpt Ref
The quarter note receives the pulse.	♩ = 60–66	Peaceful	2, 3, 4, and 5

Accompaniment

Organ (piano)

Additional Information

This canticle is in two styles: a metrical refrain and chant-like verses. See #156 for guidance in leading chant. Allow the musical phrase to follow the natural rhythm of the text.

203   At Last, Lord
Ahora, Señor

Pulse	Tempo	Style	Chpt Ref
The quarter note receives the pulse. This moderate tempo allows one to feel the quarter-note pulse, but being mindful of the larger pulse helps keep the tune moving forward.	♩ = 88–120	Walking tempo, not rushed	2, 3, and 10

Accompaniment

Melody instruments such as flute, violin, trumpet, oboe, or clarinet may double the vocal line. Piano may serve as a rhythmic instrument throughout, perhaps using a pattern such as:

204   Thankful Hearts and Voices Raise

Pulse	Tempo	Style	Chpt Ref
The half note receives the pulse.	♩ = 66–76	Joyful, light	2, 3, and 5

Accompaniment

Organ (piano). A light and slightly detached articulation works best.

Additional Information

This is an adaptation of a setting originally composed for Holy Communion Setting Three.

205   Thankful Hearts and Voices Raise

Pulse	Tempo	Style	Chpt Ref
The quarter note receives the pulse.	♩ = 120–132	Energetic, driving	2, 3, and 8

Accompaniment
Piano, keyboard, bass, drums

Additional Information
Feel strong upbeats (two and four) with hand clapping, percussion, and accents in the piano.

206   Thankful Hearts and Voices Raise

Pulse	Tempo	Style	Chpt Ref
The dotted quarter note receives the pulse.	♩. = 56–64	Vigorous, exuberant	2, 3, 6, and 9

Accompaniment
Piano and guitar or organ accompaniment is preferred. Trumpet could enhance the melody line. Guitar, bass, drums, and C instrument are possible.

207   Thankful Hearts and Voices Raise

Pulse	Tempo	Style	Chpt Ref
The dotted half note receives the pulse. Feel one full measure as the pulse.	♩. = 44–50	Dance-like, light	2, 3, and 5

Accompaniment
Organ (piano)

Additional Information
This is an adaptation of a setting originally composed for Holy Communion Setting Four.

208   Praise to You, O God of Mercy

Pulse	Tempo	Style	Chpt Ref
The quarter note receives the pulse.	♩ = 103–110	Strong	2, 3, 5, and 9

Accompaniment
Piano accompaniment is preferred. Guitar support is optional.

Additional Information
Be aware of the form: stanza 1, 2, then the bridge ("Strong is your faithfulness"), stanza 3, coda.

209 Blessed Be God, the Source of All Life

Pulse	Tempo	Style	Chpt Ref
The quarter note receives the pulse.	♩= 80–88	Warm, trusting	2, 3, 6, and 8

Accompaniment

Piano accompaniment is preferred. Organ can work. Flute, violin, or other melody instruments could be added.

210 Blessed be God, the Source of All Life

Pulse	Tempo	Style	Chpt Ref
The half note receives the pulse.	♩= 60–76	Gentle, proclamatory	2, 3, and 5

Accompaniment

Organ (piano). If sung repeatedly, flute, handbells, or other instruments could be added.

211 You Have Put On Christ

Pulse	Tempo	Style	Chpt Ref
The quarter note receives the pulse.	♩= 80–92	Cheerful, child-like	2, 3, 5, and 6

Accompaniment

Organ or piano accompaniment is preferred. Consider adding handbells and/or finger cymbals on the downbeats.

Additional Information

A light, detached articulation works best.

212 You Belong to Christ

Pulse	Tempo	Style	Chpt Ref
The half note receives the pulse. Strive for two-measure phrases.	♩= 50–66. Choose a tempo appropriate to the number of repetitions.	Stately when sung as a funeral procession; sprightly when accompanying sprinkling	2, 3, and 5

Accompaniment

The accompaniment for this acclamation is especially versatile. Possibilities include unaccompanied singing in unison or harmony, piano or organ, and/or the addition of bells, other instruments, and descants. Consider various combinations. It may be sung once or repeated with variations.

213   You Belong to Christ

Pulse	Tempo	Style	Chpt Ref
The quarter note receives the pulse. Allow the quarter note to provide energy, but use one large pulse per bar to shape the phrase. Let the syncopation, which may seem complex at first, dance within that one bar pulse.	♩ = 100–120	Joyful, driving	2, 3, and 9

Accompaniment
Piano/keyboard, guitar

214   Springs of Water, Bless the Lord

Pulse	Tempo	Style	Chpt Ref
The half note receives the pulse.	♩ = 48–60	Quietly joyful	2, 3, 4, and 5

Accompaniment
Piano (organ, guitar)

215   Blessed Be God, Who Chose You

Pulse	Tempo	Style	Chpt Ref
The dotted half note receives the pulse. Strive for four-measure phrases.	♩. = 48–52	Graceful, lilting	2, 3, 5, and 6

Accompaniment
The accompaniment for this acclamation is especially versatile. Possibilities include unaccompanied singing in unison or harmony, piano or organ, and/or the addition of bells, other instruments and descants. Consider various combinations. It may be sung once or repeated with variations.

216   Praise to You, O Christ

Pulse	Tempo	Style	Chpt Ref
The half note receives the pulse.	$\dot{\half} = 54\text{–}64$	Joyful	2, 3, and 5

Accompaniment
Organ (piano/keyboard)

217   May the God of All Grace

Pulse	Tempo	Style	Chpt Ref
The half note receives the pulse.	$\half = 44\text{–}58$	Blessing	2, 3, 5, and 6

Accompaniment
Organ (piano/keyboard)

218   You Anoint My Head

Pulse	Tempo	Style	Chpt Ref
The quarter note receives the pulse.	$\quarter = 70\text{–}86$	Flowing, Taizé-style	2, 3, 5, and 6

Accompaniment
The accompaniment for this acclamation is especially versatile. Possibilities include unaccompanied singing in unison or harmony, piano or organ, and/or the addition of bells, other instruments, and descants. Consider various combinations. It may be sung once or repeated with variations.

219   Healer of Boundless Compassion

Pulse	Tempo	Style	Chpt Ref
The half note receives the pulse.	$\half = 60\text{–}66$	Warmly	2, 3, and 5

Accompaniment
Organ (piano)

220   May the God of All Healing

Pulse	Tempo	Style	Chpt Ref
The quarter note receives the pulse.	♩ = 84–96	Hopeful, flowing, tender	2, 3, 5, and 6

Accompaniment

Piano or organ accompaniment is preferred.

Additional Information

Leading hint: Feel a stress on the dotted quarter notes of measures 4, 6, and 8, ending with conviction in the final two measures.

221   Blessed Be God, Who Forgives

Pulse	Tempo	Style	Chpt Ref
The half note receives the pulse.	♩ = 76–80	Hopeful, flowing	2, 3, 5, and 6

Accompaniment

Organ (piano)

Additional Information

This acclamation is intended for unison singing. Instruments doubling the melody or harmonies can enhance this tune on the repetitions.

222   Into Paradise May the Angels Lead You

Pulse	Tempo	Style	Chpt Ref
The half note receives the pulse.	♩ = 40–44	Reflective	2, 3, 5, and 6

Accompaniment

Piano accompaniment is preferred.

223   All of Us Go Down to the Dust

Pulse	Tempo	Style	Chpt Ref
The quarter note receives the pulse.	♩ = 50–76. Some contexts could allow for a slower tempo.	Sweeping, confident, with honesty	2, 3, and 5

Accompaniment

Organ (piano)

Additional Information

Leading hint: Keep this tune legato, always singing through the dotted quarter notes.

The alleluias of this acclamation match the alleluias of "This Is the Feast" in ELW Setting One (S101). If this acclamation is used at funerals in congregations where ELW Setting One is familiar, the alleluias will be familiar to many in the assembly.

224   Come, Let Us Sing to the Lord

Pulse	Tempo	Style	Chpt Ref
The half note receives the pulse.	♩ = 50–58. Choose a tempo that moves along but also allows the assembly to sing the text.	Lively, not rushed	2, 3, and 5

Accompaniment

Organ (piano)

Additional Information

Feel a strong pulse on the downbeat, but keep the eighth notes light. Note the instructions for measure 6 and the performance suggestions in th eaccompaniment edition.

225   Come, Ring Out Your Joy

Pulse	Tempo	Style	Chpt Ref
The half note receives the pulse.	♩ = 50–54	Upbeat, joyful	2, 3, and 8

Accompaniment

Piano accompaniment is preferred. Drums, guitars, and shakers can be added.

Additional Information

Leading hint: This setting of Psalm 95 (Venite) is in two styles: a metrical refrain and chant-like verses. See #156 for guidance in leading chant. Allow the musical phrase to follow the natural rhythm of the text.

226   Blessed Are You, Lord

Pulse	Tempo	Style	Chpt Ref
The pulse shifts between the quarter note and the dotted quarter. Like chant, it follows the natural rhythms of the text.	A flowing, not rushed tempo works best (♪ = 168–176).	Flowing, straightforward	2, 3, 4, and 5

Accompaniment

Piano accompaniment is preferred. An instrument on the melody line can support the singing.

Additional Information

Leading hint: Lead with confidence and grace, following the natural flow of the text and music.

227   We Praise You, O God

Pulse	Tempo	Style	Chpt Ref
The half note receives the pulse.	♩ = 60–68	Majestic, joyful	2, 3, and 5

Accompaniment

Organ, with brass if possible

Additional Information

Slightly detach the eighth notes.

228   We Praise You, O God

Pulse	Tempo	Style	Chpt Ref
The whole note receives the pulse. As with chant, follow the natural rhythms of the text.	○ = 52–58. Tempo will vary to accommodate the number of words/ syllables.	Dignified	3 and 4

Accompaniment

Organ accompaniment is preferred. Piano is not suited for leading this sustained style of chant.

Additional Information

Leading hint: This is an example of Anglican chant, which is best sung in harmony. Throughout the entire chant, sing the text following the natural accents, even upon reaching the half notes. They do not indicate a change to metered rhythm. As with the psalm tones, singers are encouraged to sing through to the end of the phrase, rather than slowing down when pitches change.

229   Joyous Light of Glory

Pulse	Tempo	Style	Chpt Ref
Similar to chant, the pulse alternates between groups of two and three quarter notes. (half note and dotted half) Feel this alternation in a clear and relaxed manner.	♩ = 138–160	Legato, chant-like	2, 3, and 4

Accompaniment

Organ (piano)

230   Joyous Light of Glory

Pulse	Tempo	Style	Chpt Ref
The half note receives the pulse.	♩ = 60–72	Quietly joyful	2, 3, and 9

Accompaniment

Piano, guitar, bass, drums

Additional Information

Sing the syncopations clearly, but not aggressively.

During the long-held notes in the melody, be sure the accompaniment is played rhythmically to keep the tactus clear to the singers.

231   O Gracious Light

Pulse	Tempo	Style	Chpt Ref
The half note receives the pulse.	♩ = 66–76	Legato, chant-like	2, 3, and 5

Accompaniment

Organ (piano)

232   Let My Prayer Rise Up

Pulse	Tempo	Style	Chpt Ref
The quarter note receives the pulse. Keep a sense of the dotted half note as well.	♩ = 96–102	Dancing, flowing	3, 6, and 9

Accompaniment

Piano accompaniment is preferred. Guitar support is optional.

233   Let My Prayer Arise

Pulse	Tempo	Style	Chpt Ref
The dotted half note receives the pulse.	$\mathriccol{d}$. = 42–46	Reflective, unhurried	2, 3, 4, and 8

Accompaniment
Piano or organ accompaniment is preferred.

Additional Information
This setting of Psalm 141 is in two styles: a metrical refrain and chant-like verses. See #156 for guidance in leading chant. Allow the musical phrase to follow the natural rhythm of the text.

234   My Soul Proclaims the Greatness of the Lord

Pulse	Tempo	Style	Chpt Ref
As with all chant, this setting flows according to the natural textual accents. Depending on the text, the beats will be grouped in twos or threes (counting an open note as equal to two black notes).	A fluid tempo that neither rushes nor moves too slowly works best. It should be free, yet moving forward.	Freely	2, 3, and 4

Accompaniment
While it is preferable to sing chant unaccompanied, you may need to use organ or piano for support. If keyboard is needed, keep textures thin, taking care that any accompaniment does not overshadow the melodic line.

Additional Information
See chapter 4 for further guidance in leading chant.

235   My Soul Proclaims the Greatness of the Lord

Pulse	Chpt Ref
Piano (organ)	2, 3, and 4

Additional Information
See #234 for general hints on leading chant.

Unlike other chant settings, this contemporary chant arrangement includes a detailed keyboard accompaniment. Note that the cue notes between phrases are indicated in small print in the pew edition. Be careful to play these as written in order to lead the assembly effectively.

236   Magnificat

Pulse	Tempo	Style	Chpt Ref
The quarter note receives the pulse. A strong quarter helps keep this canon together. Note that the harmonic rhythm is the half note.	♩= 84–100	Joyful, unhurried	2, 3, 4, and 6

Accompaniment

Unaccompanied singing with a flute, oboe, or other instrument to support the melody is preferred. Use keyboard only if necessary.

Additional Information

Taizé choruses are sung prayers meant to be repeated many times. See chapter 4 for further guidance in leading Taizé chant.

Approximate pronunciation: Mah-nyee-fee-kaht ah-nee-mah meh-ah. Daw-mee-noom.

237   Litany of the Saints

Accompaniment	Chpt Ref
Unaccompanied singing is preferred.	2, 3, and 4

Additional Information

Sing in a natural speech rhythm. This may mean holding onto the first note a little longer than is indicated to give the emphasis to "Lord."

Note that each stave of music includes multiple lines of text. Be sure to sing all the phrases with the same response, e.g. "Hear us, O God," before going on to the next set of text.

238   Great Litany

Accompaniment	Chpt Ref
Unaccompanied singing is preferred.	2, 3, and 4

Additional Information

Sing in a natural-speech rhythm. This may mean holding onto the first note a little longer than is indicated, to give the emphasis to "Lord."

Note that each stave of music includes multiple lines of text. Be sure to sing all the phrases with the same response, e.g. "have mercy on us," before going on to the next set of text.

Teaching hint: The F♮ in this litany can be tricky. If teaching this to a choir or the entire assembly prior to worship, be sure to lead this interval with confidence.

Hymns

239   Hark, the Glad Sound!

CHESTERFIELD

Pulse	Tempo	Style	Chpt Ref
The dotted half note receives the pulse.	𝅗𝅥. = 40–48	Lively, grand, unhurried	3 and 5

Accompaniment

Legato organ (piano) accompaniment is preferred.

Additional Information

Leading hint: Be clear and consistent when playing the first note of measure seven. Keep the pulse moving forward, yet be sure to shorten the half note and give the assembly time to breathe. You may also consider adding an extra measure.

240   Light One Candle to Watch for Messiah

TIF IN VELDELE

Pulse	Tempo	Style	Chpt Ref
The dotted quarter note receives the pulse.	♩. = 50–60	Expectant, reflective, growing energy with each stanza	3 and 6

Accompaniment

Piano or organ accompaniment is preferred. A woodwind instrument (especially clarinet) doubling the melody could enhance the singing.

Additional Information

Feel a stress on the first and fourth eighth notes of each measure while keeping the other eighths lighter. Keep the texture legato.

241   O Lord, How Shall I Meet You

WIE SOLL ICH DICH EMPFANGEN

Pulse	Tempo	Style	Chpt Ref
The half note receives the pulse.	𝅗𝅥 = 52–60	Joyful, strong, confident	3 and 5

Accompaniment

Organ (piano)

Additional Information

While many German chorales work well played slightly detached, this melody works better when sung smoothly.

242 Awake! Awake, and Greet the New Morn

REJOICE, REJOICE

Pulse	Tempo	Style	Chpt Ref
The dotted quarter note receives the pulse	♩. = 54–60	Anticipatory, jubilant	3, 6, and 9

Accompaniment

Piano with guitar accompaniment is preferred. Organ is possible.

Additional Information

Leading hint: This piece should feel dance-like, emphasizing the long-short, long-short rhythm. Be sure to detach the repeated notes.

243 Lost in the Night

LOST IN THE NIGHT

Pulse	Tempo	Style	Chpt Ref
The half note receives the pulse, yet with some flexibility in the last line. Feel a stronger pulse on the second half of each measure.	♩ = 34–38	Pleading, melancholy, quietly confident	3, 5, and 6

Accompaniment

Legato organ (piano) accompaniment is preferred, yet this could also be sung unaccompanied.

Additional Information

244 Rejoice, Rejoice, Believers

HAF TRONES LAMPA FÄRDIG

Pulse	Tempo	Style	Chpt Ref
The half note receives the pulse.	♩ = 56–68	With joyful anticipation, steady, buoyant	3 and 5

Accompaniment

Organ (piano)

Additional Information

Leading hint: Feel a strong second beat at the end of each phrase. Releasing the chord precisely on this beat helps keep the rhythm clear and steady.

245   Creator of the Stars of Night

CONDITOR ALME SIDERUM

Pulse	Tempo	Style	Chpt Ref
As with all chant, this hymn flows according to the natural textual accents. For chant, depending on the text, the beats will be grouped in twos or threes.	A fluid tempo that neither rushes nor moves too slowly works best.	With quiet awe	3 and 4

Accompaniment

While it is preferable to sing chant unaccompanied, you may need to use organ or piano for support. If keyboard is needed, be sure it does not obstruct the natural rhythm. Unison singing is preferred.

246   Hark! A Thrilling Voice is Sounding!

MERTON

Pulse	Tempo	Style	Chpt Ref
The half note receives the pulse.	♩ = 40–50. In a tune such as this, where the note values are relatively uniform, the tempo can easily drag. Be careful to feel the longer phrase.	Bright, grand, hopeful	3 and 5

Accompaniment

Organ (piano)

247   Come Now, O Prince of Peace

Ososŏ, ososŏ

OSOSŎ

Pulse	Tempo	Style	Chpt Ref
The quarter note receives the pulse, yet be aware of the strong dotted half.	♩ = 66–78	Prayerful, haunting, peaceful	3 and 12

Accompaniment

Unlike most Asian song, this hymn is intended for four-part singing. Keyboard can provide vocal support if necessary.

Additional Information

Additional instruments could include flutes, plucked string instruments, gong, finger cymbal, or triangle. In this piece, consider having one of the percussion instruments play on the last quarter of each measure and between stanzas. For guidance on specifically Asian instruments that could be employed, see chapter 12.

248　People, Look East

BESANÇON

Pulse	Tempo	Style	Chpt Ref
The dotted quarter note receives the pulse.	♩. = 70–80. This carol works best in unison; singing in harmony requires a slower tempo.	Joyful, lively, dance-like	3, 5, and 6

Accompaniment

Piano or light organ accompaniment is preferred. Flute or rhythm instruments could be added. A possible rhythm pattern would be:

Additional Information

Leading hint: Note that the first three notes are upbeats. Feel a stronger pulse on the downbeat of each measure.

249　On Jordan's Bank the Baptist's Cry

PUER NOBIS

Pulse	Tempo	Style	Chpt Ref
The dotted half note receives the pulse.	♩. = 48–56	Gently dance-like	3 and 5

Accompaniment

Legato organ (piano) accompaniment is preferred.

Additional Information

Renaissance percussion such as hand drum and tambourine could enhance the singing of this dance-like tune.

250   Blessed Be the God of Israel
FOREST GREEN

Pulse	Tempo	Style	Chpt Ref
The half note receives the pulse.	♩ = 52–64	Flowing	3, 5, and 6

Accompaniment
Organ (piano)

Additional Information
A legato or lightly lilting articulation suits this English folk tune.

251   My Soul Proclaims Your Greatness
KINGSFOLD

Pulse	Tempo	Style	Chpt Ref
The half note receives the pulse. This is a tune that might appear to have a quarter-note pulse. See pages 21–22 for further discussion on determining tactus.	♩ = 58–72. A rhythmic, moderate tempo works best.	Dance-like, lilting	3, 5, and 6

Accompaniment
Various accompaniments are possible. If leading with a piano or organ, use a lightly detached articulation and be careful that the harmonies do not prevent the melody from moving ahead. A guitar accompaniment may accentuate the folk-like character of the melody.

Additional Information
This tune works best sung in unison, particularly at a quicker tempo.

252   Each Winter As the Year Grows Older
CAROL OF HOPE

Pulse	Tempo	Style	Chpt Ref
The quarter note receives the pulse.	♩ = 74–84	Flowing, yearning	3, 5, and 6

Accompaniment
Piano or guitar accompaniment is preferred. Organ accompaniment could also be successful.

253   He Came Down

HE CAME DOWN

Pulse	Tempo	Style	Chpt Ref
The half note receives the pulse. This enables the singer to shift easily between quarter notes and triplets.	$\half = 52$–60. Be careful not to rush the triplet figures.	Joyful, unhurried	3 and 11

Accompaniment

Unaccompanied singing in four-part harmony is preferred. Percussion (drums and shakers) can be added. Keyboard support can be added if necessary.

Additional Information

Teaching hint: When learning this song, it may be helpful to have the full assembly learn the melody, gradually adding the bass, tenor, and alto lines. Percussion can then be added. This hymn can bear repetition, repeating stanzas or improvising new ones.

254   Come, Thou Long-Expected Jesus

JEFFERSON

Pulse	Tempo	Style	Chpt Ref
The quarter note receives the pulse. Early American tunes from the *Southern Harmony* tradition have a rugged quality. A quarter-note pulse helps to convey this quality.	$\quarter = 120$–132	With joyful anticipation	3 and 6

Accompaniment

Organ (piano). Singing unaccompanied in four-part harmony would work well.

255   There's a Voice in the Wilderness

ASCENSION

Pulse	Tempo	Style	Chpt Ref
The quarter note receives the pulse.	$\quarter = 112$–126	Clearly articulated, vigorous, energetic	3 and 5

Accompaniment

Organ accompaniment is preferred.

Additional Information

Leading hint: In preparing the choir to lead this, encourage them to carry energy through "crooked places," sailing through the high E♭.

256 Comfort, Comfort Now My People

FREU DICH SEHR

Pulse	Tempo	Style	Chpt Ref
The pulse shifts between the dotted half note and half note: ♩. ♩. ♪♪♪ See page 37 for further guidance in leading this rhythmic tune.	♩ = 56–70	Gentle, dance-like	3 and 5

Accompaniment

Organ (piano). Allow the accompaniment to emphasize the shifting pulse.

Additional Information

Unison singing is preferred.

257 O Come, O Come, Emmanuel

VENI, EMMANUEL

Pulse	Tempo	Style	Chpt Ref
This hymn flows according to the natural textual accents. For chant, depending on the text, the beats will be grouped in twos or threes.	A fluid tempo that neither rushes nor moves too slowly works best.	Meditative, yet moving forward on verses; refrain is jubilant.	3, 4, and 5

Accompaniment

While it is preferable to sing chant unaccompanied, you may need to use organ or piano for support. If keyboard is needed, be sure it does not obstruct the natural rhythm. Unison singing is preferred.

Additional Information

Leading hint: Consider following the notation on the last line of the phrase and carrying through from "Emmanuel" through "shall" without a breath. Then articulate a breath after "you." This emphasizes the meaning of the textual phrase.

258 Unexpected and Mysterious

ST. HELENA

Pulse	Tempo	Style	Chpt Ref
The quarter note receives the pulse.	♩ = 74–82	Expansive, lyrical	3 and 5

Accompaniment

Organ or organ with an obbligato instrument (oboe, flute, clarinet) is preferred. This can be played like a trio, with a solo instrument on the melody, the organ on the middle voice, and a string bass on the lowest voice. Note also the optional simplified accompaniment.

Additional Information

Teaching hint: Consider having a children's or adult choir sing this as an anthem before teaching it to the full assembly.

Leading hint: Always sense the longer line. Think horizontally rather than vertically.
See #587 for this tune in E major.

259 Fling Wide the Door

MACHT HOCH DIE TÜR

Pulse	Tempo	Style	Chpt Ref
The dotted half note receives the pulse.	$\dot{\half} = 50$–58. A quicker tempo preserves the dance feel.	Dance-like	3 and 5

Accompaniment
Organ (piano)

Additional Information
A detached articulation works best, with the upbeats almost staccato.

260 The King Shall Come

CONSOLATION

Pulse	Tempo	Style	Chpt Ref
The half note receives the pulse.	$\half = 46$–52	Rugged, prayerful	3 and 7

Accompaniment
Organ (piano)

Additional Information
Unison singing is preferred. Organ or piano is possible.

261 As the Dark Awaits the Dawn

LUCENT

Pulse	Tempo	Style	Chpt Ref
The half note receives the pulse.	$\half = 52$–56	Legato, contemplative	3 and 5

Accompaniment
Organ (piano)

262 Wait for the Lord

WAIT FOR THE LORD

Pulse	Tempo	Style	Chpt Ref
The half note receives the pulse.	$\half = 46$–58	Meditative, chant-like	3 and 4

Accompaniment
Unaccompanied singing in four-part harmony is preferred. Light organ, piano, or guitar can provide support. Woodwinds can play counter melodies or obbligatos. See Taizé collections in Bibliography.

Additional Information
Taizé choruses are sung prayers meant to be repeated many times. The chorus can be sung alone, or a cantor can sing the verses between repetitions of the chorus. See pages 33–34 for further guidance.

263   Savior of the Nations, Come
NUN KOMM, DER HEIDEN HEILAND

Pulse	Tempo	Style	Chpt Ref
The half note receives the pulse.	♩ = 40–48	Confident, sturdy	3 and 5

Accompaniment
Organ (piano)

264   Prepare the Royal Highway
BEREDEN VÄG FÖR HERRAN

Pulse	Tempo	Style	Chpt Ref
The dotted half note receives the pulse. Sense a stronger half note and lighter quarter note when this pattern occurs.	♩. = 60–76	Dance-like, energetic, confident	3 and 5

Accompaniment
Organ (piano)

Additional Information
Leading hint: Release the held note at the end of the first and second phrases precisely on the second full beat. This helps the assembly sense the rhythm and breathe for the next phrase.

265   The Angel Gabriel from Heaven Came
GABRIEL'S MESSAGE

Pulse	Tempo	Style	Chpt Ref
The dotted quarter note receives the pulse.	♩. = 52–60. A relaxed tempo works best.	Light, floating	3, 5, and 6

Accompaniment
Organ accompaniment is preferred.

Additional Information
Leading hint: Be sure to play the pickup notes to each phrase in time; this keeps the tempo steady. You may also consider tying some of the repeated notes in the lower three voices. See pages 38–39 for help with this organ technique.

This hymn would work well sung in alternation. See pages 45–46 for examples.

266   All Earth Is Hopeful

Toda la tierra

TODA LA TIERRA

Pulse	Tempo	Style	Chpt Ref
The quarter note receives the pulse. Feeling the quarter pulse keeps the hymn from rushing.	♩ = 84–92	Joyful, light	3 and 10

Accompaniment

Guitar and/or piano accompaniment with light percussion (conga drums, guiro, egg shakers) is preferred. A possible percussion pattern:

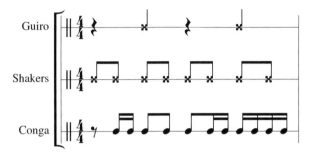

Additional Information

A light articulation will keep the hymn bright.

267   Joy to the World

ANTIOCH

Pulse	Tempo	Style	Chpt Ref
The half note receives the pulse.	♩ = 44–52	Festive, crisp, energetic	3 and 5

Accompaniment

Organ (piano)

Additional Information

The use of brass instruments can enhance this hymn.

Leading challenge: A decision will have to be made regarding the first note of measure seven. Common practice is to add two beats, thus completing the natural feel of an eight-measure phrase. The other option is to play it as written. In this case, the dotted quarter note will need to become a quarter note with a quarter rest to ensure a clear breath by the assembly. In either case, be sure to keep a steady pulse.

268   From Heaven Above

VOM HIMMEL HOCH

Pulse	Tempo	Style	Chpt Ref
The half note receives the pulse.	♩= 52–60	Joyful, strong, energetic	3 and 5

Accompaniment

Consider singing this narrative hymn in alternation with choirs, soloists, congregation, and instruments. See pages 45–46 for singing in alternation.

Additional Information

Leading hint: A characteristic of sixteenth-century chorales is their rhythmic vitality. Note that this hymn begins with an eighth-note pickup. Be sure to prepare with a breath, keep the pickup light, and feel a stress on the first quarter note.

269   Once in Royal David's City

IRBY

Pulse	Tempo	Style	Chpt Ref
The half note receives the pulse.	♩= 34–40	Expansive, flowing, gentle	3 and 5

Accompaniment

Organ (piano)

Additional Information

Consider having a soloist introduce the first stanza, gradually adding voices or harmony, including a descant on the final stanza.

270   Hark! The Herald Angels Sing

MENDELSSOHN

Pulse	Tempo	Style	Chpt Ref
The half note receives the pulse.	♩= 56–64	Lively, energetic, joyous	3 and 5

Accompaniment

Organ (piano)

Additional Information

Solo trumpet or other brass instruments could enhance this hymn.

Leading hint: The two quarter notes that begin the fourth line are commonly sung as a dotted quarter note followed by an eighth note. Be sure to play the written rhythm clearly.

271   I Am So Glad Each Christmas Eve

Jeg er så glad hver julekveld

JEG ER SÅ GLAD

Pulse	Tempo	Style	Chpt Ref
The dotted quarter note receives the pulse.	♩.= 60–66	With childlike joy, simple, lyrical	3, 5, and 6

Accompaniment
Organ (piano)

272   Lo, How a Rose E'er Blooming

ES IST EIN ROS

Pulse	Tempo	Style	Chpt Ref
The half note receives the pulse. Note the meter shifts between ²⁄₂ and ³⁄₂.	♩= 50–62	As a gentle dance	3 and 5

Accompaniment
Organ or unaccompanied four-part singing is preferred.

Additional Information
Leading hint: Enjoy, even linger on, the syncopated rhythms at the conclusion of each phrase.

273   All My Heart Again Rejoices

WARUM SOLLT ICH

Pulse	Tempo	Style	Chpt Ref
The half note receives the pulse.	♩= 62–74	Quietly joyful	3 and 5

Accompaniment
Organ (piano)

Additional Information
A legato articulation suits this chorale.

This chorale tune is easily confused with FRÖHLICH SOLL MEIN HERZE SPRINGEN, the tune used for this text in *Lutheran Book of Worship* (#46). If that might pose a problem for your assembly, make sure your introduction is clear and your choir well prepared.

274   On Christmas Night

SUSSEX CAROL

Pulse	Tempo	Style	Chpt Ref
The dotted quarter note receives the pulse.	♩.= 62–70	Dance-like, gentle	3, 5, and 6

Accompaniment
Organ (piano). A flute or other woodwind instrument on the melody would enhance this carol.

275   Angels, from the Realms of Glory

REGENT SQUARE

Pulse	Tempo	Style	Chpt Ref
The half note receives the pulse.	$\half = 50\text{–}62$	Noble, grand, festive	3 and 5

Accompaniment
Organ (piano)

276   Infant Holy, Infant Lowly

W ŻŁOBIE LEŻY

Pulse	Tempo	Style	Chpt Ref
The quarter note receives the pulse.	$\quarter = 68\text{–}78$	Lyrical	3, 5, and 6

Accompaniment
Organ or piano accompaniment is preferred. Guitar with a woodwind instrument playing the melody is also possible.

Additional Information
Leading hint: Think of this carol as a stately waltz. Imagine a strong, sweeping stride on beat one with two shorter, lighter steps on beats two and three.

277   Away in a Manger

AWAY IN A MANGER

Pulse	Tempo	Style	Chpt Ref
The dotted half note receives the pulse.	$\dottedhalf = 36\text{–}38$	Gentle, as a lullaby	3, 6, and 7

Accompaniment
Legato organ (piano) accompaniment is preferred.

278   Away in a Manger

CRADLE SONG

Pulse	Tempo	Style	Chpt Ref
The quarter note receives the pulse. Sense a strong half note followed by a lighter quarter note in each measure.	$\quarter = 78\text{–}84$	Gentle, as a lullaby	3, 6, and 7

Accompaniment
Organ (piano)

279 O Little Town of Bethlehem

ST. LOUIS

Pulse	Tempo	Style	Chpt Ref
The half note receives the pulse.	♩ = 44–56	Contemplative, serene	3 and 5

Accompaniment
Organ (piano)

280 Midnight Stars Make Bright the Skies

Mingxing canlan ye wei yang

HUAN-SHA-XI

Pulse	Tempo	Style	Chpt Ref
The quarter note receives the pulse. This pulse allows the eighth notes to have a deliberate and even pacing.	♩ = 72–96. It is best to find a tempo that allows singers to sing a phrase in one breath. Consider the second half of the tune when setting the tempo.	Quietly joyful	3 and 12

Accompaniment
This hymn is best accompanied with a flute or a violin doubling the melody, or a cello or viola playing one octave lower. The spare keyboard accompaniment provided will work on keyboard, piano, or organ. For guidance on specifically Asian instruments that could be employed, see chapter 12.

281 Silent Night, Holy Night!

Stille Nacht, heilige Nacht!

STILLE NACHT

Pulse	Tempo	Style	Chpt Ref
The dotted half or quarter note receives the pulse. A slow tempo allows one to feel the quarter-note pulse, but being mindful of the larger pulse helps keep the tune moving forward.	♩. = 80–120	Gentle, quiet	3 and 5

Accompaniment
Various accompaniments suit this carol: organ, piano, guitar, or unaccompanied singing in four-part harmony.

Additional Information
Leading hint: This tune is inspired by a traditional Austrian waltz. Keep it legato, yet allow it to dance.

282   It Came upon the Midnight Clear

CAROL

Pulse	Tempo	Style	Chpt Ref
The dotted half note receives the pulse.	$\dot{\half} = 44\text{--}50$	Flowing	3, 5, and 7

Accompaniment
Legato organ (piano) accompaniment is preferred.

283   O Come, All Ye Faithful

ADESTE FIDELES

Pulse	Tempo	Style	Chpt Ref
The half note receives the pulse.	$\half = 54\text{--}60$	Majestic, stately, grand	3 and 5

Accompaniment
Organ (piano)

Additional Information
The use of brass instruments can enhance this hymn.
Latin pronunciation: ven-EE-tay ah-doh-RAY-mus DAW-mee-noom

284   'Twas in the Moon of Wintertime

UNE JEUNE PUCELLE

Pulse	Tempo	Style	Chpt Ref
The quarter note receives the pulse.	$\quarter = 52\text{--}72$	Legato, reflective	3, 6, and 7

Accompaniment
Piano (organ). For a small assembly, this would be effective if led by acoustic guitar and recorder.

285   Peace Came to Earth

SCHNEIDER

Pulse	Tempo	Style	Chpt Ref
The half note receives the pulse.	$\half = 52\text{--}60$	Sweeping	3 and 5

Accompaniment
Organ accompaniment is preferred.

Additional Information
Leading hint: Consider breaking before the last "Immanuel" in each stanza. This will allow for a good breath to support the held higher notes.

286 Your Little Ones, Dear Lord

HER KOMMER DINE ARME SMÅ

Pulse	Tempo	Style	Chpt Ref
The quarter note receives the pulse.	♩= 88–96	Simple, childlike, gentle	3 and 6

Accompaniment

Organ (piano)

Additional Information

Articulate the repeated notes carefully. See pages 38–39 for help with playing repeated notes on the organ.

287 Let All Together Praise Our God

LOBT GOTT, IHR CHRISTEN

Pulse	Tempo	Style	Chpt Ref
The half note receives the pulse.	♩= 60–72	Strong, dance-like	3 and 5

Accompaniment

Organ (piano)

Additional Information

Articulate the repeated notes of this chorale carefully. See pages 38–39 for help with playing repeated notes on the organ.

288 Good Christian Friends, Rejoice

IN DULCI JUBILO

Pulse	Tempo	Style	Chpt Ref
The dotted quarter note receives the pulse.	♩.= 62–70	Dance-like, gentle	3, 5, and 6

Accompaniment

Organ (piano). A flute or other woodwind instrument on the melody would enhance this carol.

289 Angels We Have Heard on High

GLORIA

Pulse	Tempo	Style	Chpt Ref
The half note receives the pulse.	♩= 54–72	Joyful, flowing	3 and 5

Accompaniment

Organ (piano)

Additional Information

Consider unaccompanied singing on the refrain.

290   Go Tell It on the Mountain

GO TELL IT

Pulse	Tempo	Style	Chpt Ref
The half note or quarter note receives the pulse. A quarter note pulse can accentuate the rhythmic quality, particularly at a slower tempo.	♩ = 100–132 (♩ = 50–66). Due to their roots in oral tradition, many African American spirituals can be successful at a wide range of tempos. Knowing your context and your assembly is especially important when setting a tempo.	Joyful	3 and 8

Accompaniment

Organ or piano accompaniment is preferred

Additional Information

Especially on the refrain, accents and hand-clapping on beats two and four would be appropriate.

291   Let Our Gladness Have No End

NARODIL SE KRISTUS PÁN

Pulse	Tempo	Style	Chpt Ref
The half note receives the pulse. In the 6/4 measures of the refrain, feel a stress on beats 1, 3, and 5.	♩ = 46–52	Walking style	3 and 6

Accompaniment

Organ accompaniment is preferred. A krummhorn or similar stop reflects this Bohemian carol's folk-like origins.

Additional Information

Teaching hint: Those familiar with versions of this tune in previous hymnals will note that this version has gone back to the original pseudo-Lydian mode at the beginning of the carol (B♮, or raised fourth). This sound is characteristic of the genre.

292   Love Has Come

UN FLAMBEAU

Pulse	Tempo	Style	Chpt Ref
The dotted half note receives the pulse. The first beat of each measure is strong; two and three are light but not detached.	♩. = 54–66	Dance-like	3 and 6

Accompaniment

Organ (piano)

Additional Information

This carol can be sung in unison or in harmony. If sung in harmony, be sure that the tempo keeps moving and the dotted half pulse is maintained.

293   That Boy-Child of Mary

BLANTYRE

Pulse	Tempo	Style	Chpt Ref
The dotted quarter receives the pulse.	♩. = 56–64	Light, upbeat, lilting	3, 10, and 11

Accompaniment
Piano or guitar accompaniment is preferred. Light percussion (congas, maracas) or Orff instruments may enhance this southern African tune.

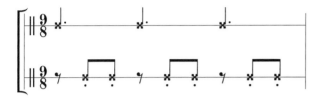

Additional Information
Leading hint: Consider having a children's choir teach this to the assembly in a dialogical fashion.

294   In the Bleak Midwinter

CRANHAM

Pulse	Tempo	Style	Chpt Ref
The half note receives the pulse.	♩ = 42–50	Gentle, sustained, prayerful	3 and 5

Accompaniment
Organ (piano)

295   Of the Father's Love Begotten

DIVINUM MYSTERIUM

Pulse	Tempo	Style	Chpt Ref
As with all chant, this hymn flows according to the natural textual accents. For chant, depending on the text, the beats will be grouped in twos or threes.	A fluid tempo that neither rushes nor moves too slowly works best.	With quiet awe	3 and 4

Accompaniment
While it is preferable to sing chant unaccompanied, you may need to use organ or piano for support. If keyboard is needed, be sure it does not obstruct the natural rhythm. Unison singing is preferred.

296   What Child Is This

GREENSLEEVES

Pulse	Tempo	Style	Chpt Ref
The dotted quarter note receives the pulse.	♩.= 42–48. Keep the tempo moving.	Simple, light	3, 5, and 6

Accompaniment

Organ accompaniment is preferred. Piano, harp, or plucked guitar are possible.

Additional Information

Leading hint: If accompanying with keyboard, it is not necessary to articulate every eighth note in the lower voices.

297   Jesus, What a Wonderful Child

WONDERFUL CHILD

Pulse	Tempo	Style	Chpt Ref
The dotted quarter note receives the pulse. Four beats to the bar, but feel every eighth note strongly to keep the rhythm strong.	♩.= 88–108	Driving, energetic	3 and 8

Accompaniment

Piano or Hammond B3 organ is preferred. Drums, bass, and guitar could be added.

Additional Information

Be very clear on the syncopations, even within the first beat. Sing "JE-sus" following the natural accents.

Leading hint: To keep the vital inner rhythms strong, consider improvising during the rests in measures 1, 2, 4, 5, and 6. See page 55 for more on this technique.

Clipping the eighth-note values is appropriate for this spirited gospel song.

298   The Bells of Christmas

Det kimer nu til julefest

DET KIMER NU TIL JULEFEST

Pulse	Tempo	Style	Chpt Ref
The dotted half note receives the pulse.	♩.= 46–52	Gently	3 and 5

Accompaniment

Organ (piano)

Additional Information

This Danish tune lends itself to singing in four-part harmony.

299   Cold December Flies Away

EL DESEMBRE CONGELAT

Pulse	Tempo	Style	Chpt Ref
The quarter note receives the pulse.	♩= 70–80. Consider the sixteenth notes in the second half when setting the tempo. If too slow, this carol loses its sprightly character. Too fast, and the assembly may stumble over the words.	Festive, with bounce	3 and 6

Accompaniment
Organ (piano). A lightly detached articulation works best.

300   The First Noel

THE FIRST NOWELL

Pulse	Tempo	Style	Chpt Ref
The quarter note receives the pulse. At a faster pulse, feel a half note followed by a quarter in each measure.	♩= 98–106	Flowing, smooth	3 and 5

Accompaniment
Organ (piano)

EPIPHANY

301   Bright and Glorious Is the Sky

DEJLIG ER DEN HIMMEL BLÅ

Pulse	Tempo	Style	Chpt Ref
The half note receives the pulse.	♩= 56–60	Simple, cheerful, bright	3, 5, and 6

Accompaniment
Organ (piano)

Additional Information
A crisp, non-legato articulation suits this tune best.

302 As with Gladness Men of Old
DIX

Pulse	Tempo	Style	Chpt Ref
The half note receives the pulse.	$\half = 52\text{–}62$	Flowing	3 and 5

Accompaniment
Organ (piano)

303 Brightest and Best of the Stars
MORNING STAR

Pulse	Tempo	Style	Chpt Ref
The half note receives the pulse.	$\half = 60\text{–}64$	Flowing	3 and 5

Accompaniment
Organ (piano)

TIME AFTER EPIPHANY

304 Christ, When for Us You Were Baptized
LOBT GOTT, IHR CHRISTEN

Pulse	Tempo	Style	Chpt Ref
The half note receives the pulse.	$\half = 60\text{–}72$	Strong, dance-like	3 and 5

Accompaniment
Organ (piano)

Additional Information
Articulate the repeated notes of this chorale carefully. See pages 38–39 for help playing repeated notes on the organ.

305 When Jesus Came to Jordan
KING'S LYNN

Pulse	Tempo	Style	Chpt Ref
The half note receives the pulse. Maintain a strong feeling of the half note.	$\half = 56\text{–}62$	Grand, stately	3, 5, and 6

Accompaniment
Organ (piano)

Additional Information
Leading hint: A marcato articulation suits this angular folk tune.

306   Come, Beloved of the Maker

JILL

Pulse	Tempo	Style	Chpt Ref
The half note receives the pulse, but also sense a comfortable quarter note. This will help the second full measure flow.	♩ = 58–66	Legato, flowing	3 and 6

Accompaniment

Organ (piano)

Additional Information

Leading hint: Treat each measure as a legato phrase.

307   Light Shone in Darkness

LUX IN TENEBRIS

Pulse	Tempo	Style	Chpt Ref
The half note receives the pulse. Stress the first beat of each measure.	♩ = 56–72	Flowing, proclamatory	3 and 6

Accompaniment

Organ or piano accompaniment. The left hand may play in a slightly detached manner. A hand drum playing a simple pattern could complement the buoyant nature of the hymn:

Additional Information

Leading hint: Allow the melody to crescendo toward the first note (C) of the fifth measure, and then again in the final two measures.

308 O Morning Star, How Fair and Bright!

WIE SCHÖN LEUCHTET

Pulse	Tempo	Style	Chpt Ref
The pulse shifts between the half note and dotted half note, producing groupings of two and three quarter notes. Keep a steady pulse.	♩ = 62–74	Vigorous, jubilant	3 and 5

Accompaniment
Organ accompaniment is preferred. An accompanying style that articulates the half and dotted half groupings will aid the singers. It can also be sung unaccompanied.

Additional Information
Leading hint: Be sure to allow the assembly to breathe between phrases, particularly before the final phrase, yet do not add extra beats or lose the pulse.

309 The Only Son From Heaven

HERR CHRIST, DER EINIG GOTTS SOHN

Pulse	Tempo	Style	Chpt Ref
Near the end, the pulse shifts between the half note and dotted half note, producing groupings of two and three quarter notes. Keep a steady pulse.	♩ = 58–72	Joyful, strong	3 and 5

Accompaniment
Organ accompaniment is preferred. An accompanying style that articulates the half and dotted half groupings will aid the singers. It can also be sung unaccompanied.

310 Songs of Thankfulness and Praise

SALZBURG

Pulse	Tempo	Style	Chpt Ref
The half note receives the pulse.	♩ = 52–62	Walking tempo	3 and 5

Accompaniment
Organ (piano)

311   Hail to the Lord's Anointed

FREUT EUCH, IHR LIEBEN

Pulse	Tempo	Style	Chpt Ref
The half note receives the pulse.	♩ = 60–66	Regal, as a processional	3 and 5

Accompaniment
Organ (piano)

Additional Information
Leading hint: Note that this chorale begins with an upbeat.

312   Jesus, Come! For We Invite You

UNION SEMINARY

Pulse	Tempo	Style	Chpt Ref
The half note receives the pulse, yet note the shifting duple/triple meter.	♩ = 54–60	Inviting, lyrical	3 and 5

Accompaniment
Organ (piano)

313   O Lord, Now Let Your Servant

KUORTANE

Pulse	Tempo	Style	Chpt Ref
The half note receives the pulse.	♩ = 50–58	Lyrical, confident	3 and 5

Accompaniment
Organ (piano)

314   Arise, Your Light Has Come

FESTAL SONG

Pulse	Tempo	Style	Chpt Ref
The half note receives the pulse.	♩ = 62–70	Strong, lively, proclamatory	3 and 5

Accompaniment
Organ (piano)

315   How Good, Lord, to Be Here!

POTSDAM

Pulse	Tempo	Style	Chpt Ref
The half note receives the pulse.	♩= 52–58	Sturdy, melodic	3 and 5

Accompaniment
Organ (piano)

316   Oh, Wondrous Image, Vision Fair

DEO GRACIAS

Pulse	Tempo	Style	Chpt Ref
The half note receives the pulse. Note the shifting accents of the melody.	♩= 44–52	Rugged, confident, majestic	3 and 5

Accompaniment
Organ accompaniment is preferred. The use of brass and/or timpani may enhance the singing of this hymn.

Additional Information
A fairly marcato articulation will enhance the rhythmic drive of the music.

317   Jesus on the Mountain Peak

BETHOLD

Pulse	Tempo	Style	Chpt Ref
The half note receives the pulse.	♩= 48–52	Grand, majestic	3 and 5

Accompaniment
Organ (piano)

318   Alleluia, Song of Gladness

PRAISE, MY SOUL

Pulse	Tempo	Style	Chpt Ref
The half note receives the pulse.	♩= 42–60	Expansive, majestic	3 and 5

Accompaniment
Organ (piano)

Additional Information
Articulate the repeated notes clearly. See pages 38–39 for help with playing repeated notes on the organ.

319   O Lord, throughout These Forty Days

CONSOLATION

Pulse	Tempo	Style	Chpt Ref
The half note receives the pulse.	♩ = 46–52	Rugged, prayerful	3 and 7

Accompaniment
Organ (piano)

Additional Information
Unison singing is preferred. Organ or piano is possible.

320   The Glory of These Forty Days

ERHALT UNS, HERR

Pulse	Tempo	Style	Chpt Ref
The half note receives the pulse.	♩ = 50–58	Strong, somber, confident	3 and 5

Accompaniment
Organ (piano)

321   Eternal Lord of Love, Behold Your Church

OLD 124TH

Pulse	Tempo	Style	Chpt Ref
The half note receives the pulse. One could also consider a broad whole-note pulse, while still keeping the internal rhythms strong.	♩ = 56–64. A brisk walking tempo works well.	Expansive, confident, sturdy	3 and 5

Accompaniment
Organ accompaniment is preferred.

Additional Information
Leading hint: Sing through the whole notes at the ends of phrases. This will keep the melody moving forward.

322   Oh, Love, How Deep

DEO GRACIAS

Pulse	Tempo	Style	Chpt Ref
The half note receives the pulse. Note the shifting accents of the melody.	♩ = 44–52	Rugged, telling the story	3 and 5

Accompaniment
Organ accompaniment is preferred.

Additional Information
A somewhat less marcato treatment than for #316 might be suitable.

323   God Loved the World

ROCKINGHAM OLD

Pulse	Tempo	Style	Chpt Ref
The dotted half note receives the pulse.	♩. = 38–42	Lyrical, noble	3 and 5

Accompaniment
Legato organ (piano) accompaniment is preferred.

324   In the Cross of Christ I Glory

RATHBUN

Pulse	Tempo	Style	Chpt Ref
The dotted half note receives the pulse.	♩. = 42–50	Flowing, noble	3 and 7

Accompaniment
Legato organ (piano) accompaniment is preferred.

325   I Want Jesus to Walk with Me

SOJOURNER

Pulse	Tempo	Style	Chpt Ref
The quarter note receives the pulse.	♩ = 76–84. See #290 for further guidance.	Confident, soulful, walking tempo	3 and 8

Accompaniment
Organ or piano accompaniment is preferred. Bass could be added. Consider singing unaccompanied if well-known.

Additional Information
Leading hint: It is appropriate feel an underlying triplet for each quarter note. The eighth notes can then be swung, rather than played as written. See the alternate accompaniment.

326 Bless Now, O God, the Journey

LLANGLOFFAN

Pulse	Tempo	Style	Chpt Ref
The dotted half note receives the pulse.	♩. = 54–58	Stately, strong	3 and 5

Accompaniment
Organ (piano)

327 Through the Night of Doubt and Sorrow

EBENEZER

Pulse	Tempo	Style	Chpt Ref
The half note receives the pulse.	♩ = 76–90	Majestic, strong, stately	3 and 5

Accompaniment
Organ (piano)

Additional Information
If sung in harmony, be careful that the harmonies do not slow the tempo.

328 Restore in Us, O God

BAYLOR

Pulse	Tempo	Style	Chpt Ref
The half note receives the pulse.	♩ = 54–60	With graceful strength	3 and 8

Accompaniment
Organ (piano)

329 As the Sun with Longer Journey

NAGEL

Pulse	Tempo	Style	Chpt Ref
The quarter note receives the pulse.	♩ = 62–66	Legato, meditative	3, 5, and 6

Accompaniment
Organ (piano)

330 Seed That in Earth Is Dying

SÅKORN SOM DØR I JORDEN

Pulse	Tempo	Style	Chpt Ref
The half note receives the pulse.	♩ = 50–56	Flowing, relaxed, confident	3 and 5

Accompaniment
Organ (piano)

331 As the Deer Runs to the River

JULION

Pulse	Tempo	Style	Chpt Ref
The dotted half or quarter note receives the pulse. A slow tempo allows one to feel the quarter-note pulse, but being mindful of the larger pulse helps keep the tune moving forward.	♩ = 78–88	Reflective	3 and 5

Accompaniment
Organ accompaniment is preferred. Carefully emphasize the pedal point on the second beat of each measure of the verse.

Additional Information
Leading challenge: This hymn requires a bit of extra practice to execute the dense inner harmonies supporting the melody.

332 I Heard the Voice of Jesus Say

THIRD MODE MELODY

Pulse	Tempo	Style	Chpt Ref
This chant-like tune has a shifting pulse. Feel an underlying half note or dotted half–note pulse.	♩ = 52–60	Intimate, contemplative	3 and 5

Accompaniment
Organ accompaniment or unaccompanied singing is preferred.

Additional Information
Unlike traditional chant, this tune sings well in harmony.

333   Jesus Is a Rock in a Weary Land

WEARY LAND

Pulse	Tempo	Style	Chpt Ref
The half note receives the pulse.	♩ = 56–66. See #290 for further guidance.	African American spiritual, with conviction	3 and 8

Accompaniment

Unaccompanied singing is preferred. Consider using a bass drum or foot stamps to maintain a steady beat. The foot stamping can alternate, beats one and three using the toe, beats two and four using the heel.

Additional Information

This is best sung with a leader singing the verses and the assembly joining on the refrain.

334   Tree of Life and Awesome Mystery

THOMAS

Pulse	Tempo	Style	Chpt Ref
The quarter note receives the pulse.	♩ = 76–86	Simply, like a folk tune	3 and 6

Accompaniment

The rolling accompaniment style lends itself to piano or guitar accompaniment. A C instrument could support the melody. If accompanied with organ, simply play the accompaniment as provided.

335   Jesus, Keep Me Near the Cross

NEAR THE CROSS

Pulse	Tempo	Style	Chpt Ref
The dotted quarter note receives the pulse. At a very slow tempo, feel an eighth-note pulse as well, to keep the inner energy going.	♩. = 38–48. This slower tempo works best if played in a swung gospel style; choose a quicker tempo if played in a revival style as written, on the organ.	Meditative, rather slow	3, 7, and 8

Accompaniment

Organ, piano or organ/piano duet accompaniment is preferred. Bass and drums could be added.

336   Lamb of God
Your Only Son
YOUR ONLY SON

Pulse	Tempo	Style	Chpt Ref
The quarter note receives the pulse.	♩ = 58–70. Be careful not to rush this song.	Reflective	3 and 9

Accompaniment

Piano, guitar, organ or praise band are all possible accompaniments. Any accompaniment should strive to support the melody.

337   Alas! And Did My Savior Bleed
MARTYRDOM

Pulse	Tempo	Style	Chpt Ref
The dotted half note receives the pulse.	♩. = 42–46	Prayerful, confident	3 and 7

Accompaniment

Legato organ (piano) accompaniment is preferred.

Additional Information

Leading hint: Some assemblies may expect the last note of the first phrase to be held an extra dotted half note (see #617). If played as written, the half note will need to be shortened in order to allow the assembly time to breathe. Know your assembly and lead either option with confidence.

338   Beneath the Cross of Jesus
ST. CHRISTOPHER

Pulse	Tempo	Style	Chpt Ref
The half note receives the pulse.	♩ = 50–54	Meditative	3 and 7

Accompaniment

Organ (piano)

339   Christ, the Life of All the Living
JESU, MEINES LEBENS LEBEN

Pulse	Tempo	Style	Chpt Ref
The half note receives the pulse.	♩ = 58–66	Calmly confident	3 and 5

Accompaniment

Organ (piano)

Additional Information

This tune is best sung smoothly in unison.

340   A Lamb Goes Uncomplaining Forth

AN WASSERFLÜSSEN BABYLON

Pulse	Tempo	Style	Chpt Ref
The half note receives the pulse.	♩ = 56–62	Stately	3 and 5

Accompaniment
Organ (piano)

Additional Information
Leading hint: Articulate precisely the ends of phrases.

341   Now Behold the Lamb

NOW BEHOLD THE LAMB

Pulse	Tempo	Style	Chpt Ref
The quarter note receives the pulse.	♩ = 56–72	Gospel, meditative	3 and 8

Accompaniment
Piano or synthesizer accompaniment is preferred. Consider adding bass, drums, and B♭ soprano saxophone.

Additional Information
If men sing the bottom notes of the chords on the treble clef, this chorus can be sung in three-part harmony.

342   There in God's Garden

SHADES MOUNTAIN

Pulse	Tempo	Style	Chpt Ref
The half note receives the pulse.	♩ = 50–56	Sturdy, confident, lyrical	3 and 5

Accompaniment
Organ (piano)

Additional Information
This tune sings well in unison or in four-part harmony.

343   My Song Is Love Unknown

LOVE UNKNOWN

Pulse	Tempo	Style	Chpt Ref
The half note receives the pulse.	♩ = 54–62	Lyrical, confident, smoothly	3 and 5

Accompaniment

Organ (piano)

Additional Information

Consider soloing out the melody or adding a solo instrument. See page 26 for help with soloing out on the organ.

See page 26 for help with soloing out on the organ.

HOLY WEEK, THREE DAYS

344   All Glory, Laud, and Honor

VALET WILL ICH DIR GEBEN

Pulse	Tempo	Style	Chpt Ref
The half note receives the pulse.	♩ = 54–66	Strong, joyful	3 and 5

Accompaniment

Organ accompaniment is preferred.

Additional Information

This hymn works well with the assembly singing the unison refrain and the choir singing the stanzas in harmony. If singing in harmony, you may wish to transpose this up to C major.

345   Jesus, I Will Ponder Now

JESU KREUZ, LEIDEN UND PEIN

Pulse	Tempo	Style	Chpt Ref
The pulse shifts between the half note and dotted half note, producing groupings of two and three quarter notes. Keep a steady pulse.	♩ = 62–68	Introspective, gentle dance	3 and 5

Accompaniment

Organ accompaniment is preferred. An accompanying style that articulates the half and dotted half groupings will aid the singers. It can also be sung unaccompanied.

346   Ride On, Ride On in Majesty!

THE KING'S MAJESTY

Pulse	Tempo	Style	Chpt Ref
The half note receives the pulse. Note the shifting meter between groups of two, three, and four quarter notes.	♩ = 52–64	Grand, stately, processional	3 and 5

Accompaniment

Organ accompaniment is preferred. A solo trumpet could enhance the melody.

Additional Information

Clear, marked articulation is needed for this rhythmic hymn.

347   Go to Dark Gethsemane

GETHSEMANE

Pulse	Tempo	Style	Chpt Ref
The half note receives the pulse.	♩ = 50–60	Somber, meditative. Note the change of mood in stanza 4.	3 and 5

Accompaniment

Organ (piano)

348   Stay with Me

STAY WITH ME

Pulse	Tempo	Style	Chpt Ref
The quarter note receives the pulse.	♩ = 64–76	Haunting	3 and 4

Accompaniment

Unaccompanied singing in four-part harmony is preferred. Light organ, piano, or guitar can provide support. Woodwinds can play counter melodies or obbligatos. See Taizé collections in Bibliography.

Additional Information

Taizé choruses are sung prayers meant to be repeated many times. The chorus can be sung alone, or a cantor can sing the verses (in Simplified Keyboard Edition) between repetitions of the chorus. See pages 33–34 for further guidance.

349 Ah, Holy Jesus
HERZLIEBSTER JESU

Pulse	Tempo	Style	Chpt Ref
The half note receives the pulse.	♩= 52–64	Unhurried, meditative	3 and 5

Accompaniment

Organ (piano). Consider singing this chorale accompanied by a solo instrument.

Additional Information

Articulate the repeated notes clearly. See page 38–39 for help with playing repeated notes on the organ.

350 They Crucified My Lord
SUFFERER

Pulse	Tempo	Style	Chpt Ref
The half note or quarter note receives the pulse. A slow tempo allows one to feel the quarter-note pulse, but being mindful of the larger pulse helps keep the tune moving forward. Be careful not to rush the eighth notes.	♩= 42–50. See #290 for further guidance.	Somber, contemplative	3 and 8

Accompaniment

Organ or piano accompaniment is preferred. This could also be sung unaccompanied in harmony.

Additional Information

Leading hint: Call and response is essential to the African American spiritual tradition. A soloist could sing each verse with the assembly joining on "not a word." If very familiar, the assembly could divide the song in various ways.

351 O Sacred Head, Now Wounded
HERZLICH TUT MICH VERLANGEN

Pulse	Tempo	Style	Chpt Ref
The quarter note receives the pulse.	♩= 64–76	Contemplative, introspective	3 and 5

Accompaniment

Organ (piano) or unaccompanied singing in four-part harmony is preferred.

352   O Sacred Head, Now Wounded

HERZLICH TUT MICH VERLANGEN

Pulse	Tempo	Style	Chpt Ref
The pulse shifts between the half note and dotted half note, producing groupings of two and three quarter notes. Keep a steady pulse.	♩ = 48–54. Have the third phrase in mind when setting the tempo.	Contemplative, introspective	3 and 5

Accompaniment
Organ accompaniment is preferred. An accompanying style that articulates the half and dotted half groupings will aid the singers. It can also be sung unaccompanied.

353   Were You There

WERE YOU THERE

Pulse	Tempo	Style	Chpt Ref
The half note receives the pulse.	♩ = 40–50. Feel an easy two beats per measure, yet never rushed. See #290 for further guidance.	Contemplative, mournful	3 and 8

Accompaniment
Organ (piano)

354   Calvary

CALVARY

Pulse	Tempo	Style	Chpt Ref
The quarter note receives the pulse.	♩ = 42–54. A slow tempo works best. See #290 for further guidance.	Somber, meditative	3 and 8

Accompaniment
Organ, piano, or unaccompanied singing is preferred.

355 Sing, My Tongue

PANGE LINGUA

Pulse	Tempo	Style	Chpt Ref
As with all chant, this hymn flows according to the natural textual accents. For chant, depending on the text, the beats will be grouped in twos or threes.	A fluid tempo that neither rushes nor moves too slowly works best.	Triumphant	3 and 4

Accompaniment

While it is preferable to sing chant unaccompanied, you may need to use organ or piano for support. If keyboard is needed, be sure it does not obstruct the natural rhythm. Unison singing is preferred.

356 Sing, My Tongue

FORTUNATUS NEW

Pulse	Tempo	Style	Chpt Ref
The quarter note receives the pulse.	♩ = 80–84	Broad, majestic	3 and 5

Accompaniment

Organ accompaniment is preferred.

357 Lamb of God, Pure and Sinless

O LAMM GOTTES, UNSCHULDIG

Pulse	Tempo	Style	Chpt Ref
The half note receives the pulse. Note the occasionally shifting pulse in the third and fourth lines. A slow tempo allows one to feel the half-note pulse, but being mindful of the larger whole note pulse helps keep the tune moving forward.	♩ = 60–69	Humble, straightforward, gentle dance	3 and 5

Accompaniment

Organ accompaniment or unaccompanied singing is preferred.

358   Great God, Your Love Has Called Us Here

RYBURN

Pulse	Tempo	Style	Chpt Ref
The dotted half note receives the primary pulse. Internally, feel the quarter to keep the rhythm alive.	♩. = 36–42	Lyrical with forward motion	3 and 5

Accompaniment

Organ accompaniment is preferred.

Additional Information

While this tune lends itself to singing in harmony, be careful that the harmony does not obstruct the forward movement of the melody.

359   Where Charity and Love Prevail

TWENTY-FOURTH

Pulse	Tempo	Style	Chpt Ref
The half note receives the pulse, yet also keep a sense of the dotted whole note (the length of one measure).	♩ = 62–70	Gently moving	3, 6, and 7

Accompaniment

Organ (piano). Unaccompanied singing in unison or in canon works well.

Additional Information

Leading challenge: When choosing a tempo, keep in mind the assembly's ability to sing through a phrase with adequate breath. This is especially important at the end of the second phrase, which ends on a high C.

360   Love Consecrates the Humblest Act

TWENTY-FOURTH

Pulse	Tempo	Style	Chpt Ref
The half note receives the pulse, yet also keep a sense of the dotted whole note (the length of one measure).	♩ = 62–70	Gently moving	3, 6, and 7

Accompaniment

Organ (piano). Unaccompanied singing in unison or in canon works well.

Additional Information

Leading challenge: When choosing a tempo, keep in mind the assembly's ability to sing through a phrase with adequate breath. This is especially important at the end of the second phrase, which ends on a high C.

361 The Day of Resurrection!

ELLACOMBE

Pulse	Tempo	Style	Chpt Ref
The half note receives the pulse.	$\half = 52-60$	Flowing	3 and 5

Accompaniment
Organ (piano)

362 At the Lamb's High Feast We Sing

SONNE DER GERECHTIGKEIT

Pulse	Tempo	Style	Chpt Ref
The half note receives the pulse, yet also feel a strong whole note pulse.	$\half = 74-80$	Energetic, strong, joyous	3 and 5

Accompaniment
A slightly detached organ accompaniment is preferred. Consider soloing out the melody. See page 26 for guidance.

Additional Information
This tune serves as a good example for the approaches to spacing between stanzas. See pages 42–43.

363 Come, You Faithful, Raise the Strain

GAUDEAMUS PARITER

Pulse	Tempo	Style	Chpt Ref
The half note receives the pulse.	$\half = 64-76$	Sprightly, dance-like	3, 5, and 6

Accompaniment
Organ (piano)

Additional Information
A legato articulation with clearly articulated repeated notes works well.

364   Christian Has Arisen, Alleluia

Mfurahini, haleluya

MFURAHINI, HALELUYA

Pulse	Tempo	Style	Chpt Ref
The dotted half note receives the pulse.	$\dot{\half} = 56\text{–}62$	Jubilant, celebrative	3 and 11

Accompaniment

Unaccompanied singing in four-part harmony with drums is preferred. Piano can provide vocal support if necessary. Here is a possible percussion pattern for two drums:

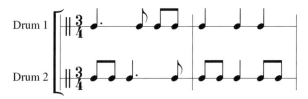

Additional Information

See pages 72–74 for comments on the text and formal structure of this African song.

365   Jesus Christ Is Risen Today

EASTER HYMN

Pulse	Tempo	Style	Chpt Ref
The half note receives the pulse.	$\half = 50\text{–}56$	Festive, crisp, grand	3 and 5

Accompaniment

Organ accompaniment is preferred. Brass instruments and/or handbells can enhance this hymn.

366   The Strife Is O'er, the Battle Done

VICTORY

Pulse	Tempo	Style	Chpt Ref
The dotted half note receives the pulse. At a broad tempo, think of a half note followed by a quarter.	$\dot{\half} = 38\text{–}44$	Victorious, flowing	3 and 5

Accompaniment

Organ accompaniment is preferred.

367   Now All the Vault of Heaven Resounds

LASST UNS ERFREUEN

Pulse	Tempo	Style	Chpt Ref
The half note receives the pulse.	♩ = 66–76	Brisk, sturdy, rhythmic	3 and 5

Accompaniment
Organ accompaniment is preferred.

Additional Information

Leading challenge: The musician needs to consider how long to hold the second melody note in the sixth full measure ("liv-**ing**"). One common practice is to hold the note for an extra half note; another is to play as written. If playing as written, consider making the B♭ a quarter note followed by a quarter rest. An A♭ passing tone in the tenor line can encourage the flow of the line. In either option, clear and consistent leadership encourages the assembly's singing.

Leading challenge: The assembly may be tempted to move too soon in the next-to-the-last measure. Be clear and exact in encouraging them to hold the melody-note F for the full three beats (six quarter notes).

368   With High Delight Let Us Unite

MIT FREUDEN ZART

Pulse	Tempo	Style	Chpt Ref
The half note receives the pulse.	♩ = 68–84	Joyful, dance-like	3 and 5

Accompaniment
Organ (piano)

Additional Information

Keep the half notes lightly articulated, giving a lift for breathing at vocal phrase endings.

Teaching hint: The rhythm for this tune is different from *LBW*, now reflecting a greater ecumenical consesus.

369   Christ the Lord Is Risen Today; Alleluia!

LLANFAIR

Pulse	Tempo	Style	Chpt Ref
The half note receives the pulse.	♩ = 64–74	Joyful, lively, dance-like	3 and 5

Accompaniment
Organ (piano)

Additional Information

Consider keeping the melody legato but the inner voices detached. This helps the assembly feel the pulse.

370   Christ Jesus Lay in Death's Strong Bands

CHRIST LAG IN TODESBANDEN

Pulse	Tempo	Style	Chpt Ref
The half note receives the pulse.	♩ = 54–60	Rugged, triumphant	3 and 5

Accompaniment

Organ (piano)

Additional Information

A characteristic of sixteenth-century chorales is their rhythmic vitality. Lead the eighth-note pickups clearly.

371   Christians, to the Paschal Victim

VICTIMAE PASCHALI

Pulse	Tempo	Style	Chpt Ref
As with all chant, this hymn flows according to the natural textual accents. For chant, depending on the text, the beats will be grouped in twos or threes.	A fluid tempo that neither rushes nor moves too slowly works best.	Flowing, yet declamatory	3 and 4

Accompaniment

Organ (piano)

Additional Information

While it is preferable to sing chant unaccompanied, you may need to use organ or piano for support. If keyboard is needed, be sure it does not obstruct the natural rhythm. Unison singing is preferred.

Leading hint: This chant works well in alternation with #372. Consider having the choir sing stanza 1 of #371, followed by the assembly singing stanza 1 of #372. Continue in this manner with the remaining stanzas.

Leading challenge: The range of this chant can be demanding for an assembly, but it is well worth learning. Consider giving them several opportunities to sing it during the Easter season.

372   Christ Is Arisen

CHRIST IST ERSTANDEN

Pulse	Tempo	Style	Chpt Ref
The half note receives the pulse.	$\half = 56–66$	Majestic, straightforward	3 and 5

Accompaniment

Organ (piano)

Additional Information

Note the shifting pulse at the ends of stanzas (alleluias). Clear articulation will accentuate the rhythmic interest.

See #371 for alternation suggestions.

373   Christ the Lord Is Risen Today!

ORIENTIS PARTIBUS

Pulse	Tempo	Style	Chpt Ref
The half note receives the pulse.	$\half = 64–72$	Crisp, exuberant, dance-like	3, 5, and 6

Accompaniment

Organ (piano)

Additional Information

Although harmony is provided, this tune sings better in unison.

374   Day of Arising

RAABE

Pulse	Tempo	Style	Chpt Ref
The dotted half or quarter note receives the pulse. A slow tempo allows one to feel the quarter-note pulse, but being mindful of the larger pulse helps keep the tune moving forward.	$\quarter = 80–100$	Broad, gentle, calm	3, 5, and 6

Accompaniment

Organ (piano)

375   Alleluia! Christ Is Arisen

¡Aleluya! Cristo resucitó

SANTO DOMINGO

Pulse	Tempo	Style	Chpt Ref
The quarter note receives the pulse. The quarter-note pulse is best supported by rhythmic divisions on percussion instruments.	♩ = 76–92	Bright, joyful	3 and 10

Accompaniment

Guitar accompaniment with percussion is preferred. Percussion instruments could include conga drums, egg shakers, tambourine, and claves, using rhythms such as these:

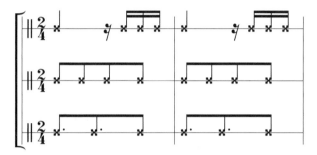

Additional Information

Piano could also be successful. A solo trumpet could enhance the melody of the refrain.

Refer to example 9, the *Danzon*, on page 66 in the Latino/Hispanic chapter.

376   Thine Is the Glory

JUDAS MACCABAEUS

Pulse	Tempo	Style	Chpt Ref
The half note receives the pulse.	♩ = 62–66	Sturdy, grand, majestic	3 and 5

Accompaniment

Organ (piano)

Additional Information

The use of brass instruments can enhance this hymn.

377   Alleluia! Jesus Is Risen!

EARTH AND ALL STARS

Pulse	Tempo	Style	Chpt Ref
The dotted half note receives the pulse.	$\downarrow. = 48–52$	Celebratory, vigorous	3 and 5

Accompaniment

Organ (piano)

Additional Information

Brass or percussion could enhance the singing of this hymn.

Leading hint: Feel a stress on beat one of each measure, with beats two and three light and nimble, as in a waltz.

378   Awake, My Heart, with Gladness

AUF, AUF, MEIN HERZ

Pulse	Tempo	Style	Chpt Ref
The dotted half note receives the pulse.	$\downarrow. = 52–60$	Dance-like, graceful	3 and 5

Accompaniment

Organ (piano)

Additional Information

Leading hint: Be careful to release the half notes at the ends of phrases clearly; this allows the assembly to breathe.

379   Now the Green Blade Rises

NOËL NOUVELET

Pulse	Tempo	Style	Chpt Ref
The half note receives the pulse.	$\downarrow = 44–50$	Dance-like, playful	3 and 6

Accompaniment

Organ (piano)

Additional Information

A light and detached articulation suits this carol.

380   Hallelujah! Jesus Lives!

FRED TIL BOD

Pulse	Tempo	Style	Chpt Ref
The half note receives the pulse. Continue to feel a strong underlying quarter note.	♩ = 52–60	Strong, joyous	3 and 5

Accompaniment
Organ (piano)

381   Peace, to Soothe Our Bitter Woes

FRED TIL BOD

Pulse	Tempo	Style	Chpt Ref
The half note receives the pulse. Continue to feel a strong underlying quarter note.	♩ = 52–60	Peaceful, assured	3 and 5

Accompaniment
Organ (piano), more legato than #380.

382   Christ Is Risen! Alleluia!

MORGENLIED

Pulse	Tempo	Style	Chpt Ref
The half note receives the pulse.	♩ = 58–66	Bright, crisp, like a fanfare	3 and 5

Accompaniment
Organ (piano)

Additional Information
The use of brass instruments can enhance this hymn.

383   Christ Is Risen! Shout Hosanna!

TURNBULL

Pulse	Tempo	Style	Chpt Ref
The quarter note receives the pulse. The moving eighth notes, prominent in the inner voices, should flow, but never feel hurried, helping to determine the quarter-note pulse.	♩ = 88–92	Grand, stately	3 and 5

Accompaniment

Organ accompaniment is preferred. If played on piano, fill in the chords and double the bass line to give it a fuller sound.

384   That Easter Day with Joy Was Bright

PUER NOBIS

Pulse	Tempo	Style	Chpt Ref
The dotted half note receives the pulse.	♩. = 48–56	Gently dance-like	3 and 5

Accompaniment

Legato organ (piano) accompaniment is preferred.

Additional Information

Renaissance percussion such as hand drum and tambourine could enhance the singing of this dance-like tune.

385   Good Christian Friends, Rejoice and Sing!

GELOBT SEI GOTT

Pulse	Tempo	Style	Chpt Ref
The dotted half note receives the pulse.	$\dot\downarrow = 48-56$	Bright, dance-like	3, 5, and 6

Accompaniment

Organ (piano)

Additional Information

Leading hint: Keeping the quarter and eighth notes light and slightly detached allows this to dance.

386, 387   O Sons and Daughters, Let Us Sing

O FILII ET FILIAE

Pulse	Tempo	Style	Chpt Ref
The dotted half note receives the pulse.	$\dot\downarrow = 46-54$	Lively, dance-like	3, 5, and 6

Accompaniment

Organ accompaniment is preferred. Handbells or instruments such as recorders and drum could enhance this tune.

Additional Information

Consider singing this longer hymn in alternation between choir or cantor and assembly. See page 45–46 for alternation suggestions.

Leading hint: Note that the rhythms of this tune differ from LBW. The refrain consists of even quarter notes in ¾ rather than a syncopated rhythm.

388   Be Not Afraid

BE NOT AFRAID

Pulse	Tempo	Style	Chpt Ref
The half note receives the pulse.	♩= 50–56	Lively	3 and 4

Accompaniment

Unaccompanied singing in four-part harmony is preferred. Light organ, piano, or guitar can provide support. Woodwinds can play counter melodies or obbligatos. See Taizé collections in Bibliography.

Additional Information

Leading hint: Unlike many Taizé chants, this chant is extroverted and syncopated. Clearly articulate at the end of measures 1, 2, 4, 5, and 6.

Taizé choruses are sung prayers meant to be repeated many times. See pages 33–34.

389   Christ Is Alive! Let Christians Sing

TRURO

Pulse	Tempo	Style	Chpt Ref
The half note receives the pulse.	♩= 76–84. This tune presents particular challenges in regard to tempo. See page 23 for further guidance.	Majestic, vigorous	3 and 5

Accompaniment

Organ (piano)

390   The Risen Christ

WOODLANDS

Pulse	Tempo	Style	Chpt Ref
The half note receives the pulse.	♩= 62–70	Majestic, energetic	3 and 5

Accompaniment

Organ accompaniment is preferred. Consider soloing out the melody. See page 26 for guidance.

Additional Information

Clearly articulate the repeated notes in this hymn, particularly the opening three notes.

391   This Joyful Eastertide

VRUECHTEN

Pulse	Tempo	Style	Chpt Ref
The half note receives the pulse. Note the shifting meter between $\frac{3}{2}$ and $\frac{3}{4}$.	♩ = 60–70	Light, celebrative	3 and 5

Accompaniment

Organ (piano). Consider singing unaccompanied in four-part harmony, always being mindful that the harmony does not slow the tempo.

392   Alleluia! Sing to Jesus

HYFRYDOL

Pulse	Tempo	Style	Chpt Ref
The half note receives the pulse.	♩ = 46–54	Strong, sturdy, lyrical	3 and 5

Accompaniment

Organ (piano)

393   A Hymn of Glory Let Us Sing!

LASST UNS ERFREUEN

Pulse	Tempo	Style	Chpt Ref
The quarter note receives the pulse.	♩ = 66–76	Brisk, sturdy, rhythmic	3 and 5

Accompaniment

Organ accompaniment is preferred.

Additional Information

Leading challenge: The musician needs to consider how long to hold the second melody note in the sixth full measure. One common practice is to hold the note for an extra quarter note; another is to play as written. If playing as written, consider making the A an eighth note followed by an eighth rest. In either option, clear and consistent leadership encourages the assembly's singing.

Leading challenge: The assembly may be tempted to move too soon in the next-to-the-last measure. Be clear and exact in encouraging them to hold the melody-note E for the full three beats.

394 Hail Thee, Festival Day!

SALVE FESTA DIES

Pulse	Tempo	Style	Chpt Ref
The half note receives the pulse	♩ = 52–60. Be careful to keep a steady tempo between the refrains and stanzas.	Grand, triumphant, march-like	3 and 5

Accompaniment

Organ accompaniment is preferred.

Additional Information

Leading challenge: This hymn is unusual in that the stanzas use two very different melodies. Well-rehearsed choir/cantor leadership will help the assembly feel more secure with the transitions. Consider also singing this in alternation between a choir/cantor and assembly.

395 Come, Holy Ghost, God and Lord

KOMM, HEILIGER GEIST, HERRE GOTT

Pulse	Tempo	Style	Chpt Ref
The half note receives the pulse.	♩ = 52–58	Jubilant, rhythmic	3 and 5

Accompaniment

Organ (piano)

Additional Information

Leading hint: A characteristic of sixteenth-century chorales is their rhythmic vitality. Note that most phrases in this hymn begin with an eighth-note pickup. Be sure to prepare with a breath, keep the pickup light, and feel a stress on the following quarter note.

396 Spirit of Gentleness

SPIRIT

Pulse	Tempo	Style	Chpt Ref
The dotted half note receives the pulse.	♩. = 40–48	Expansive, flowing	3, 6, and 9

Accompaniment

Piano (organ) or praise band are the preferred instruments.

Additional Information

The rolling accompaniment style lends itself to piano or guitar accompaniment. A C instrument could support the melody. If accompanied with organ, simply play the accompaniment as provided.

397 Loving Spirit
RESTORATION

Pulse	Tempo	Style	Chpt Ref
The half note receives the pulse.	♩ = 46–52	Rugged, prayerful	3 and 7

Accompaniment
Organ (piano)

398 Holy Spirit, Truth Divine
SONG 13

Pulse	Tempo	Style	Chpt Ref
The half note receives the pulse.	♩ = 44–50	Lyrical, flowing	3 and 5

Accompaniment
Organ (piano)

399 O Holy Spirit, Root of Life
PUER NOBIS

Pulse	Tempo	Style	Chpt Ref
The dotted half note receives the pulse.	♩. = 48–56	Gently dance-like	3 and 5

Accompaniment
Legato organ (piano) accompaniment is preferred.

Additional Information

Renaissance percussion such as hand drum and tambourine could enhance the singing of this dance-like tune.

400 God of Tempest, God of Whirlwind

CWM RHONDDA

Pulse	Tempo	Style	Chpt Ref
The half note receives the pulse.	♩ = 50–54. This tune serves as an example for tempo decisions. See page 24.	Strong, brisk	3 and 5

Accompaniment
Organ (piano)

401 Gracious Spirit, Heed Our Pleading

Njoo kwetu, Roho mwema

NJOO KWETU, ROHO MWEMA

Pulse	Tempo	Style	Chpt Ref
The quarter note receives the pulse. Lean into beats 1 and 3.	♩ = 82–92. A relaxed, unhurried tempo works best.	Confident, joyful	3 and 11

Accompaniment
Unaccompanied singing in four-part harmony with drums is preferred.

Additional Information
Piano can provide vocal support if necessary.

Keep this melody legato.

402 Eternal Spirit of the Living Christ

ADORO TE DEVOTE

Pulse	Tempo	Style	Chpt Ref
As with all chant, this hymn flows according to the natural textual accents. For chant, depending on the text, the beats will be grouped in twos or threes.	A fluid tempo that neither rushes nor moves too slowly works best.	Prayer to the Counselor	3 and 4

Accompaniment
While it is preferable to sing chant unaccompanied, you may need to use organ or piano for support. If keyboard is needed, be sure it does not obstruct the natural rhythm. Unison singing is preferred.

403   Like the Murmur of the Dove's Song

BRIDEGROOM

Pulse	Tempo	Style	Chpt Ref
The quarter note receives the pulse, but also sense the dotted half. A slower tempo allows one to feel the quarter-note pulse, but being mindful of the larger pulse helps keep the tune moving forward.	♩ = 82–98	Flowing, reflective	3, 5, and 6

Accompaniment
Organ (piano)

Additional Information
Teaching hint: When learning this hymn, consider teaching the syncopation in the last phrase ("come . . .").

404   Come, Gracious Spirit, Heavenly Dove

HERR JESU CHRIST, MEINS

Pulse	Tempo	Style	Chpt Ref
The dotted half note receives the pulse.	♩. = 44–50	Simply, moving forward	3 and 5

Accompaniment
Organ (piano)

Additional Information
Leading hint: Be aware of the syncopation in the first bar of the second system and articulate clearly.

405   O Spirit of Life

O HEILIGER GEIST

Pulse	Tempo	Style	Chpt Ref
The quarter note receives the pulse.	♩ = 72–92. A slower tempo works best when singing in harmony.	Confident, prayerful	3 and 5

Accompaniment
Organ accompaniment or unaccompanied singing in four-part harmony is preferred.

406   Veni Sancte Spiritus / Holy Spirit, Come to Us

TAIZÉ VENI SANCTE

Pulse	Tempo	Style	Chpt Ref
The dotted quarter note receives the pulse.	♩. = 40–48	Contemplative, pleading	3 and 4

Accompaniment

Unaccompanied singing in four-part harmony is preferred. Light organ, piano, or guitar can provide support. Woodwinds can play counter melodies or obbligatos. See Taizé collections in Bibliography.

Additional Information

Taizé choruses are sung prayers meant to be repeated many times. The ostinato can be sung alone, or a cantor can sing verses over it. Verses are available in the accompaniment edition of Service Music and Hymns and in the Simplified Keyboard Accompaniment Edition. See pages 33–34 for further guidance.

407   O Living Breath of God

Soplo de Dios viviente

VÅRVINDAR FRISKA

Pulse	Tempo	Style	Chpt Ref
The quarter note receives the pulse. Feel an added weight on the first beat of each measure.	♩ = 80–100	Joyful, prayerful	3 and 10

Accompaniment

Guitar accompaniment with percussion is preferred. Percussion instruments could include conga drums, egg shakers, tambourine, and claves, using rhythms such as these:

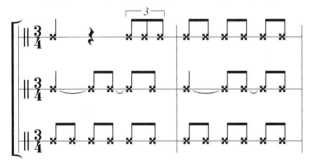

Piano could also be successful.

Additional Information

Play with a separation between quarter notes, with lightness on beats two and three.
This could also be rendered as a *Bolero*. See example on page 66.

This song is a joyful invitation. Lead it in the spirit of reverence and prayer.

408   Come, Thou Almighty King

ITALIAN HYMN

Pulse	Tempo	Style	Chpt Ref
The dotted half note receives the pulse.	♩.= 38–46	Vigorous, strong, forward-moving	3 and 5

Accompaniment
Organ (piano)

409   Kyrie! God, Father

KYRIE, GOTT VATER

Pulse	Tempo	Style	Chpt Ref
The half note receives the pulse.	♩ = 60–68	Strong, chant-like	3, 4, and 5

Accompaniment
Organ (piano)

Additional Information
Like chant, this chorale shifts meter; follow the natural stresses of the text.

410   All Glory Be to God on High

ALLEIN GOTT IN DER HÖH

Pulse	Tempo	Style	Chpt Ref
The dotted half note receives the pulse.	♩.= 50–60. If taken too fast, this hymn can become breathless and difficult to sing.	Dance-like, with energy	3 and 5

Accompaniment
Organ (piano)

Additional Information
A slightly detached articulation suits this dance-like tune.

411   We All Believe in One True God

WIR GLAUBEN ALL

Pulse	Tempo	Style	Chpt Ref
The half note receives the pulse.	♩ = 66–80	Bold, proclamatory, chant-like	3 and 5

Accompaniment

Organ accompaniment or unaccompanied voices is preferred. Piano would not carry the strength of this tune.

Additional Information

Some separation between half notes can help hold singers together.

412   Come, Join the Dance of Trinity

KINGSFOLD

Pulse	Tempo	Style	Chpt Ref
The half note receives the pulse. Because of the text's reference to dance, the half note will keep it lighter than a quarter-note tactus.	♩ = 58–72. A rhythmic, moderate tempo works best.	Dance-like, lilting	3, 5, and 6

Accompaniment

Various accompaniments are possible. If leading with a piano or organ, use a lightly detached articulation and be careful that the harmonies do not prevent the melody from moving ahead. A guitar accompaniment may accentuate the folk-like character of the melody.

413   Holy, Holy, Holy, Lord God Almighty!

NICAEA

Pulse	Tempo	Style	Chpt Ref
The half note receives the pulse.	♩ = 52–58	Majestic, noble	3 and 5

Accompaniment

Organ (piano)

Additional Information

In stanza two, the first two melody notes on "seraphim" are often treated as a dotted quarter and eighth. Decide ahead how you want to lead it, and articulate clearly.

414   Holy God, We Praise Your Name

GROSSER GOTT

Pulse	Tempo	Style	Chpt Ref
The half note receives the pulse.	$\dot{\half} = 36\text{--}40$	Grand, majestic	3 and 5

Accompaniment
Organ (piano)

415   Father Most Holy

CHRISTE SANCTORUM

Pulse	Tempo	Style	Chpt Ref
The half note receives the pulse.	$\half = 54\text{--}58$	Lyrical, energized	3 and 5

Accompaniment
Organ (piano)

FESTIVALS, COMMEMORATIONS

416   At the Name of Jesus

KING'S WESTON

Pulse	Tempo	Style	Chpt Ref
The half note receives the pulse.	$\half = 76\text{--}88$	Majestic, broad, stately	3 and 5

Accompaniment
Organ accompaniment is preferred.

Additional Information
There is sometimes a tendency to treat the first two melody notes as pickups. Note that they fall, rather, at the beginning of the measure and so should be stressed.

417   In His Temple Now Behold Him

REGENT SQUARE

Pulse	Tempo	Style	Chpt Ref
The half note receives the pulse.	$\half = 52\text{--}60$	Noble, grand, festive	3 and 5

Accompaniment
Organ (piano)

418   Rejoice in God's Saints

LAUDATE DOMINUM

Pulse	Tempo	Style	Chpt Ref
The quarter note receives the pulse.	♩ = 96–108	Victorious, strong	3 and 5

Accompaniment
Organ (piano)

Additional Information
Leading hint: The opening note is an upbeat. Feel the stress on the first full downbeat.

419   For All the Faithful Women

KUORTANE

Pulse	Tempo	Style	Chpt Ref
The half note receives the pulse.	♩ = 50–58	Lyrical, confident	3 and 5

Accompaniment
Organ (piano)

Additional Information
Note that this hymn may alternatively be sung to KING'S LYNN (#420).

420   By All Your Saints

KING'S LYNN

Pulse	Tempo	Style	Chpt Ref
The half note receives the pulse. Maintain a strong feeling of the half note.	♩ = 56–62	Grand, stately	3, 5, and 6

Accompaniment
Organ (piano)

Additional Information
Leading hint: A marcato articulation suits this angular folk tune. Note that this hymn may alternatively be sung to KUORTANE (#421).

421   By All Your Saints

KUORTANE

Pulse	Tempo	Style	Chpt Ref
The half note receives the pulse.	♩ = 50–58	Lyrical, confident	3 and 5

Accompaniment

Organ (piano)

Additional Information

Note that this hymn may alternatively be sung to KING'S LYNN (#420).

422   For All the Saints

SINE NOMINE

Pulse	Tempo	Style	Chpt Ref
The half note receives the pulse.	♩ = 54–60	Majestic, energetic, forward-moving	3 and 5

Accompaniment

Organ accompaniment is preferred.

Additional Information

Consider having a choir sing one or all of stanzas 3–5 in harmony. To reflect the different character of these stanzas, consider a change in organ registration or instrumentation. Consider soloing out the melody. See page 26 for help with soloing out.

423   Shall We Gather at the River

HANSON PLACE

Pulse	Tempo	Style	Chpt Ref
The quarter note receives the pulse.	♩ = 84–100	Inviting, affirmative	3 and 7

Accompaniment

Organ (piano). Singing unaccompanied in four-part harmony would work well.

Additional Information

Leading hint: The dotted eighth/sixteenth patterns can be treated as triplets or sung exactly as notated.

424   Ye Watchers and Ye Holy Ones

LASST UNS ERFREUEN

Pulse	Tempo	Style	Chpt Ref
The half note receives the pulse.	♩ = 66–76	Brisk, sturdy, rhythmic	3 and 5

Accompaniment

Organ accompaniment is preferred.

Additional Information

Leading challenge: The musician needs to consider how long to hold the second melody note in the sixth full measure. One common practice is to hold the note for an extra half note; another is to play it as written. If playing as written, consider making the B♭ a quarter note followed by a quarter rest. An A♭ passing tone in the tenor line can encourage the flow of the line. In either option, clear and consistent leadership encourages the assembly's singing.

Leading challenge: The assembly may be tempted to move too soon in the next-to-the-last measure. Be clear and exact in encouraging them to hold the melody-note F for the full three beats (six quarter notes).

425   Behold the Host Arrayed in White

DEN STORE HVIDE FLOK

Pulse	Tempo	Style	Chpt Ref
The dotted half note receives the pulse. Sense two broad beats per measure, like a tolling bell.	♩. = 34–40	With graceful breadth	3, 5, and 6

Accompaniment

Organ accompaniment is preferred.

426   Sing with All the Saints in Glory

MISSISSIPPI

Pulse	Tempo	Style	Chpt Ref
The quarter note receives the pulse.	♩ = 72–80	Joyful, exuberant	3 and 5

Accompaniment

Organ or piano accompaniment is preferred.

427   For All Your Saints, O Lord

FESTAL SONG

Pulse	Tempo	Style	Chpt Ref
The half note receives the pulse.	𝅗𝅥 = 62–70	Strong, lively, proclamatory	3 and 5

Accompaniment
Organ (piano)

428   Give Thanks For Saints

REPTON

Pulse	Tempo	Style	Chpt Ref
The half note receives the pulse.	𝅗𝅥 = 42–48	Lyrical, sustained	3 and 5

Accompaniment
Organ (piano)

429   In Our Day of Thanksgiving

ST. CATHERINE'S COURT

Pulse	Tempo	Style	Chpt Ref
The dotted half note receives the pulse.	𝅗𝅥. = 32–38	Stately, broadly	3 and 5

Accompaniment
Organ (piano)

Additional Information
The Simplified Keyboard Accompaniment Edition has an accompaniment in C major.

430   Rejoice, for Christ is King!

LAUS REGIS

Pulse	Tempo	Style	Chpt Ref
The half note receives the pulse.	𝅗𝅥 = 60–76	Broad, celebratory, majestic	3 and 5

Accompaniment
Organ or piano accompaniment is preferred.

Additional Information
Organ (piano)

431   O Christ, What Can It Mean for Us
ALL SAINTS NEW

Pulse	Tempo	Style	Chpt Ref
The half note receives the pulse.	$\half = 54-60$	Bold, walking style	3 and 5

Accompaniment
Organ (piano)

432   The Head That Once Was Crowned
ST. MAGNUS

Pulse	Tempo	Style	Chpt Ref
The half note receives the pulse.	$\half = 54-60$	Bold, regal	3 and 5

Accompaniment
Organ (piano)

END TIME

433   Blessing, Honor, and Glory
BLESSING, HONOR, AND GLORY

Pulse	Tempo	Style	Chpt Ref
The half note receives the pulse.	$\half = 54-64$	Strong, majestic	3 and 9

Accompaniment
Piano and guitar or worship band is the preferred accompaniment. If using worship band, consider saxophone or flute on the melody, acoustic guitar on rhythm, electric guitar on power chords (full chords on the down beat), and bass on the root.

434   Jesus Shall Reign
DUKE STREET

Pulse	Tempo	Style	Chpt Ref
The half note receives the pulse.	$\half = 64-70$	Stately, bright, victorious	3 and 5

Accompaniment
Organ (piano)

Additional Information
This tune serves as a good example for the approaches to spacing between phrases. See pages 40–42.

435 Lo! He Comes with Clouds Descending

HELMSLEY

Pulse	Tempo	Style	Chpt Ref
The half note receives the pulse.	$\half = 52–60$	Triumphant, majestic	3 and 5

Accompaniment
Organ (piano)

Additional Information
Even in a dry acoustic, this tune needs a slower tempo that will allow it to open up.

436 Wake, Awake, for Night is Flying

WACHET AUF

Pulse	Tempo	Style	Chpt Ref
The half note receives the pulse, with the exception of the phrase at "Rise and prepare," which is treated ♩ ♩ ♩. ♩. ♩	$\half = 60–72$	Bold, vigorous, exultant	3 and 9

Accompaniment
Organ accompaniment is preferred; unaccompanied voices is possible. Piano will not carry this tune well. If playing on piano, consider adding a solo instrument such as trumpet or oboe to the melody.

437 On Jordan's Stormy Bank I Stand

PROMISED LAND

Pulse	Tempo	Style	Chpt Ref
The half note receives the pulse.	$\half = 56–62$	March-like	3 and 7

Accompaniment
Organ (piano) or robust unaccompanied singing.

Additional Information
This tune is known in both major and minor versions. If you want to try it in minor, simply pretend that the key signature is one sharp instead of three flats; you may also want to sharp the Ds.

438 My Lord, What a Morning

BURLEIGH

Pulse	Tempo	Style	Chpt Ref
The half note receives the pulse.	$\half = 38$–52, but feel a strong internal quarter note for energy. See # 290 for further guidance.	Introspective on refrain and proclamatory on verses; or upbeat and spirited	3 and 8

Accompaniment
Unaccompanied singing or piano is preferred. Organ or piano accompaniment can also be successful.

Additional Information
This spiritual can be sung in very different ways, from very slowly to quite upbeat.

439 Soon and Very Soon

VERY SOON

Pulse	Tempo	Style	Chpt Ref
The half note receives the pulse.	$\half = 52$–60. It is best to choose a moderate tempo that helps feel strong upbeats on the second and fourth quarter notes. Be careful not to rush.	Lively, uplifting	3 and 8

Accompaniment
Piano, keyboard, or unaccompanied singing in four-part harmony is preferred. Drum set and hand clapping on the upbeats could enhance the singing. A slower tempo allows for greater keyboard improvisation. See the alternate accompaniment for an example.

Additional Information
A slightly detached articulation suits this tune.

440 In Peace and Joy I Now Depart

MIT FRIED UND FREUD

Pulse	Tempo	Style	Chpt Ref
The pulse shifts—half note at the beginning, yet a dotted-half or quarter-note pulse will be necessary later due to the complex rhythms. Certainly feel six quarter notes at the beginning of the third phrase.	$\half = 48$–50	With peace, joy, and rhythmic vitality	3 and 5

Accompaniment
Organ accompaniment is preferred.

441   Oh, Happy Day When We Shall Stand

LOBT GOTT, IHR CHRISTEN

Pulse	Tempo	Style	Chpt Ref
The half note receives the pulse.	♩ = 60–72	Strong, dance-like	3 and 5

Accompaniment

Organ (piano)

Additional Information

Articulate the repeated notes of this chorale carefully. See pages 38–39 for help playing repeated notes on the organ.

HOLY BAPTISM

442   All Who Believe and Are Baptized

ES IST DAS HEIL

Pulse	Tempo	Style	Chpt Ref
The half note receives the pulse.	♩ = 48–56	Sturdy, grand	3 and 5

Accompaniment

Organ (piano)

Additional Information

Leading hint: Treat the first quarter note in each phrase as a pickup.

443   Dearest Jesus, We Are Here

LIEBSTER JESU, WIR SIND HIER

Pulse	Tempo	Style	Chpt Ref
The half note receives the pulse.	♩ = 40–50. Strive for a tempo that allows for comfortable quarter and half notes.	Gentle, peaceful	3 and 5

Accompaniment

Organ (piano)

Additional Information

A legato articulation suits this chorale.

444   Cradling Children in His Arm

GAUDEAMUS PARITER

Pulse	Tempo	Style	Chpt Ref
The half note receives the pulse.	♩ = 64–76	Warm, dance-like	3, 5, and 6

Accompaniment

Organ (piano)

Additional Information

A legato articulation with clearly articulated repeated notes works well.

445   Wash, O God, Our Sons and Daughters

BEACH SPRING

Pulse	Tempo	Style	Chpt Ref
The half note receives the pulse.	♩ = 76–92	Hopeful, declarative	3 and 7

Accompaniment

Organ (piano)

Additional Information

This American tune works well sung in canon. A treble string or woodwind instrument could enhance the singing.

A legato articulation with clearly articulated repeated notes is appropriate. See pages 38–39 for help with playing repeated notes on the organ.

446   I'm Going on a Journey

WET SAINTS

Pulse	Tempo	Style	Chpt Ref
The quarter note or half note receives the pulse. A slow tempo allows one to feel the quarter-note pulse, but being mindful of the larger pulse helps keep the tune moving forward.	♩ = 90–100. A relaxed tempo is preferred.	Easy, with a swing	3, 7, and 9

Accompaniment

Piano/keyboard accompaniment is preferred. Consider also a jazz combo, adding bass and trap set.

Additional Information

Leading hint: The swinging eighths are essential to the blues-jazz style of this hymn. Jazz, like the African American spiritual, depends on improvisation. Do not take all pitches and rhythmic details too seriously. The pianist could add echoes of the melody in the right hand between phrases if the pulse remained steady. In addition, the last notes of phrases could hang on a bit and then diminish. See page 55 for more on improvisation in this style.

Leading hint: Due to the frequent entrances of the vocal line, a skilled cantor/soloist can be very helpful in teaching and leading this song.

447 O Blessed Spring

BERGLUND

Pulse	Tempo	Style	Chpt Ref
The half note receives the pulse.	♩ = 52–72	Lyrical, meditative	3 and 5

Accompaniment

Organ (piano)

Additional Information

Leading hint: Keep the singing of this tune legato, and sing to the ends of phrases.

448 This Is the Spirit's Entry Now

LAND OF REST

Pulse	Tempo	Style	Chpt Ref
The dotted half note receives the pulse.	♩. = 42–48	Gentle, folk-like	3, 6, and 7

Accompaniment

Unaccompanied singing, organ, or piano preferred. This tune also works well in canon at the measure. The second voice enters on the last beat of the first measure.

Additional Information

Leading hint: Be careful not to accent the upbeat to each measure.

449 We Know That Christ Is Raised

ENGELBERG

Pulse	Tempo	Style	Chpt Ref
The half note or quarter note receives the pulse. A slow tempo allows one to feel the quarter-note pulse, but being mindful of the larger pulse helps keep the tune moving forward.	♩ = 50–60	Strong, flowing	3 and 5

Accompaniment

Organ (piano)

Additional Information

Consider adding a trumpet to the melody or soloing out with a reed stop on the organ. See page 26 for help with soloing out.

450   I Bind unto Myself Today

ST. PATRICK'S BREASTPLATE

Pulse	Tempo	Style	Chpt Ref
The dotted half note receives the pulse on stanzas 1–3 and 5; the quarter note receives the pulse on stanza 4.	♩. = 42–46; for stanza 4, ♩ = 78–88. In theory this hymn could be sung at one tempo, but the fourth stanza becomes too fast for the text. The other stanzas need to have an energetic swing.	Joyful, rugged, bold	3 and 5

Accompaniment
Organ accompaniment is preferred.

Additional Information
Leading challenge: The transition from stanza 3 to stanza 4 and back to stanza 5 can be tricky. After stanza 3, be sure to leave enough space to change the tempo for stanza 4. Because of the different music for stanza 4, it works well to have a choir sing that stanza.

451   We Are Baptized in Christ Jesus

OUIMETTE

Pulse	Tempo	Style	Chpt Ref
The quarter note or half note receives the pulse. A slow tempo allows one to feel the quarter-note pulse, but being mindful of the larger pulse helps keep the tune moving forward.	♩ = 100–120	Warm, lilting	3 and 6

Accompaniment
Piano (organ) and/or guitar is preferred. Woodwinds could enhance the melody line.

452   Awake, O Sleeper, Rise from Death

AZMON

Pulse	Tempo	Style	Chpt Ref
The quarter note receives the pulse. Feel an accent on the first beat of each measure.	♩ = 88–102	Sturdy, joyful	3 and 5

Accompaniment
Organ (piano)

Additional Information
Leading hint: A rather detached articulation suits this tune.

453   Baptized and Set Free

BAPTIZED AND SET FREE

Pulse	Tempo	Style	Chpt Ref
The dotted half receives the pulse.	♩.= 38–46	Flowing, with rhythm	3, 6, and 9

Accompaniment
Piano (organ) or praise band are the preferred instruments.

454   Remember and Rejoice

ST. THOMAS

Pulse	Tempo	Style	Chpt Ref
The half note receives the pulse.	♩= 54–60	Affirmative, straightforward, joyful	3 and 5

Accompaniment
Organ (piano)

455   Crashing Waters at Creation

STUTTGART

Pulse	Tempo	Style	Chpt Ref
The half note receives the pulse.	♩= 52–60	Strong, steady, lyrical	3 and 5

Accompaniment
Organ (piano)

Additional Information
Articulate the repeated notes clearly. See pages 38–39 for help with playing repeated notes on the organ.

456   Baptized in Water

BUNESSAN

Pulse	Tempo	Style	Chpt Ref
The dotted half note receives the pulse.	♩.= 48–58	Simple, flowing, joyful	3 and 6

Accompaniment
Piano (organ). Plucked guitar would also work.

Additional Information
Leading hint: Note that the first three beats are an upbeat to the downbeat of the first measure.

457　Waterlife

SPIRIT LIFE

Pulse	Tempo	Style	Chpt Ref
The quarter note receives the pulse.	♩ = 110–125	Light, dance-like	3 and 9

Accompaniment

Worship band is preferred. See #433 for detailed suggestions. Piano works best with a flute supporting the melody.

Additional Information

Leading hint: Sing the ⁷₄ meter as you would speak it. A drummer accenting beats six and seven can help ease singing in this meter.

458　Praise and Thanksgiving Be to God

CHRISTE SANCTORUM

Pulse	Tempo	Style	Chpt Ref
The half note receives the pulse.	♩ = 54–58	Lyrical, energized	3 and 5

Accompaniment

Organ (piano)

459　Wade in the Water

WADE IN THE WATER

Pulse	Tempo	Style	Chpt Ref
The half note receives the pulse, yet be mindful of the internal syncopated rhythms.	♩ = 54–66. See #290 for further guidance.	Lively, with a groove	3 and 8

Accompaniment

Piano accompaniment is preferred. Drums and handclapping on beats 2 and 4 could enhance this tune.

Additional Information

Leading hint: Consider swinging the eighth notes in an easy triplet (♫ = ♩ ♪). Improvisation characterizes these spirituals. Do not take all the pitches and rhythmic details too seriously.

460 Now the Silence
NOW

Pulse	Tempo	Style	Chpt Ref
The dotted quarter note receives the pulse.	♩.= 56–60	Broad, gentle, not dance-like	3 and 5

Accompaniment

Organ (piano)

461 All Who Hunger, Gather Gladly
HOLY MANNA

Pulse	Tempo	Style	Chpt Ref
The half note receives the pulse.	♩= 60–68	Declarative, joyful	3 and 7

Accompaniment

Piano or accompaniment is preferred. Other possible instruments include flute, Orff instruments, or guitar.

Additional Information

A slightly detached accompaniment helps this dance.

462 Now We Join in Celebration
SCHMÜCKE DICH

Pulse	Tempo	Style	Chpt Ref
The meter shifts between the half note and dotted half note. The dotted half note pulse occurs in the third phrase only (♩. ♩. ♩ ♩ ♩).	♩= 54–60	Broad, quietly joyful	3 and 5

Accompaniment

Organ (piano)

Additional Information

A legato articulation works best, with a slight strengthening at the beginning of each half note.

463   Lord, Who the Night You Were Betrayed

SONG 1

Pulse	Tempo	Style	Chpt Ref
The half note receives the pulse.	♩ = 52–58	Smooth, walking tempo	3 and 5

Accompaniment
Organ (piano)

464   Bread of Life, Our Host and Meal

JESUS, FEED US

Pulse	Tempo	Style	Chpt Ref
The half note receives the pulse.	♩ = 46–50	Simple, joyful, unhurried	3 and 6

Accompaniment
Piano or guitar accompaniment is preferred, but organ accompaniment would also be successful.

465   As the Grains of Wheat

AS THE GRAINS

Pulse	Tempo	Style	Chpt Ref
The quarter note receives the pulse.	♩ = 86–92	Lyrical	3, 6, and 9

Accompaniment
The rolling accompaniment style lends itself to piano or guitar accompaniment. A C instrument could support the melody. If accompanied with organ, hold beats one and three as a half note in the pedal, and treat the left-hand part as E ♪ ♪ ♫.

466   In the Singing

BREAD OF PEACE

Pulse	Tempo	Style	Chpt Ref
The half note receives the pulse.	♩ = 40–50	Legato, reflective, subtle	3 and 6

Accompaniment
Piano accompaniment is preferred. A flute could enhance the melody line. Keyboard, bass and guitar could also be successful. A simple accompaniment works best.

467   We Place upon Your Table, Lord

DISTRESS

Pulse	Tempo	Style	Chpt Ref
The half note receives the pulse, yet also keep a sense of the dotted whole note (the length of one measure).	$\half = 64–74$	Gently moving	3 and 7

Accompaniment

Organ (piano). Unaccompanied singing in unison works well.

Additional Information

Leading challenge: When choosing a tempo, keep in mind the assembly's ability to sing through a phrase with adequate breath. This is especially important at the end of the third phrase, which ends on a high C.

468   Around You, O Lord Jesus

O JESU, ÄN DE DINA

Pulse	Tempo	Style	Chpt Ref
The dotted half note receives the pulse.	$\half. = 52–58$	Gentle, lilting, lyrical	3, 5 and 6

Accompaniment

Legato organ (piano) accompaniment is preferred.

469   By Your Hand You Feed Your People

CAMROSE

Pulse	Tempo	Style	Chpt Ref
The quarter note receives the pulse.	$\quarter = 82–86$	Broadly, simply	3 and 6

Accompaniment

Piano or organ accompaniment is preferred. Guitar support is optional.

470   Draw Us in the Spirit's Tether

UNION SEMINARY

Pulse	Tempo	Style	Chpt Ref
The half note receives the pulse, yet note the shifting duple/triple meter.	♩ = 54–60	Trusting, lyrical	3 and 5

Accompaniment

Organ (piano)

471   Let Us Break Bread Together

BREAK BREAD TOGETHER

Pulse	Tempo	Style	Chpt Ref
The half note receives the pulse.	♩ = 46–58. See #290 for further guidance.	Reflective	3 and 8

Accompaniment

Organ or piano accompaniment is preferred. Consider singing unaccompanied.

Additional Information

Leading hint: This spiritual can be sung slowly unaccompanied, or in a New Orleans jazz style with improvisational piano, clarinet, bass, and drums.

472   Eat This Bread

Jesus Christ, Bread of Life

BERTHIER

Pulse	Tempo	Style	Chpt Ref
The half note receives the pulse.	♩ = 38–44	Simply	3 and 4

Accompaniment

Unaccompanied singing in four-part harmony is preferred. Light organ, piano, or guitar can provide support. Woodwinds can play counter melodies or obbligatos. See Taizé collections in Bibliography.

Additional Information

Taizé choruses are sung prayers meant to be repeated many times. The chorus can be sung alone, or a cantor can sing the verses between repetitions of the chorus. See pages 33–34 for further guidance.

Note that the two texts are alternate ones; choose one or the other.

473 Holy, Holy, Holy
Santo, santo, santo
ARGENTINE SANTO

Pulse	Tempo	Style	Chpt Ref
The half note receives the pulse.	$\half = 48-60$	Subdued, joyful	3, 6, and 10

Accompaniment

Guitar and/or piano with light percussion (egg shakers and congas) is preferred.

Additional Information

If playing on keyboard, be sure to tie the inner voices.

This sings well in four-part harmony. Since the women's tessitura is low, consider having altos sing the melody and sopranos sing the alto or tenor line up an octave.

474 Bread of Life from Heaven
ARGENTINE SANTO / BREAK NOW THE BREAD

Pulse	Tempo	Style	Chpt Ref
The half note receives the pulse.	$\half = 44-48$	Legato, folk-like	3, 6, and 10

Accompaniment

Guitar supported by piano or organ is the preferred accompaniment. The dotted quarter, eighth-note rhythm pattern should be prominent in the guitar.

475 Lord, Enthroned in Heavenly Splendor
BRYN CALFARIA

Pulse	Tempo	Style	Chpt Ref
The half note receives the pulse, yet think of most measures as a whole note followed by a half note.	$\half = 70-80$	Strong, majestic	3 and 5

Accompaniment

Organ accompaniment is preferred. Solo trumpet on the melody would be a fine addition.

476   Thee We Adore, O Savior
ADORO TE DEVOTE

Pulse	Tempo	Style	Chpt Ref
As with all chant, this hymn flows according to the natural textual accents. For chant, depending on the text, the beats will be grouped in twos or threes.	A fluid tempo that neither rushes nor moves too slowly works best.	Meditative	3 and 4

Accompaniment

While it is preferable to sing chant unaccompanied, you may need to use organ or piano for support. If keyboard is needed, be sure it does not obstruct the natural rhythm. Unison singing is preferred.

477   I Received the Living God
LIVING GOD

Pulse	Tempo	Style	Chpt Ref
The quarter note receives the pulse, yet also sense the dotted half note. A slow tempo allows one to feel the quarter-note pulse, but being mindful of the larger pulse helps keep the tune moving forward.	♩ = 66–76	Joyful, flowing	3, 6, and 7

Accompaniment

Piano (organ)

Additional Information

Consider having a cantor/choir sing the stanzas, and the assembly joining on the refrain.

478   Father, We Thank You
RENDEZ À DIEU

Pulse	Tempo	Style	Chpt Ref
The half note receives the pulse.	♩ = 56–66	Stately at a slower tempo, lilting at a quicker tempo	3 and 5

Accompaniment

Organ (piano)

479 We Come to the Hungry Feast

HUNGRY FEAST

Pulse	Tempo	Style	Chpt Ref
Feel a gently syncopated half-note pulse	♩= 40–48. Consider a carefully led rubato in the final four measures.	Longing, hopeful	3 and 6

Accompaniment

Piano or guitar accompaniment is preferred. Consider adding a solo instrument to the melody line.

Additional Information

Leading hint: Feel the syncopated rhythm, yet keep this tune unhurried and legato.

480 O Bread of Life from Heaven

O WELT, ICH MUSS DICH LASSEN

Pulse	Tempo	Style	Chpt Ref
The quarter note receives the pulse.	♩= 58–68	Prayerful, gentle	3 and 5

Accompaniment

Organ accompaniment is preferred. Consider also accompanying this with string instruments. This may also be sung unaccompanied if led by a choir.

481 Come to the Table

COME TO THE TABLE

Pulse	Tempo	Style	Chpt Ref
The dotted quarter note receives the pulse.	♩.= 52–56	Legato, reflective	3 and 9

Accompaniment

Unaccompanied singing in four-part harmony is preferred. Light piano, organ, or guitar is also successful. It is not necessary to play all the repeated notes. Any accompaniment should not obscure the vocal lines.

482 I Come with Joy

DOVE OF PEACE

Pulse	Tempo	Style	Chpt Ref
The dotted quarter note receives the pulse.	♩.= 68–78	Dance-like, not rushed	3, 6, and 7

Accompaniment

Piano or organ accompaniment is preferred. A single melodic instrument or tambourine could enhance this tune.

Additional Information

This tune can be sung in canon. The second voice enters on beat six of the first full measure ("a"). (A light, detached articulation will keep this dance-like.)

483 Here Is Bread

HERE IS BREAD

Pulse	Tempo	Style	Chpt Ref
The half note receives the pulse.	♩ = 40–48	Legato, contemplative	3 and 9

Accompaniment

Piano/guitar or worship band is the preferred accompaniment. If using worship band, consider a C instrument on melody and acoustic guitar on rhythm. Electric guitar can lightly improvise, with electric or string bass on root.

484 You Satisfy the Hungry Heart

Gift of Finest Wheat

BICENTENNIAL

Pulse	Tempo	Style	Chpt Ref
The quarter note receives the pulse. Note the mixed meter of this hymn.	♩ = 80–88	Warm, flowing	3 and 6

Accompaniment

Organ (piano). Consider soloing out the melody. See pages 26–27 for help on soloing out.

Additional Information

This communion hymn can work well with a choir/cantor singing the verses and the assembly joining on the refrain.

485 I Am the Bread of Life

I AM THE BREAD

Pulse	Tempo	Style	Chpt Ref
The half note receives the pulse.	♩ = 44–50	Gentle on verses, confident on refrain	3, 5, and 9

Accompaniment

Piano/guitar or worship band is the preferred accompaniment. If using worship band, consider a C instrument on melody and acoustic guitar on rhythm. Electric guitar can lightly improvise, with electric or string bass on root. Organ accompaniment is also possible.

Additional Information

Four-part harmony works well on the refrain. Consider using a cantor/soloist on the verses.

Quiet verses lead to a sturdy refrain. A legato feel should be present throughout.

486   God Extends an Invitation

Nuestro Padre nos invita

NUESTRO PADRE

Pulse	Tempo	Style	Chpt Ref
The dotted quarter note receives the pulse.	♩.= 56–68	Celebrative, grateful	3 and 10

Accompaniment

Piano and/or guitar accompaniment with light percussion is preferred (shakers, claves, guiro).

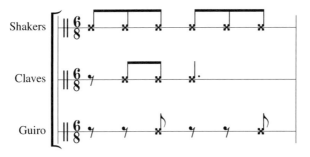

Additional Information

This can also be sung like a *Cueca or Vals* (see examples 7 and 12, page 68).

487   What Feast of Love

GREENSLEEVES

Pulse	Tempo	Style	Chpt Ref
The dotted quarter note receives the pulse.	♩.= 42–48. Keep the tempo moving.	Simple, light	3, 5, and 6

Accompaniment

Organ accompaniment is preferred. Piano, harp, or plucked guitar are possible.

Additional Information

Leading hint: If accompanying with keyboard, it is not necessary to articulate every eighth note in the lower voices.

488   Soul, Adorn Yourself with Gladness

SCHMÜCKE DICH

Pulse	Tempo	Style	Chpt Ref
The meter shifts between the half note and dotted half note. The dotted half-note pulse occurs in the third phrase only (♩. ♩. ♩ ♩ ♩).	♩ = 54–60	Broad, quietly joyful	3 and 5

Accompaniment

Organ (piano)

Additional Information

A legato articulation works best, with a slight strengthening at the beginning of each half note.

489   Soul, Adorn Yourself with Gladness

Vengo a ti, Jesús amado

CANTO AL BORINQUEN

Pulse	Tempo	Style	Chpt Ref
The pulse shifts between the quarter note and dotted quarter note. For examples of the dotted quarter pulse, see measure three.	♩ = 90–110. Once an assembly is familiar with the text, this can go quite fast.	Light, joyful. The shift from major to minor adds a joyous character to each refrain.	3 and 10

Accompaniment

Guitar and/or piano accompaniment with light percussion is preferred.

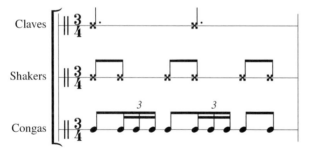

A flute or other solo instrument could enhance the melody line. Also see the *Bolero* rhythm, example 2, page 67.

490   Let All Mortal Flesh Keep Silence
PICARDY

Pulse	Tempo	Style	Chpt Ref
The half note receives the pulse.	♩ = 60–70	Mysterious, meditative	3 and 5

Accompaniment

Organ (piano)

Additional Information

As an alternative accompaniment, consider singing with handbells.

491   Come, Let Us Eat
A VA DE

Pulse	Tempo	Style	Chpt Ref
The half note receives the pulse. Feel weight on the first beat of every measure.	♩ = 44–52	Joyful, subdued. This song can be sung quietly or exuberantly, depending on the tempo and tone of the leader.	3 and 11

Accompaniment

Unaccompanied singing is preferred. African drums can be added. If using light keyboard accompaniment, take care that it does not obscure the vocal line.

Additional Information

Leading hint: The call-and-response nature of this tune makes it especially suitable for communion; printed materials are not needed. A single-voice leader can begin, with the assembly responding, or high voices can sing the leader part, with the low voices responding.

492   Eat This Bread, Drink This Cup
STONERIDGE

Pulse	Tempo	Style	Chpt Ref
The half note receives the pulse.	♩ = 44–48.	Legato, gently flowing	3, 6, and 9

Accompaniment

Piano/guitar or worship band is the preferred accompaniment. If using worship band, consider a C instrument on melody and acoustic guitar on rhythm. Electric guitar can lightly improvise, with electric or string bass on root.

493   Taste and See
TASTE AND SEE

Pulse	Tempo	Style	Chpt Ref
The half note receives the pulse.	$\half$ = 48–60. Choosing a tempo for this tune can be challenging. If too slow the refrain feels ponderous; too fast, and the verses are frantic. Strive for a relaxed, unhurried pace.	Freely, reflective	3 and 8

Accompaniment

Piano accompaniment is preferred; Bass and trap set could be added. The pianist can freely "fill in" or improvise during the refrain. See page 55 for further guidance on improvisation.

494   For the Bread Which You Have Broken
OMNI DIE

Pulse	Tempo	Style	Chpt Ref
The half note receives the pulse.	$\half$ = 58–66	Introspective, prayerful, flowing	3 and 5

Accompaniment

Organ (piano)

495   We Who Once Were Dead
MIDDEN IN DE DOOD

Pulse	Tempo	Style	Chpt Ref
The quarter note receives the pulse. The alternation between $\frac{4}{4}$ and $\frac{5}{4}$ is integral to this tune.	$\quarter$ = 72–92	Lively	3 and 5

Accompaniment

Organ (piano)

Additional Information

Leading hint: This hymn needs a sturdy character to its presentation that emphasizes its rhythmic character.

496   One Bread, One Body

ONE BREAD, ONE BODY

Pulse	Tempo	Style	Chpt Ref
The half note receives the pulse.	♩ = 48–56	Legato, gently flowing	3 and 9

Accompaniment

Piano/guitar or worship band is the preferred accompaniment. If using worship band, consider a C instrument on melody and acoustic guitar on rhythm. Electric guitar can lightly improvise, with electric or string bass on root.

Additional Information

Leading hint: Sing through the longer-held notes.

497   Strengthen for Service, Lord

BUCKHURST RUN

Pulse	Tempo	Style	Chpt Ref
The quarter note receives the pulse.	♩ = 56–68. It is important to achieve a sense of flow while also giving the assembly a chance to sing the text.	Reflective, hopeful	3 and 5

Accompaniment

Organ (piano). A single instrument could be added to enhance the melody.

Additional Information

Leading hint: Play this chant-like tune as legato as possible.

498   United at the Table

Unidos en la fiesta

UNIDOS EN LA FIESTA

Pulse	Tempo	Style	Chpt Ref
The dotted half note receives the pulse, but a sense of the quarter note helps with the text.	♩. = 56–72	Lively, festive	3 and 10

Accompaniment

Guitar with percussion (conga drum, shakers, claves, tambourine, guiro) is the preferred accompaniment.

Piano with maracas is also successful. Also see the *Vals* rhythm, example 12, page 68.

Additional Information

Although scored for unison voices, lower voices can sing a third below the melody on the refrain

499   O Lord, We Praise You

GOTT SEI GELOBET UND GEBENEDEIET

Pulse	Tempo	Style	Chpt Ref
The quarter note receives the pulse, yet sense the larger half note pulse as well.	♩ = 74–90	Marcato, sturdy, rhythmic	3 and 5

Accompaniment

Organ (piano)

500 Now We Remain

NOW WE REMAIN

Pulse	Tempo	Style	Chpt Ref
The dotted half note receives the pulse.	♩.= 40–46	Legato, gently flowing	3, 6, and 9

Accompaniment

Piano/guitar or worship band is the preferred accompaniment. If using worship band, consider a C instrument on melody and acoustic guitar on rhythm. Electric guitar can lightly improvise, with electric or string bass on root.

501 Come with Us, O Blessed Jesus

WERDE MUNTER

Pulse	Tempo	Style	Chpt Ref
The dotted half note receives the pulse.	♩.= 42–50	Lyric, flowing	3 and 5

Accompaniment

Legato organ (piano) accompaniment is preferred.

502 The King of Love My Shepherd Is

ST. COLUMBA

Pulse	Tempo	Style	Chpt Ref
Either the dotted half note or quarter could receive the pulse. If keeping a quarter-note pulse, feel an emphasis on the first beat of each measure.	♩= 84–108	Flowing, lyrical, confident	3, 5, and 6

Accompaniment

Organ or piano accompaniment is preferred. A treble solo instrument can enhance this Irish pastorale.

503 A Mighty Fortress Is Our God
EIN FESTE BURG

Pulse	Tempo	Style	Chpt Ref
This rhythmic chorale shifts between a half-note and dotted-half-note pulse. See page 38 for a diagram of this rhythm.	♩ = 78–90	Grand, strong, rugged	3 and 5

Accompaniment

Organ (piano) in a slightly detached style is preferred.

Additional Information

Note that this chorale begins on the upbeat. Be sure to prepare with a breath, keep the pickup light, and feel a stress on the first quarter note.

504, 505 A Mighty Fortress Is Our God
EIN FESTE BURG

Pulse	Tempo	Style	Chpt Ref
The half note receives the pulse.	♩ = 48–54	Confident, sturdy, strong	3 and 5

Accompaniment

Organ (piano). Brass instruments could enhance the singing of this chorale.

Additional Information

See #509 for this tune in the key of D major.

506 The Word of God Is Source and Seed
GAUDEAMUS DOMINO

Pulse	Tempo	Style	Chpt Ref
The dotted half note receives the pulse. Throughout, sense a strong half followed by a quarter.	♩. = 52–58	Flowing	3 and 5

Accompaniment

Organ (piano)

Additional Information

Leading challenge: The melisma of the last phrase ("Do-") may prove challenging. Careful articulation by the organist is essential.

Latin pronunciation: gow-deh-ah-moos daw-mee-noh.

507   O God of Light

ATKINSON

Pulse	Tempo	Style	Chpt Ref
The half note receives the pulse.	♩ = 56–68	Bright, bold	3 and 5

Accompaniment

Organ (piano). Brass would be a welcome addition.

508   As Rain from the Clouds

AFTON WATER

Pulse	Tempo	Style	Chpt Ref
The dotted half note receives the pulse.	♩. = 38–44	Gently flowing	3 and 6

Accompaniment

Piano or organ accompaniment is preferred.

Additional Information

Teaching hint: Consider teaching the descending-seventh leap of the final phrase.

509   God's Word Is Our Great Heritage

EIN FESTE BURG

Pulse	Tempo	Style	Chpt Ref
The half note receives the pulse.	♩ = 48–54	Confident, sturdy, strong	3 and 5

Accompaniment

Organ (piano). Brass instruments could enhance the singing of this chorale.

Additional Information

See #504 for this tune in the key of C major.

510   Word of God, Come Down on Earth

LIEBSTER JESU, WIR SIND HIER

Pulse	Tempo	Style	Chpt Ref
The half note receives the pulse.	♩ = 40–50. Strive for a tempo that allows for comfortable quarter and half notes.	Gentle, peaceful	3 and 5

Accompaniment

Organ (piano)

Additional Information

A legato articulation suits this chorale melody.

511 Thy Strong Word

EBENEZER

Pulse	Tempo	Style	Chpt Ref
The half note receives the pulse.	♩= 76–90	Majestic, strong, stately	3 and 5

Accompaniment

Organ (piano)

Additional Information

If sung in harmony, be careful that the harmonies do not slow the tempo.

512 Lord, Let My Heart Be Good Soil

GOOD SOIL

Pulse	Tempo	Style	Chpt Ref
The quarter note receives the pulse.	♩= 80–86	Prayerful, gentle	3 and 9

Accompaniment

Worship band accompaniment is preferred. See #483 for detailed suggestions. Piano alone will also work. A simple and unobtrusive accompaniment suits this song.

513 Listen, God Is Calling

Neno lake Mungu

NENO LAKE MUNGU

Pulse	Tempo	Style	Chpt Ref
The quarter note receives the pulse.	♩= 84–100	Rhythmic, joyful	3 and 11

Accompaniment

Unaccompanied singing in four-part harmony is preferred. African drums or conga drums can be added.

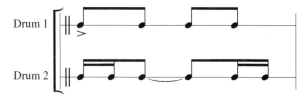

Additional Information

Leading hint: This joyful call-and-response song needs to stay within the rhythmic framework. Do not add extra time between the refrain and the verses. Note that the last note of the first refrain and of the verse is a quarter value.

514 O Word of God Incarnate

MUNICH

Pulse	Tempo	Style	Chpt Ref
The half note receives the pulse.	♩ = 50–58	Flowing, with quiet confidence	3 and 5

Accompaniment
Organ (piano)

515 Break Now the Bread of Life

BREAD OF LIFE

Pulse	Tempo	Style	Chpt Ref
The half note receives the pulse.	♩ = 58–64	Simply, lyrical	3, 5 and 7

Accompaniment
Organ (piano)

516 Almighty God, Your Word Is Cast

ST. FLAVIAN

Pulse	Tempo	Style	Chpt Ref
The half note receives the pulse.	♩ = 52–60	Introspective, solid	3 and 5

Accompaniment
Organ (piano)

517 Lord, Keep Us Steadfast in Your Word

ERHALT UNS, HERR

Pulse	Tempo	Style	Chpt Ref
The half note receives the pulse.	♩ = 50–58	Strong, somber, confident	3 and 5

Accompaniment
Organ (piano)

518   We Eat the Bread of Teaching

WISDOM'S FEAST

Pulse	Tempo	Style	Chpt Ref
The quarter note receives the pulse.	♩ = 84–96	With gentle joy	3 and 6

Accompaniment

Piano or guitar accompaniment is preferred. Organ is also possible.

519   Open Your Ears, O Faithful People

YISRAEL V 'ORAITA

Pulse	Tempo	Style	Chpt Ref
The quarter note receives the pulse.	♩ = 60–84. If familiar, consider taking the refrain more quickly than the verses, or start the whole song slowly, gradually building tempo throughout.	Dance-like	3 and 6

Accompaniment

Piano accompaniment is preferred. Adding a clarinet on the melody, and also tambourine, could enhance this tune.

520   Dearest Jesus, at Your Word

LIEBSTER JESU, WIR SIND HIER

Pulse	Tempo	Style	Chpt Ref
The half note receives the pulse.	♩ = 40–50. Strive for a tempo that allows for comfortable quarter and half notes.	Gentle, peaceful	3 and 5

Accompaniment
Organ (piano)

Additional Information
A legato articulation suits this chorale.

521   O Day of Rest and Gladness

ELLACOMBE

Pulse	Tempo	Style	Chpt Ref
The half note receives the pulse.	♩ = 52–60	Flowing	3 and 5

Accompaniment
Organ (piano)

522   As We Gather at Your Table

IN BABILONE

Pulse	Tempo	Style	Chpt Ref
The half note receives the pulse.	♩ = 46–52	Lyrical	3 and 7

Accompaniment
Organ (piano)

523   Let Us Go Now to the Banquet
Vamos todos al banquete
VAMOS TODOS AL BANQUETE

Pulse	Tempo	Style	Chpt Ref
The quarter note receives the pulse. ♩ = 100–116		Simple, lively	3 and 10

Accompaniment

Guitar with percussion (conga drum, shakers, claves, tambourine, guiro) is the preferred accompaniment.

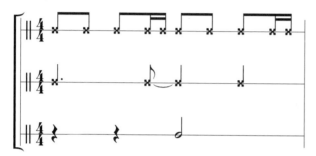

Accordion is a possible addition. See also the *Corrida* or *Danzon* rhythms, examples 6 and 9, page 67.

Additional Information

Although scored for unison voices, lower voices can sing a third below the melody on the refrain.

524   What Is This Place
KOMT NU MET ZANG

Pulse	Tempo	Style	Chpt Ref
The half note receives the pulse.	♩ = 58–66	Dance-like, deliberate, energetic	3, 5, and 6

Accompaniment

This hymn sings best unaccompanied in four-part harmony. Organ or piano accompaniment is possible.

Additional Information

A light marcato articulation works best.

525   You Are Holy

Du är helig

DU ÄR HELIG

Pulse	Tempo	Style	Chpt Ref
The half note receives the pulse. Syncopation against the quarter note is critical to effective singing.	♩ = 62–80. Setting the tempo from the half note will help the feel of the hymn.	Joyful, rhythmic	3, 9, and 10

Accompaniment

Piano accompaniment with light percussion (shakers and claves) is preferred.

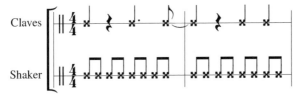

A solo instrument on the melody allows the piano to concentrate on the rhythm and the bass.

Additional Information

Leading hint: This song works well in canon. Part 1 can be sung simultaneously with part 2. The accompaniment can play either part, since the harmonies are the same. It is recommended that you sing the entire song once together before splitting into two parts. After you have repeated it numerous times, the instrumentalists can strongly slow it down and add a fermata to the end of either section.

This tune can have a samba or pop/rock feel.

526   God Is Here!

ABBOT'S LEIGH

Pulse	Tempo	Style	Chpt Ref
The dotted half note receives the pulse.	♩. = 36–42	Grand, noble	3 and 5

Accompaniment

Organ (piano)

Additional Information

Teaching hint: Teach/lead clearly the descending major sixth in the next-to-last measure of the refrain. Assemblies tend to sing an E instead of the C. If singing this in harmony, be careful that the harmony does not slow the tempo.

527 Lord Jesus Christ, Be Present Now

HERR JESU CHRIST, DICH ZU UNS WEND

Pulse	Tempo	Style	Chpt Ref
The pulse shifts between the dotted half note and half note. See #308.	♩= 68–88	Dance-like, firm	3 and 5

Accompaniment

Organ or piano accompaniment is preferred. See the alternate accompaniment provided for piano. Using this accompaniment may require a slower tempo.

528 Come and Fill Our Hearts

Confitemini Domino

CONFITEMINI DOMINO

Pulse	Tempo	Style	Chpt Ref
The quarter note receives the pulse, yet feel the larger dotted half as well.	♩= 68–76	Contemplative	3 and 4

Accompaniment

Unaccompanied singing in four-part harmony is preferred. Light organ, piano, or guitar can provide support. Woodwinds can play counter melodies or obbligatos. See Taizé collections in Bibliography.

Additional Information

Taizé choruses are sung prayers meant to be repeated many times. See pages 33–34 for further guidance. Latin pronunciation: kawn-fee-teh-mee-nee daw-mee-noh.

529 Jesus, We Are Gathered

Jesu, tawa pano

JESU, TAWA PANO

Pulse	Tempo	Style	Chpt Ref
The quarter note receives the pulse.	♩= 80–92	Reflective or joyful	3 and 4

Accompaniment

Unaccompanied singing in four-part harmony is preferred. Light piano and/or percussion can be added.

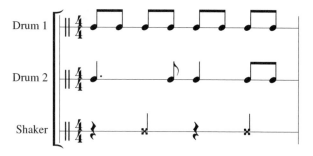

Additional Information

This song may be slower and quieter, or louder and more energetic, depending upon its function in the service. Approximate Shona pronunciation: Jeh-soo tah-wah pah-noh moo zee-tah reh-nyoo.

530 Here, O Lord, Your Servants Gather

Sekai no tomo to te o tsunagi

TŌKYŌ

Pulse	Tempo	Style	Chpt Ref
The half note or quarter note receives the pulse. A slow tempo allows one to feel the quarter-note pulse, but being mindful of the larger pulse helps keep the tune moving forward.	♩ = 84–100	Flowing, quietly joyful	3 and 12

Accompaniment
Unaccompanied unison singing is preferred, perhaps with flute doubling the melody. If piano or other keyboard is used, keep the accompaniment light and spare. A finger cymbal can play on beat three or four of the vocal line.

Additional Information
Teaching hint: Unison instruments can introduce the melody, with the provided accompaniment added on later stanzas.

531 The Trumpets Sound, the Angels Sing

The Feast Is Ready

THE FEAST IS READY

Pulse	Tempo	Style	Chpt Ref
The half note receives the pulse.	♩ = 64–76	Energetic, exuberant	3, 9, and 10

Accompaniment
Piano or worship band, with strong percussion, is the preferred accompaniment. Brass is very fitting.

Additional Information
Leading hint: A strong sense of the downbeat is needed, since the phrases begin on the offbeat. Be careful not to rush the triplets of the refrain.

532 Gather Us In

GATHER US IN

Pulse	Tempo	Style	Chpt Ref
The dotted quarter note receives the pulse.	♩. = 60–68	Lively, dance-like	3, 6, and 9

Accompaniment
Piano with guitar accompaniment is preferred. Organ is possible.

533   Open Now Thy Gates of Beauty

UNSER HERRSCHER

Pulse	Tempo	Style	Chpt Ref
Either the half note or quarter note receives the pulse. A slow tempo allows one to feel the quarter-note pulse, but being mindful of the larger pulse helps keep the tune moving forward.	♩ = 56–62; ♩ = 100–116	Lyrical, with breadth	3 and 4

Accompaniment
Organ (piano)

534   Savior, Again to Your Dear Name

ELLERS

Pulse	Tempo	Style	Chpt Ref
The half note receives the pulse.	♩ = 56–66	Lyrical, prayerful, warm	3 and 4

Accompaniment
Organ (piano)

535   Hallelujah! We Sing Your Praises

Haleluya! Pelo tsa rona

HALELUYA! PELO TSA RONA

Pulse	Tempo	Style	Chpt Ref
The quarter note receives the pulse. The rhythmic singing emphasizes the first beat and the syncopation on the second beat.	♩ = 96–112	Lively, strong	3 and 11

Accompaniment
Unaccompanied singing in four-part harmony is preferred. Keyboard can provide vocal support if necessary.

Additional Information
This song consists of many shorter phrases. Be sure to honor the rests and give the assembly time to breathe.

536   God Be with You Till We Meet Again

GOD BE WITH YOU

Pulse	Tempo	Style	Chpt Ref
The half note receives the pulse.	♩ = 42–48. This is often sung as if in the fifth system, measure one, there were a fermata on the second beat ("meet" on the C).	Assured	3, 7, and 8

Accompaniment
Organ, piano, or organ/piano duet accompaniment is preferred. Bass and drums can be added.

537   On Our Way Rejoicing

HERMAS

Pulse	Tempo	Style	Chpt Ref
The half note receives the pulse.	♩ = 60–76	Brisk, joyful, confident	3 and 5

Accompaniment
Organ (piano)

Additional Information
Note that this setting has a singable four-part harmony. Once learned, consider singing unaccompanied.

538   The Lord Now Sends Us Forth

Enviado soy de Dios

ENVIADO

Pulse	Tempo	Style	Chpt Ref
The quarter note receives the pulse.	♩ = 84–92	Lively, joyful	3 and 10

Accompaniment
Guitar and/or piano accompaniment with percussion (claves, egg shakers, guiro, conga drum) is preferred.

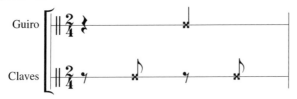

Bass could be added. The rhythm of the left-hand piano part could also be a rhythm for a conga drum. See also the *Danzon* rhythm, example 9, page 66.

539 Abide, O Dearest Jesus

CHRISTUS, DER IST MEIN LEBEN

Pulse	Tempo	Style	Chpt Ref
The half note receives the pulse.	♩ = 52–62	Prayerful, calm	3 and 5
Accompaniment			

Organ (piano)

540 Go, Make Disciples

GO, MAKE DISCIPLES

Pulse	Tempo	Style	Chpt Ref
The quarter note receives the pulse.	♩ = 90–96	Driving rock feel	3 and 9
Accompaniment			

Worship band is preferred. Piano and guitar are optional. This song is more effective with a rhythm section.

541 O Jesus, Blessed Lord

UD GÅR DU NU PÅ LIVETS VEJ

Pulse	Tempo	Style	Chpt Ref
The half note receives the pulse.	♩ = 50–54	Sincere, simple, joyful	3, 5, and 6
Accompaniment			

Organ (piano)

542 O Living Bread from Heaven

AURELIA

Pulse	Tempo	Style	Chpt Ref
The half note receives the pulse.	♩ = 52–58	Confident, firm	3 and 5
Accompaniment			

Organ (piano)

Additional Information

Articulate the repeated melody notes clearly. See pages 38–39 for help with playing repeated notes on the organ.

543   Go, My Children, with My Blessing

AR HYD Y NOS

Pulse	Tempo	Style	Chpt Ref
Either the half or quarter note receives the pulse. If using the half note, be careful not to rush. If using the quarter note, take care not to make the tune march-like.	♩ = 84–90; ♩ = 40–48	Lyrical	3 and 5

Accompaniment
Organ (piano)

544   Praise the Lord, Rise Up Rejoicing

ALLES IST AN GOTTES SEGEN

Pulse	Tempo	Style	Chpt Ref
The half note receives the pulse.	♩ = 56–64	Confident, steady, joyful	3 and 5

Accompaniment
Organ (piano)

Additional Information
Articulate the repeated melody notes clearly. See pages 38–39 for help with playing repeated notes on the organ.

545   Lord, Dismiss Us with Your Blessing

SICILIAN MARINERS

Pulse	Tempo	Style	Chpt Ref
The half note receives the pulse.	♩ = 48–54	Lyrical	3 and 5

Accompaniment
Organ (piano)

546   To Be Your Presence

ENGELBERG

Pulse	Tempo	Style	Chpt Ref
The half note or quarter note receives the pulse. A slow tempo allows one to feel the quarter-note pulse, but being mindful of the larger pulse helps keep the tune moving forward.	♩ = 50–60	Strong, flowing	3 and 5

Accompaniment
Consider adding a trumpet to the melody or soloing out with a reed stop on the organ. See pages 26–27 for help with soloing out.

547   Sent Forth by God's Blessing

THE ASH GROVE

Pulse	Tempo	Style	Chpt Ref
The dotted half note receives the pulse.	♩. = 42–50	Energetic, flowing	3, 5, and 6

Accompaniment
Organ (piano)

Additional Information
Leading hint: Keep the eighth notes light, always moving to the next downbeat.

548   Rise, O Church, like Christ Arisen

SURGE ECCLESIA

Pulse	Tempo	Style	Chpt Ref
The half note receives the pulse.	♩ = 64–70	Broad, forward-moving	3 and 5

Accompaniment
Organ accompaniment is preferred.

Additional Information
Leading hint: This hymn's accompaniment supports a natural crescendo through the two alleluias that lead to the high D at the beginning of the last phrase.

549   Send Me, Jesus

Thuma mina, Nkosi yam

THUMA MINA, NKOSI YAM

Pulse	Tempo	Style	Chpt Ref
The quarter note receives the pulse. The rhythmic singing emphasizes the first beat and the syncopation on the second beat.	♩ = 102–116	Joyful, rhythmic	3 and 11

Accompaniment

Unaccompanied singing in four-part harmony is preferred. Keyboard can provide vocal support if necessary.

550   On What Has Now Been Sown

DARWALL'S 148TH

Pulse	Tempo	Style	Chpt Ref
The half note receives the pulse.	♩ = 64–74	Joyful, lyrical, walking style	3 and 5

Accompaniment

Organ (piano)

Additional Information

Consider playing the opening leaps as a marcato fanfare, yet keeping the stepwise motion legato.

551   The Spirit Sends Us Forth to Serve

CHESTERFIELD

Pulse	Tempo	Style	Chpt Ref
The dotted half note receives the pulse.	♩. = 40–48	Lively, grand, unhurried	3 and 5

Accompaniment

Legato organ (piano) accompaniment is preferred.

Additional Information

Leading hint: Be clear and consistent when playing the first note of measure seven. Keep the pulse moving forward, yet be sure to shorten the half note and give the assembly time to breathe. You may also consider adding an extra measure.

552   Blessed Be the God of Israel

MERLE'S TUNE

Pulse	Tempo	Style	Chpt Ref
The half note receives the pulse.	♩= 58–70	Calm, confident	3 and 6

Accompaniment
Organ (piano)

553   Christ, Whose Glory Fills the Skies

RATISBON

Pulse	Tempo	Style	Chpt Ref
The half note receives the pulse.	♩= 58–66	Lyrical, joyful	3 and 5

Accompaniment
Organ (piano)

Additional Information
Articulate the repeated melody notes clearly. See pages 38–39 for help with playing repeated notes on the organ.

554   Lord, Your Hands Have Formed

GAYOM NI HIGAMI

Pulse	Tempo	Style	Chpt Ref
The quarter note or half note receives the pulse. A slow tempo allows one to feel the quarter-note pulse, but being mindful of the larger pulse helps keep the tune moving forward. Similar to chant, the pulse is flexible, never rigid.	♩= 44–54	Simple, calm, reflective	3 and 12

Accompaniment
Unaccompanied unison singing is preferred, perhaps with flute doubling the melody. If piano or other keyboard is used, keep the accompaniment light and spare. A finger cymbal can play on beat two of the vocal line.

Additional Information
Teaching hint: The grace note in the melody indicates vocal slide, beginning on the beat and sliding for the duration of the quarter note. See page 77 for more on this feature of Asian melodies.

555   Oh, Sing to God Above

Cantemos al Señor

ROSAS

Pulse	Tempo	Style	Chpt Ref
The dotted quarter note receives the pulse.	♩.= 66–82	Joyous, spirited	3 and 10

Accompaniment

Piano/guitar accompaniment with percussion instruments is preferred (maracas, conga, clave, tambourine.

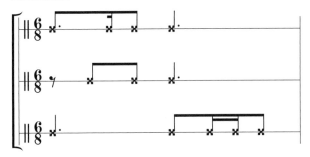

See also the *Vals* rhythm, example 12, page 67.

556   Morning Has Broken

BUNESSAN

Pulse	Tempo	Style	Chpt Ref
The dotted half note receives the pulse.	♩.= 48–58	Simple, flowing, joyful	3 and 6

Accompaniment

Piano (organ). Plucked guitar would also work.

Additional Information

Leading hint: Note that the first three beats are an upbeat to the downbeat of the first measure.

557   Awake, My Soul, and with the Sun

MORNING HYMN

Pulse	Tempo	Style	Chpt Ref
The half note receives the pulse.	♩ = 52–58	Lilting, steady	3 and 5

Accompaniment
Organ (piano)

558   Lord God, We Praise You

CHRISTE SANCTORUM

Pulse	Tempo	Style	Chpt Ref
The half note receives the pulse.	♩ = 54–58	Lyrical, energized	3 and 5

Accompaniment
Organ (piano)

559   O Splendor of God's Glory Bright

SPLENDOR PATERNAE

Pulse	Tempo	Style	Chpt Ref
As with all chant, this hymn flows according to the natural textual accents. For chant, depending on the text, the beats will be grouped in twos or threes.	A fluid tempo that neither rushes nor moves too slowly works best.	With quiet awe	3 and 4

Accompaniment
While it is preferable to sing chant unaccompanied, you may need to use organ or piano for support. If keyboard is needed, be sure it does not obstruct the natural rhythm. Unison singing is preferred.

560   Christ, Mighty Savior

INNISFREE FARM

Pulse	Tempo	Style	Chpt Ref
The quarter or dotted quarter note receives the pulse. Maintain a strong sense of the underlying eighth note. Think of this as a chant melody, with twos and threes.	♩ = 56–68	Expansive, chant-like, quiet energy	3, 4, and 5

Accompaniment

Legato organ accompaniment is preferred. A string orchestra also works well.

Additional Information

Teaching hint: Consider learning this hymn by first speaking the text in rhythm.

561   Joyous Light of Heavenly Glory

JOYOUS LIGHT

Pulse	Tempo	Style	Chpt Ref
The quarter note receives the pulse, but also feel the broad dotted half.	♩ = 78–84	Legato, gently flowing	3 and 6

Accompaniment

Piano accompaniment is preferred. Guitar support optional.

562   O Radiant Light, O Sun Divine

JESU DULCIS MEMORIA

Pulse	Tempo	Style	Chpt Ref
As with all chant, this hymn flows according to the natural textual accents. For chant, depending on the text, the beats will be grouped in twos or threes.	A fluid tempo that neither rushes nor moves too slowly works best.	With quiet awe	3 and 4

Accompaniment

While it is preferable to sing chant unaccompanied, you may need to use organ or piano for support. If keyboard is needed, be sure it does not obstruct the natural rhythm. Unison singing is preferred.

563 O Light Whose Splendor Thrills

ST. CLEMENT

Pulse	Tempo	Style	Chpt Ref
The dotted half note receives the pulse.	♩.= 36–40. With this slow primary pulse, feel the quarter note pulse internally to keep the rhythm moving ahead.	Lyrical, smooth, flowing	3 and 5

Accompaniment

Legato organ (piano) accompaniment is preferred.

564 God, Who Made the Earth and Heaven

AR HYD Y NOS

Pulse	Tempo	Style	Chpt Ref
Either the half or quarter note receives the pulse. If using the half note, be careful not to rush. If using the quarter note, take care not to make the tune march-like.	♩= 84–90; ♩= 40–48	Lyrica	3 and 5

Accompaniment

Organ (piano)

565 All Praise to Thee, My God, This Night

TALLIS' CANON

Pulse	Tempo	Style	Chpt Ref
The half note receives the pulse.	♩= 48–62	Sturdy, confident, calm	3 and 5

Accompaniment

Organ (piano)

Additional Information

Two ways of singing this in canon are possible. An assembly may sing it as a perpetual canon without stopping between stanzas, or complete each stanza before continuing with the next one.

566   When Twilight Comes

DAPIT HAPON

Pulse	Tempo	Style	Chpt Ref
The quarter note receives the pulse.	♩ = 68–76	Quiet, calm, introspective	3 and 12

Accompaniment

Guitar is the preferred accompaniment. Piano could be used, but be careful not to obscure the melody. Regarding this hymn, see also page 78.

567   To You, before the Close of Day

JAM LUCIS

Pulse	Tempo	Chpt Ref
As with all chant, this hymn flows according to the natural textual accents. For chant, depending on the text, the beats will be grouped in twos or threes.	A fluid tempo that neither rushes nor moves too slowly works best.	3 and 4

Accompaniment

While it is preferable to sing chant unaccompanied, you may need to use organ or piano for support. If keyboard is needed, be sure it does not obstruct the natural rhythm. Unison singing is preferred.

Additional Information

Leading hint: Since this is a chant, the eighth rests preceding the phrases indicate a pause for breathing; they are not strictly-metered breaks.

568   Now Rest beneath Night's Shadow

O WELT, ICH MUSS DICH LASSEN

Pulse	Tempo	Style	Chpt Ref
The half note receives the pulse.	♩ = 60–72	Gentle, forward-moving	3 and 5

Accompaniment

Organ (piano)

569   The Day You Gave Us, Lord, Has Ended
ST. CLEMENT

Pulse	Tempo	Style	Chpt Ref
The dotted half note receives the pulse.	$\dot{\half} = 36$–40. With this slow primary pulse, feel the quarter-note pulse internally to keep the rhythm moving ahead.	Lyrical, smooth, flowing	3 and 5

Accompaniment
Legato organ (piano) accompaniment is preferred.

570   Now the Day Is Over
MERRIAL

Pulse	Tempo	Style	Chpt Ref
The half note receives the pulse.	$\half = 44$–50	Quiet, meditative	3 and 5

Accompaniment
Organ (piano)

Additional Information
Articulate the repeated notes clearly. See pages 38–39 for help with playing repeated notes on the organ.

571   O Trinity, O Blessed Light
O HEILIGE DREIFALTIGKEIT

Pulse	Tempo	Style	Chpt Ref
The half note receives the pulse.	$\half = 50$–58	Stately, yet introspective	3 and 5

Accompaniment
Organ (piano)

Additional Information
Leading hint: Keep in mind that the first note in each phrase is a pickup, and do not let the held dotted half notes at the ends of phrases become stagnant. Feel a legato, forward motion throughout.

572   Now It Is Evening
BOZEMAN

Pulse	Tempo	Style	Chpt Ref
The quarter note receives the pulse.	$\quarter = 84$–98	Smooth, contemplative jazz ballad	3, 7, and 9

Accompaniment
Electric piano accompaniment is preferred. Organ and piano work well. The use of soprano saxophone on the melody could enhance this hymn.

573   My Soul Now Magnifies the Lord

ICH HEB MEIN AUGEN SEHNLICH AUF

Pulse	Tempo	Style	Chpt Ref
The dotted half note receives the pulse.	$\dot{\half} = 58–68$	Vigorous, dance-like	3 and 5

Accompaniment

Organ (piano)

Additional Information

A slightly detached articulation works well. Note that this chorale begins on the upbeat. Feel a strong accent on the first half note.

VOCATION, MINISTRY

574   Here I Am, Lord

HERE I AM, LORD

Pulse	Tempo	Style	Chpt Ref
The half note receives the pulse.	$\half = 52–60$	Gently on verses, confidently on refrains	3, 6, and 9

Accompaniment

Piano and/or guitar accompaniment is preferred. If leading with a worship band, see #483 for further suggestions.

Additional Information

Leading hint: Consider having a soloist sing the verses with the full assembly joining on the refrain. This practice highlights the dialogical quality of this song.

575   In Christ Called to Baptize

ST. DENIO

Pulse	Tempo	Style	Chpt Ref
The dotted half note receives the pulse.	$\dot{\half} = 38–44$	Sturdy, forward-moving	3 and 5

Accompaniment

Organ (piano)

Additional Information

Articulate the repeated notes clearly. See pages 38–39 for help playing repeated notes on the organ.

576   We All Are One In Mission

KUORTANE

Pulse	Tempo	Style	Chpt Ref
The half note receives the pulse.	♩= 50–58	Lyrical, confident	3 and 5

Accompaniment

Organ (piano)

577   Creator Spirit, Heavenly Dove

VENI CREATOR SPIRITUS

Pulse	Tempo	Style	Chpt Ref
As with all chant, this hymn flows according to the natural textual accents. For chant, depending on the text, the beats will be grouped in twos or threes.	A fluid tempo that neither rushes nor moves too slowly works best.	Peaceful, prayerful	3 and 4

Accompaniment

While it is preferable to sing chant unaccompanied, you may need to use organ or piano for support. If keyboard is needed, be sure it does not obstruct the natural rhythm. Unison singing is preferred.

Additional Information

The primary accompaniment has passing tones at the ends of phrases. These keep the movement flowing, but may cause confusion as to when to breathe. This can be dealt with in one of two ways: either slow down those two eighth notes a tiny bit, break, and go on with the next phrase; or omit the passing tone.

578   Creator Spirit, Heavenly Dove

KOMM, GOTT SCHÖPFER

Pulse	Tempo	Style	Chpt Ref
The half note receives the pulse, yet recall this chorale's chant origins (it is based on #577). Play the natural rhythms of the text.	♩= 50–66	Prayerful	3 and 5

Accompaniment

Organ accompaniment or unaccompanied singing is preferred.

579 Lord, You Give the Great Commission

ABBOT'S LEIGH

Pulse	Tempo	Style	Chpt Ref
The dotted half note receives the pulse.	$\dot{\half}$ = 36–42	Grand, noble	3 and 5

Accompaniment

Organ (piano)

Additional Information

Teaching hint: Teach/lead clearly the descending major sixth in the next-to-last measure of the refrain. Assemblies tend to sing an E instead of the C. If singing this in harmony, be careful that the harmony does not slow the tempo.

580 How Clear Is Our Vocation, Lord

REPTON

Pulse	Tempo	Style	Chpt Ref
The half note receives the pulse.	$\half$ = 42–48	Lyrical, sustained	3 and 5

Accompaniment

Organ (piano)

581 You Are Mine

YOU ARE MINE

Pulse	Tempo	Style	Chpt Ref
The half note receives the pulse.	$\half$ = 40–48	Legato, confident, contemplative	3 and 9

Accompaniment

Piano accompaniment is preferred. Guitar or worship band is also possible. See #483 for further suggestions.

582 Holy Spirit, Ever Dwelling

IN BABILONE

Pulse	Tempo	Style	Chpt Ref
The half note receives the pulse.	$\half$ = 46–52	Lyrical	3 and 7

Accompaniment

Organ (piano)

583   Take My Life, That I May Be

Toma, oh Dios, mi voluntad

TOMA MI VOLUNTAD

Pulse	Tempo	Style	Chpt Ref
The half note receives the pulse.	♩ = 60–70	Light, rhythmic	3 and 10

Accompaniment

Guitar with percussion (conga drum, shakers, claves, tambourine, guiro) is the preferred accompaniment. Piano with maracas is also successful.

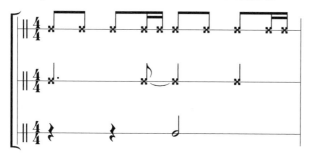

See also the *Balada* rhythm, example 1, page 66.

584   The Son of God, Our Christ

SURSUM CORDA

Pulse	Tempo	Style	Chpt Ref
The half note receives the pulse.	♩ = 58–66	Straightforward, flowing	3 and 5

Accompaniment

Organ (piano)

MARRIAGE

585   Hear Us Now, Our God and Father

HYFRYDOL

Pulse	Tempo	Style	Chpt Ref
The half note receives the pulse.	♩ = 46–54	Strong, sturdy, lyrical	3 and 5

Accompaniment

Organ (piano)

586   This Is a Day, Lord, Gladly Awaited
BUNESSAN

Pulse	Tempo	Style	Chpt Ref
The dotted half note receives the pulse.	$\dot{\half} = 48$–58	Simple, flowing, joyful	3 and 6

Accompaniment

Piano (organ). Plucked guitar would also work.

Additional Information

Leading hint: Note that the first three beats are an upbeat to the downbeat of the first measure.

GRACE, FAITH

587   There's a Wideness in God's Mercy
ST. HELENA

Pulse	Tempo	Style	Chpt Ref
The quarter note receives the pulse.	$\quarter = 74$–82	Expansive, lyrical	3 and 5

Accompaniment

Organ or organ with an obbligato instrument (oboe, flute, clarinet) is preferred. This can be played like a trio, with a solo instrument on the melody, the organ on the middle voice, and a string bass on the lowest voice. Note also the optional simplified accompaniment.

Additional Information

Teaching hint: Consider having a children's or adult choir sing this as an anthem before teaching it to the full assembly.

Leading hint: Always sense the longer line. Think horizontally rather than vertically.

See #258 for this tune in E♭ major.

---

588   There's a Wideness in God's Mercy
LORD, REVIVE US

Pulse	Tempo	Style	Chpt Ref
The half note receives the pulse.	$\half = 50$–56	Lyrical, yet rugged	3 and 7

Accompaniment

Piano (organ). A slightly detached accompaniment suits this early North American tune.

589   All Depends on Our Possessing

ALLES IST AN GOTTES SEGEN

Pulse	Tempo	Style	Chpt Ref
The half note receives the pulse.	♩ = 56–64	Confident, steady, joyful	3 and 5

Accompaniment

Organ (piano)

Additional Information

Articulate the repeated melody notes clearly. See pages 38–39 for help with playing repeated notes on the organ.

590   Salvation unto Us Has Come

ES IST DAS HEIL

Pulse	Tempo	Style	Chpt Ref
The half note receives the pulse.	♩ = 52–58	Dance-like, bold, energetic	3 and 5

Accompaniment

Organ (piano)

Additional Information

A slightly marcato touch in the accompaniment aids the rhythmic singing.

Leading hint: Note the beginning of each phrase on the upbeat. Be sure to prepare with a breath, keep the pickup light, and feel a stress on the first quarter note.

See the treatment of this tune on pages 36–37.

591   That Priceless Grace

THAT PRICELESS GRACE

Pulse	Tempo	Style	Chpt Ref
The half note receives the pulse.	♩ = 44–52	Meditative, unhurried	3 and 11

Accompaniment

Piano accompaniment is preferred. Flute, guitar and/or drums can be added.

592   Just As I Am, without One Plea

WOODWORTH

Pulse	Tempo	Style	Chpt Ref
The dotted half note receives the pulse.	$\dot{\hspace{0.1em}}$ = 36–42	Meditative, sincere	3, 7, and 8

Accompaniment

Legato organ (piano) accompaniment is preferred.

Additional Information

This American gospel tune lends itself to four-part harmony.

593   Drawn to the Light

LA CROSSE

Pulse	Tempo	Style	Chpt Ref
The tactus is the dotted half note, yet feel the quarter note to keep the energy going.	$\dot{\hspace{0.1em}}$ = 53–58	Lyrica	3 and 6

Accompaniment

Piano (organ) and/or guitar is preferred. Woodwinds could enhance the melody line.

594   Dear Christians, One and All, Rejoice

NUN FREUT EUCH

Pulse	Tempo	Style	Chpt Ref
The half note receives the pulse.	$\dot{\hspace{0.1em}}$ = 54–60	Joyful, with rhythmic vitality	3 and 5

Accompaniment

Organ (piano)

Additional Information

Leading hint: A characteristic of sixteenth-century chorales is their rhythmic vitality. Note that this hymn begins with an eighth-note pickup. Be sure to prepare with a breath, keep the pickup light, and feel a stress on the first quarter note.

595   Jesus Loves Me!

JESUS LOVES ME

Pulse	Tempo	Style	Chpt Ref
The quarter note receives the pulse.	♩ = 48–66	Simple, gentle, flowing; or energetic, robust	3 and 7

Accompaniment
Organ, piano, or unaccompanied singing is preferred.

596   My Hope Is Built on Nothing Less

THE SOLID ROCK

Pulse	Tempo	Style	Chpt Ref
The quarter note or dotted half note receives the pulse. A slow tempo allows one to feel the quarter-note pulse, but being mindful of the larger pulse helps keep the tune moving forward. Accentuate the pattern of two eighth notes followed by two quarter notes.	♩ = 76–84	Strong, driving	3 and 5

Accompaniment
Organ (piano)

597   My Hope Is Built on Nothing Less

MELITA

Pulse	Tempo	Style	Chpt Ref
The half note receives the pulse.	♩ = 46–54	Strong, confident, prayerful	3 and 5

Accompaniment
Organ (piano)

598   For by Grace You Have Been Saved
ARMOLAULU

Pulse	Tempo	Style	Chpt Ref
The quarter note receives the pulse.	♩= 76–94	Gently rhythmic	3 and 9

Accompaniment

Piano, guitar, or worship band are the preferred accompaniments. Organ is also possible. Light percussion on trap set can add rhythmic interest. See #483 for further suggestions, but note that these are different meters.

CONFESSION, FORGIVENESS

599   Lord Jesus, Think on Me
SOUTHWELL

Pulse	Tempo	Style	Chpt Ref
The half note receives the pulse.	♩= 48–56	Introspective, confident	3 and 5

Accompaniment

Organ (piano)

600   Out of the Depths I Cry to You
AUS TIEFER NOT

Pulse	Tempo	Style	Chpt Ref
The half note receives the pulse.	♩= 46–50	Serious, penitential, yet still rhythmic	3 and 5

Accompaniment

Organ (piano)

Additional Information

Leading hint: As with other rhythmic chorales, this tune needs a firm, rhythmic pulse. Yet the gravity of this text and tune gives it a more legato, penitential spirit.

601   Savior, When in Dust to You
ABERYSTWYTH

Pulse	Tempo	Style	Chpt Ref
The half note receives the pulse.	$\half = 42$–50	Stately, somber, prayerful	3 and 5

Accompaniment

Organ (piano)

602   Your Heart, O God, Is Grieved
Vieme to, Pane Bože náš

ZNÁME TO, PANE BOŽE NÁŠ

Pulse	Tempo	Style	Chpt Ref
The half note receives the pulse. Note that the opening measures are sung more freely in chant style. In measure two, consider the A ("have") as an upbeat.	$\half = 46$–52	Contemplative, penitential	3, 4, and 5

Accompaniment

Organ (piano) or unaccompanied singing is preferred. A choir could sing the opening phrase in harmony, with the assembly continuing in unison or harmony.

603   God, When Human Bonds Are Broken
MERTON

Pulse	Tempo	Style	Chpt Ref
The half note receives the pulse.	$\half = 40$–50. In a tune such as this where the note values are relatively uniform, the tempo can easily drag. Be careful to feel the longer phrase.	Imploring, trusting	3 and 5

Accompaniment

Organ (piano)

604   O Christ, Our Hope

LOBT GOTT, IHR CHRISTEN

Pulse	Tempo	Style	Chpt Ref
The half note receives the pulse.	♩ = 60–72	Strong, dance-like	3 and 5

Accompaniment
Organ (piano)

Additional Information
Articulate the repeated notes of this chorale carefully. See pages 38–39 for help playing repeated notes on the organ.

605   Forgive Our Sins As We Forgive

DETROIT

Pulse	Tempo	Style	Chpt Ref
The half note receives the pulse.	♩ = 66–78	Pleading, simple	3, 6, and 7

Accompaniment
Organ, piano, or guitar accompaniment is preferred. This melody is best played smoothly; the accompaniment may be slightly detached.

606   Our Father, We Have Wandered

HERZLICH TUT MICH VERLANGEN

Pulse	Tempo	Style	Chpt Ref
The quarter note receives the pulse.	♩ = 64–76	Contemplative, introspective	3 and 5

Accompaniment
Organ (piano) or unaccompanied singing in four-part harmony is preferred.

607   Come, Ye Disconsolate

CONSOLATOR

Pulse	Tempo	Style	Chpt Ref
The quarter note or half note receives the pulse. A slow tempo allows one to feel the quarter-note pulse, but being mindful of the larger pulse helps keep the tune moving forward.	♩ = 84–100	Comforting, expansive	3, 7, and 8

Accompaniment
Consider two options for accompaniment: A piano or organ can lead in a straightforward manner, or the piano can feel a triple pulse and adapt this hymn to a $\frac{12}{8}$ gospel style.

Additional Information
This sings well in four-part harmony.

608   Softly and Tenderly Jesus Is Calling

THOMPSON

Pulse	Tempo	Style	Chpt Ref
The dotted quarter note receives the pulse. A slow tempo allows one to feel the eighth-note pulse, but being mindful of the larger pulse helps keep the tune moving forward.	♪ = 80–96	Legato, meditative, tender	3 and 7

Accompaniment
Piano, organ, or singing unaccompanied is preferred.

609   Chief of Sinners Though I Be

GETHSEMANE

Pulse	Tempo	Style	Chpt Ref
The half note receives the pulse.	♩ = 50–60	Trusting, with quiet awe	3 and 5

Accompaniment
Organ (piano)

610   O Christ, the Healer, We Have Come
DISTRESS

Pulse	Tempo	Style	Chpt Ref
The half note receives the pulse, yet also keep a sense of the dotted whole note (the length of one measure).	♩ = 64–74	Prayerful, interceding	3 and 7

Accompaniment

Organ (piano). Unaccompanied singing in unison works well.

Additional Information

Leading challenge: When choosing a tempo, keep in mind the assembly's ability to sing through a phrase with adequate breath. This is especially important at the end of the third phrase, which ends on a high C.

611   I Heard the Voice of Jesus Say
KINGSFOLD

Pulse	Tempo	Style	Chpt Ref
The half note receives the pulse. This is a tune that might seem to have a quarter-note pulse. See pages 21–22 for further discussion on determining tactus.	♩ = 58–72. The text suggests a slower tempo than with other uses of this tune.	Comforting	3, 5, and 6

Accompaniment

Various accompaniments are possible. If leading with a piano or organ, use a lightly detached articulation and be careful that the harmonies do not prevent the melody from moving ahead. A guitar accompaniment may accentuate the folk-like character of the melody.

612   Healer of Our Every Ill
HEALER OF OUR EVERY ILL

Pulse	Tempo	Style	Chpt Ref
The half note or quarter note receives the pulse. A slow tempo allows one to feel the quarter-note pulse, but being mindful of the larger pulse helps keep the tune moving forward.	♩ = 42–46	Devotional, lyrical	3, 6, and 9

Accompaniment

Piano accompaniment with guitar support is preferred.

613　Thy Holy Wings

BRED DINA VIDA VINGAR

Pulse	Tempo	Style	Chpt Ref
The half note receives the pulse.	$\half = 46-58$	Simple, tender, with quiet confidence	3 and 6

Accompaniment

Piano or organ accompaniment is preferred. The provided alternate accompaniment works best on piano. An obbligato instrument such as flute can enhance this gentle tune.

614　There Is a Balm in Gilead

BALM IN GILEAD

Pulse	Tempo	Style	Chpt Ref
The half note receives the pulse.	$\half = 40-50$. This should be led freely with rubato. See #290 for further guidance.	Legato, reflective	3 and 8

Accompaniment

Organ (piano)

615　In All Our Grief

FREDERICKTOWN

Pulse	Tempo	Style	Chpt Ref
The half note receives the pulse.	$\half = 48-54$	Reflective, strong, lyrical	3 and 5

Accompaniment

Organ (piano)

Additional Information

Leading hint: The opening E of the melody is the second beat of a $\frac{6}{4}$ measure. Consider playing a C in the bass before the first note to start the singing.

616   Jesus, Remember Me

REMEMBER ME

Pulse	Tempo	Style	Chpt Ref
The quarter note receives the pulse.	♩ = 66–80	Meditative	3 and 4

Accompaniment
Unaccompanied singing in four-part harmony is preferred. Light organ, piano, or guitar can provide support. Woodwinds can play counter melodies or obbligatos. See Taizé collections in Bibliography.

Additional Information
Taizé choruses are sung prayers meant to be repeated many times. See pages 33–34 for further guidance.

617   We Come to You for Healing, Lord

MARTYRDOM

Pulse	Tempo	Style	Chpt Ref
The dotted half note receives the pulse.	♩. = 42–46	Prayerful, confident	3 and 7

Accompaniment
Legato organ (piano) accompaniment is preferred.

HOPE, ASSURANCE

618   Guide Me Ever, Great Redeemer

CWM RHONDDA

Pulse	Tempo	Style	Chpt Ref
The half note receives the pulse.	♩ = 50–54. This tune serves as an example for tempo decisions. See page 24.	Strong, brisk	3 and 5

Accompaniment
Organ (piano)

Additional Information
The harmonization is a traditional one, meant for singing in harmony. The optional alto and bass notes near the end could be led by the choir.

619   I Know That My Redeemer Lives!

DUKE STREET

Pulse	Tempo	Style	Chpt Ref
The half note receives the pulse.	♩ = 64–70	Stately, bright, victorious	3 and 5

Accompaniment

Organ (piano)

Additional Information

This tune serves as a good example for the approaches to spacing between phrases. See pages 40–42.

A longer text like this is a good opportunity for singing stanzas in alternation. See pages 45–46.

620   How Sweet the Name of Jesus Sounds

ST. PETER

Pulse	Tempo	Style	Chpt Ref
The half note receives the pulse.	♩ = 48–54	Stately, lyrical	3 and 5

Accompaniment

Organ (piano)

Additional Information

This wedding of tune and text presents challenges for musical phrasing. See pages 43–44 for further discussion of this hymn.

A longer text like this is a good opportunity for singing stanzas in alternation. See pages 45–46.

621   Jesus Lives, My Sure Defense

JESUS, MEINE ZUVERSICHT

Pulse	Tempo	Style	Chpt Ref
The half note receives the pulse.	♩ = 54–60. Choose a tempo that allows the assembly to breathe comfortably at the end of each line.	Confident, victorious	3 and 5

Accompaniment

Organ (piano)

Additional Information

This chorale sings best in unison.

Sing this as three five-measure phrases.

An assembly that is unfamiliar with this tune will need careful introduction to the G♯ in the last phrase.

622   Neither Death nor Life

NEITHER DEATH NOR LIFE

Pulse	Tempo	Style	Chpt Ref
The quarter note or dotted half note receives the pulse. A slow tempo allows one to feel the quarter note pulse, but being mindful of the larger pulse helps keep the tune moving forward.	♩= 92–98	Brisk, energetic	3 and 9

Accompaniment

Piano, supported by gospel organ, guitar, and percussion (trap set) is the preferred accompaniment. Piano alone is possible.

Additional Information

The rests in the melody are critical to the rhythm of this gospel-like tune.

Leading hint: Allow this gospel style tune to swing. A strong cantor or soloist with the ability to improvise on the verses will add to the gospel feel. See page 56 for further guidance in improvisation in this style.

623   Rock of Ages, Cleft for Me

TOPLADY

Pulse	Tempo	Style	Chpt Ref
The half note receives the pulse.	♩= 62–76. Find a tempo that suits the introspective nature of the text but doesn't drag.	Hopeful, confident	3 and 7

Accompaniment

Organ (piano)

Additional Information

Part of the interest in this tune comes from the alternation between the dotted pattern ♩. ♪ and the straight one ♩ ♩ . Pay attention to that.

624   Jesus, Still Lead On

SEELENBRÄUTIGAM

Pulse	Tempo	Style	Chpt Ref
The half note receives the pulse.	♩ = 64–72	Lyrical, sturdy	3 and 5

Accompaniment

Organ (piano)

Additional Information

Leading hint: Though they are notated as downbeats, the two quarter notes seem to function best as pickups to the half notes. Honor the full duration of the dotted whole notes. A legato articulation works best.

625   Come, We That Love the Lord

We're Marching to Zion

MARCHING TO ZION

Pulse	Tempo	Style	Chpt Ref
The dotted quarter note receives the pulse.	♩. = 56–66. Allow the refrain, particularly the final ♫ pattern, to set the pulse.	Moving, energetic	3, 7 and 8

Accompaniment

Organ (piano). This American revival tune has a call-and-response character. Consider having a small group sing the stanzas, with the assembly joining on the refrain.

626   By Gracious Powers

TELOS

Pulse	Tempo	Style	Chpt Ref
The half note receives the pulse.	♩ = 60–72	Pensive, quietly confident	3 and 5

Accompaniment

Organ (piano)

Additional Information

Watch the breathing at the ends of the first and third staves—make those quarters quite short.

Carefully prepare this with the choir ahead of time, especially the C♮ in the third line coming shortly after a C♯.

627　O Day Full of Grace

DEN SIGNEDE DAG

Pulse	Tempo	Style	Chpt Ref
The half note receives the pulse.	$\half = 44$–50	Crisp, majestic, flowing	3 and 5

Accompaniment

Organ (piano)

Additional Information

Note that the text on the right-hand page substitutes for stanzas 2–4 printed on the left-hand page.

628　Jerusalem, My Happy Home

LAND OF REST

Pulse	Tempo	Style	Chpt Ref
The dotted half note receives the pulse.	$\half. = 42$–56	With anticipation, folk-like	3, 6, and 7

Accompaniment

Unaccompanied singing, organ, or piano preferred. This tune also works well in canon at the measure. The second voice enters on the last beat of the first measure.

Additional Information

Leading hint: Be careful not to accent the upbeat to each measure.

629　Abide with Me

EVENTIDE

Pulse	Tempo	Style	Chpt Ref
The half note receives the pulse.	$\half = 44$–56	Confident, quietly strong	3 and 5

Accompaniment

Organ (piano). This tune works well unaccompanied in four-part harmony.

630   In Heaven Above

I HIMMELEN, I HIMMELEN

Pulse	Tempo	Style	Chpt Ref
The dotted half note receives the pulse.	$\dot{\half} = 40–48$	Lyrical, forward-moving, gentle	3 and 6

Accompaniment
Organ (piano)

Additional Information
Leading hint: Feel the mid-measure pulse on the tied note at the end of each phrase so that the rhythmic flow is not short-changed. Consider repeating the bass note A on beats three and four of the $\frac{6}{4}$ measure.

631   Love Divine, All Loves Excelling

HYFRYDOL

Pulse	Tempo	Style	Chpt Ref
The half note receives the pulse.	$\half = 46–54$	Strong, lyrical	3 and 5

Accompaniment
Organ (piano)

632   O God, Our Help in Ages Past

ST. ANNE

Pulse	Tempo	Style	Chpt Ref
Either the half note or quarter note receives the pulse. A slower tempo allows one to feel the quarter-note pulse, but being mindful of the larger pulse helps keep the tune moving forward.	$\half = 40–52;\ \quarter = 80–104$	Stately, confident	3 and 5

Accompaniment
Organ (piano)

633   We've Come This Far by Faith

THIS FAR BY FAITH

Pulse	Tempo	Style	Chpt Ref
The quarter note receives the pulse.	♩ = 78–96	With fervor, soulful, deliberate	3 and 8

Accompaniment

Piano/organ accompaniment with drums and/or handclapping is preferred. Claps (or drumbeats) could come on beats two and four.

634   All Hail the Power of Jesus' Name!

CORONATION

Pulse	Tempo	Style	Chpt Ref
The half note receives the pulse.	♩ = 52–68	Strong, sturdy	3 and 7

Accompaniment

Organ (piano)

Additional Information

This early American tune works well unaccompanied in four-part harmony.

635   We Walk by Faith

SHANTI

Pulse	Tempo	Style	Chpt Ref
The quarter note receives the pulse.	♩ = 72–76	Gentle, lyrical	3 and 6

Accompaniment

Piano or organ accompaniment is preferred. Guitar support is optional.

636   How Small Our Span of Life

KINGSFOLD

Pulse	Tempo	Style	Chpt Ref
The half note receives the pulse. This is a tune that might seem to have a quarter-note pulse. See pages 21–22 for further discussion on determining tactus.	♩ = 58–72. A rhythmic, moderate tempo works best.	Gentle, with praise	3, 5, and 6

Accompaniment

Various accompaniments are possible. If leading with a piano or organ, use a lightly detached articulation and be careful that the harmonies do not prevent the melody from moving ahead. A guitar accompaniment may accentuate the folk-like character of the melody.

637   Holy God, Holy and Glorious

NELSON

Pulse	Tempo	Style	Chpt Ref
The quarter note receives the pulse.	♩ = 76–90. Take care to stretch slightly at the ends of phrases and in preparation for the high E♭ in the second line.	Awe-filled, flowing	3 and 5

Accompaniment

Legato organ accompaniment is preferred.

Additional Information

Leading hint: Note the shift in the numbers of beats per measure. Remember to sing through the phrases, keeping the quarter note constant.

638   Blessed Assurance

ASSURANCE

Pulse	Tempo	Style	Chpt Ref
The dotted quarter note receives the pulse, yet always feel the underlying eighth note.	♩. = 48–68	Joyful, energetic	3, 7, and 8

Accompaniment

Piano (organ). This gospel tune lends itself to singing in four-part harmony.

Additional Information

Leading hint: Allow the melody to flow in a legato style, but consider detaching the repeated notes.

See page 57 for further comments on this tune.

639 When We Are Living

Pues si vivimos

SOMOS DEL SEÑOR

Pulse	Tempo	Style	Chpt Ref
The half note receives the pulse. At a slower tempo, the quarter note could receive the pulse.	♩= 48–60	Lyrical, prayerful	3 and 10

Accompaniment

Piano and/or guitar accompaniment with light percussion (conga drum and egg shakers) is preferred.

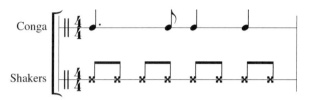

See also the *Bolero* rhythm, example 2, page 66.

Additional Information

Harmony in thirds could be improvised.

640 Our Father, by Whose Name

RHOSYMEDRE

Pulse	Tempo	Style	Chpt Ref
The half note receives the pulse.	♩= 54–62	Lyrical, assured	3 and 5

Accompaniment

Organ (piano)

Additional Information

Articulate the repeated notes clearly. See pages 38–39 for help playing repeated notes on the organ.

641 All Are Welcome

TWO OAKS

Pulse	Tempo	Style	Chpt Ref
The half note receives the pulse.	♩= 48–52. A strong, joyful tempo works best.	Easily flowing	3, 6, and 9

Accompaniment

Organ or piano accompaniment is preferred. Guitar support is optional.

642 Ubi caritas et amor
Where True Charity and Love Abide

TAIZÉ UBI CARITAS

Pulse	Tempo	Style	Chpt Ref
The quarter note receives the pulse.	♩= 58–70	Contemplative	3 and 4

Accompaniment

Unaccompanied singing in four-part harmony is preferred. Light organ, piano, or guitar can provide support. Woodwinds can play counter melodies or obbligatos. See Taizé collections in Bibliography.

Additional Information

Taizé choruses are sung prayers meant to be repeated many times. The chorus can be sung alone, or a cantor can sing the verses above the second half of the chorus. (Verses are available in the accompaniment edition of Service Music and Hymns and in the Simplified Keyboard Accompaniment Edition.) See pages 33–34 for further guidance.

The Latin is given priority in the layout of this piece. Latin pronunciation: oo-bee kah-ree-tahs et ah-more deh-oos ee-bee est.

643 We Are All One in Christ
Somos uno en Cristo

SOMOS UNO

Pulse	Tempo	Style	Chpt Ref
The quarter note receives the pulse. At a quicker tempo, feel the half-note pulse.	♩= 88–108. If assembly knows this well, it could move more quickly. Be sure to feel the syncopations.	Light, lively	3 and 10

Accompaniment

Guitar and/or piano accompaniment with light percussion (conga drums, egg shakers, and tambourine) is preferred.

See also the *Corrido* rhythm, example 6, page 66.

644   Although I Speak with Angel's Tongue

O WALY WALY

Pulse	Tempo	Style	Chpt Ref
The quarter note receives the pulse.	♩ = 66–80	Smooth, flowing, straightforward	3, 6, and 7

Accompaniment

Piano (organ)

Additional Information

Leading hint: Keep the phrases alive, especially through the held notes.

645   Christ Is Made the Sure Foundation

WESTMINSTER ABBEY

Pulse	Tempo	Style	Chpt Ref
Either the dotted half or quarter note receives the pulse. When keeping a quarter-note pulse, feel a half-note/quarter-note pattern for each measure.	♩. = 38–44	Majestic, grand	3 and 5

Accompaniment

Organ (piano)

646   The Peace of the Lord

La paz del Señor

LA PAZ DEL SEÑOR

Pulse	Tempo	Style	Chpt Ref
The dotted half note receives the pulse.	♩. = 52–58	Quietly joyful, waltz-like	3 and 10

Accompaniment

Guitar and/or piano accompaniment is preferred. Tambourine could be added on beats two and three.

647   Glorious Things of You Are Spoken

BLAENWERN

Pulse	Tempo	Style	Chpt Ref
The dotted half note receives the pulse.	$\dot{\half} = 38\text{--}46$	Majestic, stately	3 and 5

Accompaniment
Organ (piano)

648   Beloved, God's Chosen

ANDREW'S SONG

Pulse	Tempo	Style	Chpt Ref
The dotted half or quarter note receives the pulse. A slow tempo allows one to feel the quarter-note pulse, but being mindful of the larger pulse helps keep the tune moving forward.	$\quarter = 76\text{--}92$	Gentle, lyrical	3 and 6

Accompaniment
Piano accompaniment is preferred. Organ is possible, but consider soloing out the melody. See pages 26–27 for help with soloing out.

Additional Information
Leading challenge: The leaps in the final extended phrase can pose a challenge. Consider having a choir or soloist introduce the first two stanzas, with the assembly joining on the final stanza.

Leading hint: If using the interlude between stanzas, be sure to give a clear indication for the assembly's entrance by breaking the sound. If used as an introduction, be consistent by including it between stanzas.

649 Behold, How Pleasant
Miren qué bueno

MIREN QUÉ BUENO

Pulse	Tempo	Style	Chpt Ref
The quarter note receives the pulse.	♩ = 80–94	Light, joyful	3 and 10

Accompaniment

Guitar and/or piano accompaniment with light percussion (claves, shakers, conga drum, guiro) is preferred.

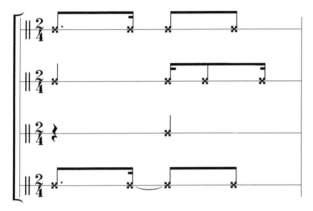

See also the *Danza* rhythm, example 8, page 66.

650 In Christ There Is No East or West

MCKEE

Pulse	Tempo	Style	Chpt Ref
The half note receives the pulse.	♩ = 44–58	Grand, majestic	3, 5, and 8

Accompaniment

Organ or piano accompaniment is preferred. This hymn, based on an African American spiritual, can be swung in ¹²⁄₈ or played as written.

Additional Information

If leading this with more of a swing, adding other instruments, including bass and drums, may be effective.

651   Oh, Praise the Gracious Power

CHRISTPRAISE RAY

Pulse	Tempo	Style	Chpt Ref
The half note receives the pulse.	♩ = 52–60	3 and 5	Joyous, majestic

Accompaniment

Organ (piano)

Additional Information

Leading hint: Note how the text builds in stanzas six and seven.

Teaching hint: Consider teaching the assembly the refrain and having a choir sing the stanzas. Once familiar, consider singing in alternation.

652   Built on a Rock

KIRKEN DEN ER ET GAMMELT HUS

Pulse	Tempo	Style	Chpt Ref
The dotted half note receives the pulse.	♩. = 38–48	Rugged, energetic, powerful	3 and 5

Accompaniment

Organ (piano). The use of brass instruments could enhance this tune.

Additional Information

Leading hint: Either a more detached or a legato articulation would work with this tune. If singing in unison, consider a slightly detached accompaniment that accentuates the feeling of one broad beat per measure. If sung in harmony, consider a more legato articulation.

653   Where True Charity and Love Abide

UBI CARITAS

Pulse	Tempo	Style	Chpt Ref
As with all chant, this hymn flows according to the natural textual accents. For chant, depending on the text, the beats will be grouped in twos or threes.	A fluid tempo that neither rushes nor moves too slowly works best.	In peaceful trust	3 and 4

Accompaniment

While it is preferable to sing chant unaccompanied, you may need to use organ or piano for support. If keyboard is needed, be sure it does not obstruct the natural rhythm. Unison singing is preferred.

654   The Church's One Foundation

AURELIA

Pulse	Tempo	Style	Chpt Ref
The half note receives the pulse.	♩= 52–58	Confident, firm	3 and 5

Accompaniment
Organ (piano)

Additional Information
Articulate the repeated melody notes clearly. See pages 38–39 for help with playing repeated notes on the organ.

655   Son of God, Eternal Savior

IN BABILONE

Pulse	Tempo	Style	Chpt Ref
The half note receives the pulse.	♩= 46–52	Lyrical	3 and 7

Accompaniment
Organ (piano)

656   Blest Be the Tie That Binds

DENNIS

Pulse	Tempo	Style	Chpt Ref
The dotted half note receives the pulse.	♩.= 36–40	Lyrical, forward-moving	3, 5, and 7

Accompaniment
Organ (piano)

657 Rise, O Sun of Righteousness

SONNE DER GERECHTIGKEIT

Pulse	Tempo	Style	Chpt Ref
The half note receives the pulse, yet also feel a strong whole-note pulse.	♩ = 74–80	Energetic, strong, joyous	3 and 5

Accompaniment

A slightly detached organ accompaniment is preferred. Consider soloing out the melody. See pages 26–27 for guidance.

Additional Information

This tune serves as a good example for the approaches to spacing between stanzas. See pages 42–43.

658 O Jesus, Joy of Loving Hearts

WALTON

Pulse	Tempo	Style	Chpt Ref
The dotted half note receives the pulse.	♩. = 44–56	Lilting, assured	3 and 5

Accompaniment

Organ (piano)

659 Will You Let Me Be Your Servant

THE SERVANT SONG

Pulse	Tempo	Style	Chpt Ref
The half note receives the pulse.	♩ = 50–58	3 and 6	Legato, easily flowing

Accompaniment

Unaccompanied singing in four-part harmony is preferred. Light piano, guitar, or organ accompaniment is possible.

Additional Information

Take note of the second-to-last measure, the only place where it shifts from $\frac{4}{4}$ to $\frac{3}{4}$.

660 Lift High the Cross

CRUCIFER

Pulse	Tempo	Style	Chpt Ref
The half note receives the pulse.	♩ = 58–64	Processional style, stately	3 and 5

Accompaniment

Organ accompaniment is preferred. Consider soloing out the melody on the refrain. See pages 26–27 for help with soloing out.

Additional Information

Leading hint: Consider the different musical character between the refrain and stanzas. The refrain sings better in unison; the stanzas work well in harmony.

661 I Love to Tell the Story

HANKEY

Pulse	Tempo	Style	Chpt Ref
The half note receives the pulse.	♩ = 98–110	Confident, joyful	3 and 7

Accompaniment

Organ (piano)

662 Christ Is the King!

BEVERLY

Pulse	Tempo	Style	Chpt Ref
The half note receives the pulse.	♩ = 54–60	Confident, joyful	3 and 5

Accompaniment

Organ accompaniment is preferred. Consider soloing out the melody. See pages 26–27 for help with soloing out.

663 Spread, Oh, Spread, Almighty Word

GOTT SEI DANK

Pulse	Tempo	Style	Chpt Ref
The half note receives the pulse.	♩ = 50–56	Direct, bright, vigorous	3 and 5

Accompaniment

Organ (piano)

Additional Information

Consider singing this simple tune in harmony, unaccompanied.

664 Heaven Is Singing for Joy

El cielo canta alegría

ALEGRÍA

Pulse	Tempo	Style	Chpt Ref
The quarter note receives the pulse.	♩ = 84–90. Take care that the sixteenth notes are not too fast, nor the quarter notes too slow.	Lively, energetic	3 and 10

Accompaniment

Guitar and/or piano accompaniment with light percussion (claves, shakers, conga drum, guiro) is preferred.

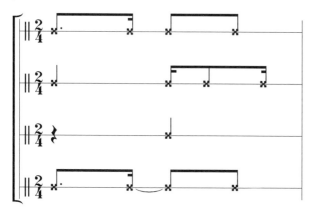

See also the *Carnavalito* rhythm, example 5, page 66.

665   Rise, Shine, You People!

WOJTKIEWIECZ

Pulse	Tempo	Style	Chpt Ref
The half note receives the pulse.	♩ = 60–66	Vigorous	3 and 5

Accompaniment

Organ (piano)

Additional Information

The first and third phrases benefit from a crisp, marcato articulation. Think fanfare.

666   What Wondrous Love Is This

WONDROUS LOVE

Pulse	Tempo	Style	Chpt Ref
The half note receives the pulse.	♩ = 54–70. If led carefully, the tempo could gradually increase in each stanza.	Flowing, rugged	3 and 7

Accompaniment

Unison unaccompanied singing works well with this tune. Keep the melody prominent. Organ or piano possible. A choir could lead a stanza in harmony.

Additional Information

Leading hint: Note the change of mood with each stanza. Consider this hymn as a crescendo.

667   Take Up Your Cross, the Savior Said

BOURBON

Pulse	Tempo	Style	Chpt Ref
The half note receives the pulse, yet also keep a sense of the dotted whole note (the length of one measure).	♩ = 64–74	Sturdy, rugged	3 and 7

Accompaniment

Organ (piano). Unaccompanied singing in unison or in canon works well.

668   O Zion, Haste

ANGELIC SONGS

Pulse	Tempo	Style	Chpt Ref
The half note receives the pulse.	♩ = 74–88	Sturdy, jubilant	3 and 5

Accompaniment

Organ (piano)

669   Rise Up, O Saints of God!
FESTAL SONG

Pulse	Tempo	Style	Chpt Ref
The half note receives the pulse.	♩ = 62–70	Strong, lively, proclamatory	3 and 5

Accompaniment
Organ (piano)

670   Build Us Up, Lord
BUILD US UP

Pulse	Tempo	Style	Chpt Ref
The quarter note or dotted half note receives the pulse. A slow tempo allows one to feel the quarter-note pulse, but being mindful of the larger pulse helps keep the tune moving forward.	♩. = 104–112	Gospel	3 and 9

Accompaniment
Piano, supported by gospel organ, guitar, and percussion (trap set) is the preferred accompaniment. Piano alone is possible.

Additional Information
The rests in the melody are critical to the rhythm of this gospel-like tune.

Leading hint: Allow this gospel-style tune to swing. A strong cantor or soloist with the ability to improvise on the verses will add to the gospel feel. See page 55 for further guidance in improvisation in this style.

671   Shine, Jesus, Shine
SHINE, JESUS, SHINE

Pulse	Tempo	Style	Chpt Ref
The half note receives the pulse.	♩ = 60–70	Energetic	3 and 9

Accompaniment
Worship band or piano accompaniment is preferred. See #433 for further suggestions. A trap set or other percussion could enhance this energetic song.

Additional Information
Leading hint: Be sure to keep a steady pulse between the verses and the refrain.

672   Signs and Wonders
FREU DICH SEHR

Pulse	Tempo	Style	Chpt Ref
The pulse shifts between the dotted half note and half note: ♩. ♩. ♪♪♪ See page 37 for further guidance in leading this rhythmic tune.	♩ = 56–70	Dance-like	3 and 5

Accompaniment
Organ (piano). Allow the accompaniment to emphasize the shifting pulse.

673   God, Whose Almighty Word
ITALIAN HYMN

Pulse	Tempo	Style	Chpt Ref
The dotted half note receives the pulse.	♩. = 38–46	Vigorous, strong, forward-moving	3 and 5

Accompaniment
Organ (piano)

674   Let Us Talents and Tongues Employ
LINSTEAD

Pulse	Tempo	Style	Chpt Ref
The half note receives the pulse. A quarter-note pulse could be employed if the tune remains buoyant.	♩ = 64–74	Light, energetic	3 and 10

Accompaniment
Piano and/or guitar accompaniment with conga drums, shakers and claves is preferred.

Alternate percussion options include maracas and tambourine.

675 O Christ, Our Light, Our Radiance True

O JESU CHRISTE, WAHRES LICHT

Pulse	Tempo	Style	Chpt Ref
The dotted half note receives the pulse.	$\dot{\half} = 40$–50	Confident, lyrical	3 and 5

Accompaniment
Organ (piano)

676 Lord, Speak to Us, That We May Speak

CANONBURY

Pulse	Tempo	Style	Chpt Ref
The half note receives the pulse.	$\half = 46$–52	Straightforward, walking style	3 and 5

Accompaniment
Organ (piano)

677 This Little Light of Mine

THIS JOY

Pulse	Tempo	Style	Chpt Ref
The half note receives the pulse.	$\half = 88$–100	Energetic, upbeat	3 and 8

Accompaniment
Piano, organ, or unaccompanied singing is preferred. Hand clapping may be added on beats two and four.

Additional Information
A light, detached articulation works best.

678   God, Whose Giving Knows No Ending

RUSTINGTON

Pulse	Tempo	Style	Chpt Ref
The half note receives the pulse.	♩=46–52	Sturdy, lyrical	3 and 5

Accompaniment

Organ (piano)

Additional Information

Articulate the repeated melody notes clearly. See pages 38–39 for help with playing repeated notes on the organ.

679   For the Fruit of All Creation

AR HYD Y NOS

Pulse	Tempo	Style	Chpt Ref
Either the half or quarter note receives the pulse. If using the half note, be careful not to rush. If using the quarter note, take care not to make the tune march-like.	♩= 84–90; ♩= 40–48	Lyrical	3 and 5

Accompaniment

Organ (piano)

680   We Plow the Fields and Scatter

Aramos nuestros campos

SAN FERNANDO

Pulse	Tempo	Style	Chpt Ref
The quarter note receives the pulse.	♩= 84–100	Joyful	3 and 10

Accompaniment

Guitar and/or piano accompaniment with light percussion (claves, shakers, conga drum, guiro) is preferred.

681   We Plow the Fields and Scatter

WIR PFLÜGEN

Pulse	Tempo	Style	Chpt Ref
The half note receives the pulse.	♩= 56–64	Joyful	3 and 5

Accompaniment

Organ (piano)

682 To God Our Thanks We Give

REAMO LEBOGA

Pulse	Tempo	Style	Chpt Ref
The dotted quarter note receives the pulse. Feel extra weight at the beginning of each beat.	♩.= 62–80	Walking pace, gracious	3 and 11

Accompaniment

Unaccompanied singing in four-part harmony is preferred; the harmony is integral to this song. Piano can provide vocal support if necessary. Light percussion (shaker and drum) can be added.

Additional Information

Leading hint: Most of the assembly's entrances occur off the beat. Encourage their entrances by carrying the dotted half notes through and releasing them precisely on beat four. Keep the eighth notes light and dance-like.

683 The Numberless Gifts of God's Mercies

JAG KAN ICKE RÄKNA DEM ALLA

Pulse	Tempo	Style	Chpt Ref
The quarter note receives the pulse.	♩= 88–100	Cheerful, flowing	3 and 6

Accompaniment

Organ (piano)

Additional Information

Leading hint: Most of the assembly's entrances occur off the beat. Encourage their entrances by carrying the dotted half notes through and releasing them precisely on beat four. Keep the eighth notes light and dance-like.

684 Creating God, Your Fingers Trace

PROSPECT

Pulse	Tempo	Style	Chpt Ref
The dotted half note receives the pulse.	♩.= 34–42	Flowing, meditative	3, 6, and 7

Accompaniment

Organ (piano). At a quicker tempo, consider singing unaccompanied in unison.

Additional Information

This tune works well as a canon at two measures. The second voice enters on the third beat of the second measure ("your").

685   Take My Life, That I May Be

PATMOS

Pulse	Tempo	Style	Chpt Ref
The half note receives the pulse.	♩ = 48–56	Lyrical, flowing	3 and 5

Accompaniment

Organ (piano)

Additional Information

Consider singing this simple tune unaccompanied in four-part harmony.

686   We Give Thee but Thine Own

HEATH

Pulse	Tempo	Style	Chpt Ref
The half note receives the pulse.	♩ = 60–70	With motion	3 and 5

Accompaniment

Organ (piano)

687   Come to Us, Creative Spirit

CASTLEWOOD

Pulse	Tempo	Style	Chpt Ref
The quarter note receives the pulse.	♩ = 70–86	Lyrical, forward-moving	3 and 6

Accompaniment

Organ (piano). A flute on the melody could enhance the singing.

688   Lord of Light

ABBOT'S LEIGH

Pulse	Tempo	Style	Chpt Ref
The dotted half note receives the pulse.	♩. = 36–42	Grand, noble	3 and 5

Accompaniment

Organ (piano)

Additional Information

Teaching hint: Teach-lead clearly the descending major sixth in the next-to-last measure of the refrain. Assemblies tend to sing an E instead of the C. If singing this in harmony, be careful that the harmony does not slow the tempo.

689 Praise and Thanksgiving

BUNESSAN

Pulse	Tempo	Style	Chpt Ref
The dotted half note receives the pulse.	♩.= 48–58	Simple, flowing, joyful	3 and 5

Accompaniment

Piano (organ). Plucked guitar would also work.

Additional Information

Leading hint: Note that the first three beats are an upbeat to the downbeat of the first measure.

690 We Raise Our Hands to You, O Lord

VI REKKER VÅRE HENDER FREM

Pulse	Tempo	Style	Chpt Ref
The quarter note receives the pulse. Note the shifting meter; measure three is in $\frac{4}{4}$.	♩= 76–84	Simple, direct, tender	3 and 5

Accompaniment

Piano (organ)

Additional Information

Leading hint: Consider this tune as two long phrases; the eighth rests and the releases from the dotted quarter notes propel the melody forward. In the second system, you may want to stretch slightly on the ascending leaps to the high Ds.

691 Accept, O Lord, the Gifts We Bring

BARBARA ALLEN

Pulse	Tempo	Style	Chpt Ref
The quarter note receives the pulse.	♩= 84–98	Flowing, direct	3, 6, and 7

Accompaniment

Organ (piano)

Additional Information

Leading hint: Consider this folk tune as two legato phrases.

692   We Are an Offering

OFFERING

Pulse	Tempo	Style	Chpt Ref
The half note or quarter note receives the pulse. A slower tempo allows one to feel the quarter-note pulse, but being mindful of the larger pulse helps keep the tune moving forward.	♩ = 60–70	Legato, expansive	3 and 9

Accompaniment

Worship band or piano/guitar accompaniment is preferred.

693   Come, Ye Thankful People, Come

ST. GEORGE'S, WINDSOR

Pulse	Tempo	Style	Chpt Ref
The half note receives the pulse.	♩ = 56–64	Strong, joyful	3 and 5

Accompaniment

Organ (piano)

694   Sing to the Lord of Harvest

WIE LIEBLICH IST DER MAIEN

Pulse	Tempo	Style	Chpt Ref
The half note receives the pulse.	♩ = 52–64	Joyful, exuberant	3 and 5

Accompaniment

Organ (piano)

Additional Information

Unison singing keeps this tune flowing.

695   As Saints of Old

FOREST GREEN

Pulse	Tempo	Style	Chpt Ref
The half note receives the pulse.	♩ = 52–64	Flowing	3, 5, and 6

Accompaniment

Organ (piano)

Additional Information

A legato or lightly lilting articulation suits this English folk tune.

696   Jesus Calls Us; o'er the Tumult
GALILEE

Pulse	Tempo	Style
The half note receives the pulse.	$\half = 66-80$	Lyrical

Accompaniment
Organ (piano)

Additional Information
Leading hint: Play this hymn legato with lightly detached repeated notes.

LAMENT

697   Just a Closer Walk with Thee
CLOSER WALK

Pulse	Tempo	Style	Chpt Ref
The quarter note receives the pulse.	$\quarter = 58-68$	Confident, prayerful	3, 7 and 8

Accompaniment
Organ (piano). Singing unaccompanied in four-part harmony would work well.

698   How Long, O God
LAND OF REST

Pulse	Tempo	Style	Chpt Ref
The dotted half note receives the pulse.	$\half. = 42-48$	Yearning	3 and 6

Accompaniment
Unaccompanied singing, organ, or piano preferred. This tune also works well in canon at the measure. The second voice enters on the last beat of the first measure.

Additional Information
Leading hint: Be careful not to accent the upbeat to each measure.

699 In Deepest Night

DEEP BLUE

Pulse	Tempo	Style	Chpt Ref
The half note receives the pulse.	♩ = 50–56. This may be sung freely with rubato. In measure seven, on the words "quietly," "mournfully," and "faithfully," take a rallentando and decrescendo into the G major chord in measure eight.	Smooth, reflective	3 and 5

Accompaniment

Piano (organ)

Additional Information

Leading hint: Articulate clearly the descending melody of the last phrase.
Teaching hint: Teach the change of tonality in the third system.

700 Bring Peace to Earth Again

PACE MIO DIO

Pulse	Tempo	Style	Chpt Ref
The quarter note receives the pulse.	♩ = 66–80	Prayerful, pleading	3, 5, and 6

Accompaniment

Piano or organ accompaniment is preferred.

Additional Information

Very slight articulations, especially on descending chromatic lines, can be effective.

701 Once We Sang and Danced

KAS DZIEDĀJA

Pulse	Tempo	Style	Chpt Ref
The quarter note receives the pulse.	♩ = 72–84	Mournful, longing	3 and 6

Accompaniment

Organ or piano accompaniment is preferred. A solo instrument such as oboe or violin could enhance the singing.

702   You, Dear Lord

Tú, Señor, que brillas

TÚ SEÑOR

Pulse	Tempo	Style	Chpt Ref
The half note receives the pulse.	♩ = 68–76	Sad but hopeful	3 and 10

Accompaniment
Guitar and/or piano accompaniment with light percussion (claves, shakers, conga drum) is preferred.

703   O God, Why Are You Silent

HERZLICH TUT MICH VERLANGEN

Pulse	Tempo	Style	Chpt Ref
The quarter note receives the pulse.	♩ = 64–76	Contemplative, introspective	3 and 5

Accompaniment
Organ (piano) or unaccompanied singing in four-part harmony is preferred.

704   When Pain of the World Surrounds Us

CALLED TO FOLLOW

Pulse	Tempo	Style	Chpt Ref
The half or quarter note receives the pulse. While the harmony dictates a half-note tactus, the mood and a slower tempo may suggest a quarter-note tactus.	♩ = 52–58; ♩ = 104–116	Confident	3, 6, and 9

Accompaniment
Organ, piano, and guitar are possible accompaniments.

705 God of Grace and God of Glory

CWM RHONDDA

Pulse	Tempo	Style	Chpt Ref
The half note receives the pulse.	♩ = 50–54. This tune serves as an example for tempo decisions. See page 24.	Strong, brisk	3 and 5

Accompaniment

Organ (piano)

706 The People Walk

Un pueblo que camina

UN PUEBLO QUE CAMINA

Pulse	Tempo	Style	Chpt Ref
The dotted quarter note receives the pulse.	♩. = 84–96	Purposeful	3 and 10

Accompaniment

Guitar and/or piano accompaniment with light percussion (claves, shakers, conga drum) is preferred.

707 Lord of Glory, You Have Bought Us

HYFRYDOL

Pulse	Tempo	Style	Chpt Ref
The half note receives the pulse.	♩ = 46–54	Strong, sturdy, lyrical	3 and 5

Accompaniment

Organ (piano)

708 Jesu, Jesu, Fill Us with Your Love

CHEREPONI

Pulse	Tempo	Style	Chpt Ref
The dotted quarter note receives the pulse.	♩.= 58–70	Lilting, calm	3 and 10

Accompaniment

Piano with light hand percussion (shaker, African drum) is preferred.

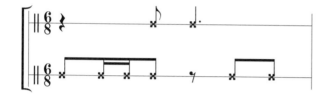

Additional Information

Unaccompanied singing or organ can also be successful.
In Ghana, the first word would be pronounced "yay-soo."

709 When Our Song Says Peace

JENKINS

Pulse	Tempo	Style	Chpt Ref
The quarter note receives the pulse.	♩= 96–104	Militant until last three measures, then gentle and legato	3 and 5

Accompaniment

Organ or piano accompaniment is preferred. The use of brass instruments could enhance the singing of this hymn. A marcato articulation suits the march-like quality of this hymn.

Additional Information

Leading hint: This hymn can have bold, march-like spirit until the last three measures, which should settle into a gentler legato.

710 Let Streams of Living Justice

THAXTED

Pulse	Tempo	Style	Chpt Ref
The quarter note receives the pulse, yet feel the large, soaring phrases.	♩= 70–80	Broad, majestic, forward-moving	3 and 5

Accompaniment

Organ accompaniment is preferred.

Additional Information

Teaching hint: The length and range of this tune can be challenging for some assemblies. Consider introducing it first as a choral anthem.

711   O Day of Peace

JERUSALEM

Pulse	Tempo	Style	Chpt Ref
The quarter note receives the pulse, yet feel the large, soaring phrases.	♩ = 58–64	Broad, lyrical, yearning	3 and 5

Accompaniment

Organ accompaniment is preferred.

712   Lord, Whose Love in Humble Service

BEACH SPRING

Pulse	Tempo	Style	Chpt Ref
The half note receives the pulse.	♩ = 76–92	Hopeful, declarative	3 and 7

Accompaniment

Organ (piano)

Additional Information

This American tune works well sung in canon. A treble string or woodwind instrument could enhance the singing.

A legato articulation with clearly articulated repeated notes is appropriate. See pages 38–39 for help with playing repeated notes on the organ.

713   O God of Every Nation

LLANGLOFFAN

Pulse	Tempo	Style	Chpt Ref
The dotted half note receives the pulse.	♩ = 54–58	Stately, strong	3 and 5

Accompaniment

Organ (piano)

714   O God of Mercy, God of Light

JUST AS I AM

Pulse	Tempo	Style	Chpt Ref
The dotted half note receives the pulse.	♩. = 38–42	Lyrical, flowing	3 and 5

Accompaniment

Legato organ (piano) accompaniment is preferred.

715   Christ, Be Our Light

CHRIST, BE OUR LIGHT

Pulse	Tempo	Style	Chpt Ref
The dotted half note receives the pulse.	♩.= 48–56	Verses: yearning and gracious; refrain: buoyant and hopeful	3 and 6

Accompaniment
Piano/guitar. Organ or praise band are also possible.

Additional Information
Leading hint: A distinctive feature of this hymn is its alternation between minor and major keys. A B-major chord (instead of G) in the measure between the refrain and verses can assist with this transition.

716   Lord of All Nations, Grant Me Grace

BEATUS VIR

Pulse	Tempo	Style	Chpt Ref
The dotted half note receives the pulse, but keep the quarter note in mind in the measures that contain the ♩ ♩ (short-long) rhythmic pattern.	♩.= 36–42	Reflective, yet with rhythmic vitality	3 and 5

Accompaniment
Organ (piano)

717   Let Justice Flow like Streams

ST. THOMAS

Pulse	Tempo	Style	Chpt Ref
The half note receives the pulse.	♩= 54–60	Affirmative, straightforward, joyful	3 and 5

Accompaniment
Organ (piano)

718 In a Lowly Manger Born

MABUNE

Pulse	Tempo	Style	Chpt Ref
The quarter note receives the pulse.	♩ = 56–68	Calm, gracious	3 and 12

Accompaniment

Unaccompanied singing is preferred. If using keyboard to accompany, keep it light and gentle. Flute doubling the melody would be effective.

Additional Information

Finger cymbals, triangles, or small gongs could be added at the ends of phrases. See section in the Asian chapter, page 77.

719 Where Cross the Crowded Ways of Life

WALTON

Pulse	Tempo	Style	Chpt Ref
The dotted half note receives the pulse.	♩. = 44–56	Hopeful	3 and 5

Accompaniment

Organ (piano)

720 We Are Called

WE ARE CALLED

Pulse	Tempo	Style	Chpt Ref
The dotted half note receives the pulse. Feel a clear quarter-note pulse on the pickups to the first, fifth, and ninth measures of the refrain ("We are").	♩. = 38–42	Lively, gospel style	3, 8, and 9

Accompaniment

Piano and/or guitar accompaniment or worship band is preferred.

Additional Information

See #433 for worship band suggestions. A solo instrument such as a trumpet or saxophone can enhance the melody. Trap set is optional.

Teaching hints: Note how the text matches with the melody in the verses. The tied sixteenth notes of the third phrase can be especially challenging.

721   Goodness Is Stronger than Evil

GOODNESS IS STRONGER

Pulse	Tempo	Style	Chpt Ref
The dotted quarter note receives the pulse.	♩.= 48–66	Celebratory, easily flowing	3 and 6

Accompaniment

Unaccompanied singing in four-part harmony is preferred. Organ or piano is possible, yet be sure to give prominence to the vocal lines.

Additional Information

Leading hint: Repetition is essential to this South African freedom chant.

722   O Christ, Your Heart, Compassionate

ELLACOMBE

Pulse	Tempo	Style	Chpt Ref
The half note receives the pulse.	♩= 52–60	Flowing	3 and 5

Accompaniment

Organ (piano)

723   Canticle of the Turning

STAR OF COUNTY DOWN

Pulse	Tempo	Style	Chpt Ref
The half note receives the pulse. At a quicker tempo, one could feel a single broad pulse to the bar, with strong downbeats and dancing upbeats.	♩= 64–84. While a quicker tempo fits the spirit of this dance, consider the assembly's familiarity with the text and tune.	Dance-like, decisive, with a light bounce	3 and 6

Accompaniment

Piano (organ) or guitar accompaniment is preferred. A fiddle or reed instrument could enhance this rousing Irish tune.

724   All Who Love and Serve Your City

NEW ORLEANS

Pulse	Tempo	Style	Chpt Ref
The quarter note receives the pulse.	♩= 60–76	Legato, slowly, thoughtful	3 and 5

Accompaniment

Organ accompaniment is preferred. A dark, thicker registration suits this hymn.

Additional Information

Leading hint: Play the A natural on the final chord in every stanza.

725   When the Poor Ones
Cuando el pobre

EL CAMINO

Pulse	Tempo	Style	Chpt Ref
The dotted quarter note receives the pulse.	♩.= 56–68	Hopeful	3 and 10

Accompaniment

Piano and/or guitar accompaniment with light percussion is preferred (shakers, claves, guiro). A light, articulated accompaniment works best.

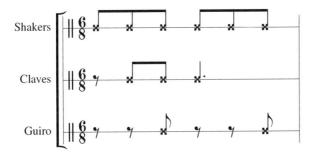

Additional Information

Notice that the two-against-three layering of rhythms is built into this melody. See page 66 for information about this.

726   Light Dawns on a Weary World

TEMPLE OF PEACE

Pulse	Tempo	Style	Chpt Ref
The half note receives the pulse.	♩ = 50–54. Despite the half-quarter beginning, be aware of the eighth notes throughout the tune as you set the tempo.	Inviting, flowing	3 and 6

Accompaniment

Piano or guitar accompaniment is preferred. Organ or praise band are also possible. The verses can be accompanied more lightly than the refrain.

Additional Information

Teaching hint: When introducing this tune, consider teaching the descending sixths of the refrain first.

727   Lord Christ, When First You Came to Earth

MIT FREUDEN ZART

Pulse	Tempo	Style	Chpt Ref
The half note receives the pulse.	♩ = 68–84	Vigorous, trusting	3 and 5

Accompaniment

Organ (piano)
Keep the half notes lightly articulated, giving a lift for breathing at vocal phrase endings.

Additional Information

Teaching hint: The rhythm for this tune is different from *LBW*, now reflecting greater ecumenical consensus.

728   Blest Are They

BLEST ARE THEY

Pulse	Tempo	Style	Chpt Ref
The dotted half note receives the pulse.	♩. = 40–44	Forward-moving	3, 6, and 9

Accompaniment

Piano and/or guitar accompaniment is preferred. Organ or worship band is possible. See #433 for worship band suggestions. An organist will need to adapt the arpeggiated accompaniment to a chordal style.

729   The Church of Christ, in Every Age

WAREHAM

Pulse	Tempo	Style	Chpt Ref
The dotted half note receives the pulse.	♩. = 40–46	Strong, forward-moving	3 and 5

Accompaniment

Organ (piano)

730 Lord Our God, with Praise We Come

ROMEDAL

Pulse	Tempo	Style	Chpt Ref
The half note receives the pulse, yet consider each measure as a half note followed by a whole note. Feel the stress on the second beat or whole note.	♩ = 80–88	Firm, broad, trusting	3 and 6

Accompaniment
Organ (piano)

731 Earth and All Stars!

EARTH AND ALL STARS

Pulse	Tempo	Style	Chpt Ref
The dotted half note receives the pulse.	♩. = 48–52	Celebratory, vigorous	3 and 5

Accompaniment
Organ (piano). Brass or percussion could enhance the singing of this hymn.

Additional Information
Leading hint: Feel a stress on beat one of each measure, with beats two and three light and nimble, as in a waltz.

732 Borning Cry

WATERLIFE

Pulse	Tempo	Style	Chpt Ref
The quarter note or half note receives the pulse. A slow tempo allows one to feel the quarter-note pulse, but being mindful of the larger pulse helps keep the tune moving forward.	♩ = 100–120	Gentle, story-telling	3 and 6

Accompaniment
Piano (organ) and/or guitar is preferred. Woodwinds could enhance the melody line.

Additional Information
Leading hint: Each stanza of this hymn flows immediately into the next. At the repeat sign, consider bending the tempo slightly, which allows the assembly to breathe.

733   Great Is Thy Faithfulness

FAITHFULNESS

Pulse	Tempo	Style	Chpt Ref
The quarter note receives the pulse. Feel an emphasis on the first beat of each measure.	♩ = 90–102	Robust, praise	3 and 7

Accompaniment

Organ, piano, or unaccompanied singing is preferred. Consider having a quartet sing the stanzas, with the assembly joining on the refrain.

Additional Information

Leading hint: This tune flows, yet keep the ♪. ♪ patterns crisp like a fanfare.

734   God, Whose Farm Is All Creation

HARVEST GIFTS

Pulse	Tempo	Style	Chpt Ref
The quarter note receives the pulse.	♩ = 86–100	Prayerful	3 and 5

Accompaniment

A very legato organ (piano) accompaniment is preferred.

735   Mothering God, You Gave Me Birth

NORWICH

Pulse	Tempo	Style	Chpt Ref
The dotted half note receives the pulse.	♩. = 50–56	Gently moving	3 and 6

Accompaniment

Organ or piano accompaniment is preferred.

Additional Information

Leading hint: Note that the melody keeps aiming higher in each phrase until measure ten, where it begins to descend.

736   God, the Sculptor of the Mountains

JENNINGS-HOUSTON

Pulse	Tempo	Style	Chpt Ref
The dotted quarter note receives the pulse; keep a strong sense of the internal rhythms.	♩. = 64–68. This is a slow gospel-jazz style and should not be played too quickly.	Gospel	3 and 8

Accompaniment
Piano accompaniment is preferred. This can also work well on organ.

Additional Information
Leading hint: The walking bass line characterizes this hymn. Keep the bass line "walking" (D, G, F♯, E) in the last bar to lead directly into the next stanza.

737   He Comes to Us as One Unknown

REPTON

Pulse	Tempo	Style	Chpt Ref
The half note receives the pulse.	♩ = 42–48	Lyrical, sustained	3 and 5

Accompaniment
Organ (piano)

738   God Created Heaven and Earth

TŌA-SĪA

Pulse	Tempo	Style	Chpt Ref
The quarter note receives the pulse.	♩ = 64–78	Calm, confident	3 and 12

Accompaniment
Unaccompanied unison singing would be possible, perhaps with a flute doubling the melody. If keyboard is needed for support, use piano gently. Consider adding finger cymbals at the end of each vocal phrase or on beat one of each measure.

739   Touch the Earth Lightly

TENDERNESS

Pulse	Tempo	Style	Chpt Ref
The dotted half note receives the pulse.	♩. = 48–52	Flowing, waltz-like	3 and 6

Accompaniment
Organ, piano, or guitar accompaniment is preferred. Keeping in mind this tune's title and tune name, keep the accompaniment simple and supportive, never overpowering.

740   God of the Sparrow

ROEDER

Pulse	Tempo	Style	Chpt Ref
The quarter note receives the pulse.	♩= 86–90	Broad, lyrical	3 and 6

Accompaniment
Organ (piano)

PRAYER

741   Your Will Be Done

Mayenziwe

MAYENZIWE

Pulse	Tempo	Style	Chpt Ref
The quarter note receives the pulse.	♩= 76–90	Legato, prayerful	3 and 11

Accompaniment
Unaccompanied singing in four-part harmony is preferred. The harmony is integral to this song. Piano can provide vocal support if necessary. Light hand percussion (shaker, djembe, bell) could be added.

742   What a Friend We Have in Jesus

CONVERSE

Pulse	Tempo	Style	Chpt Ref
The half note receives the pulse.	♩= 40–50. Due to this hymn's held notes and slow harmonic rhythm, a nicely moving tempo works best.	Gracious, warm, but moving	3 and 7

Accompaniment
Piano or organ accompaniment is preferred. The alternate accompaniment works well on piano. Note that this accompaniment fills in the harmony. See page 56 for more on this technique.

Additional Information
Leading hint: Another approach to this tune would be to take it at a slower tempo and swing it as if it were in ¹²/₈ (♫ = ♩ ♪).

743   Now to the Holy Spirit Let Us Pray

NUN BITTEN WIR

Pulse	Tempo	Style	Chpt Ref
The half note receives the pulse.	♩ = 70–84	Sturdy, prayerful	3 and 5

Accompaniment
Organ (piano)

Additional Information
A slightly marcato articulation will support the singing.

744   Lord, Be Glorified

BE GLORIFIED

Pulse	Tempo	Style	Chpt Ref
The half note receives the pulse.	♩ = 40–50	Legato, simple, devotional	3, 8, and 9

Accompaniment
Unaccompanied singing in four-part harmony or an arpeggiated piano accompaniment is preferred.

Additional Information
Leading hint: Additional verses could be improvised for this sung prayer.

745   Lord, Teach Us How to Pray Aright

SONG 67

Pulse	Tempo	Style	Chpt Ref
The half note receives the pulse.	♩ = 48–56	Stately, penitential	3 and 5

Accompaniment
Organ (piano)

746, 747   Our Father, God in Heaven Above

VATER UNSER

Pulse	Tempo	Style	Chpt Ref
The half note receives the pulse.	♩ = 46–54	Prayerful, sturdy	3 and 5

Accompaniment
Organ (piano)

748　O God in Heaven

HALAD

Pulse	Tempo	Style	Chpt Ref
The quarter note receives the pulse.	♩ = 64–74	Meditative	3 and 12

Accompaniment

Unlike most Asian song, this Filipino tune can be sung unaccompanied in four-part harmony. Use piano support if necessary.

749　O God of Love, O King of Peace

ERHALT UNS, HERR

Pulse	Tempo	Style	Chpt Ref
The half note receives the pulse.	♩ = 50–58	Somber, imploring	3 and 5

Accompaniment

Organ (piano)

750　Lord, Thee I Love with All My Heart

HERZLICH LIEB

Pulse	Tempo	Style	Chpt Ref
The half note receives the pulse.	♩ = 40–48. An ideal tempo is one that moves forward without feeling rushed.	Prayerful, confident	3 and 5

Accompaniment

Organ (piano)

Additional Information

Leading hint: Consider alternating voices on the middle stanza, with all joining at "Lord Jesus Christ." A similar effect can be achieved with a fuller organ registration.

751　O Lord, Hear My Prayer

The Lord Is My Song

HEAR MY PRAYER

Pulse	Tempo	Style	Chpt Ref
The half note receives the pulse.	♩ = 36–42	Contemplative	3 and 4

Accompaniment

Unaccompanied singing in four-part harmony is preferred. Light organ, piano, or guitar can provide support. Woodwinds can play counter melodies or obbligatos. See Taizé collections in Bibliography.

Additional Information

Taizé choruses are sung prayers meant to be repeated many times. See pages 33–34 for further guidance.

752   Lord, Listen to Your Children Praying

CHILDREN PRAYING

Pulse	Tempo	Style	Chpt Ref
The half note receives the pulse. A slow tempo allows one to feel the quarter-note pulse, but being mindful of the larger pulse helps keep the tune moving forward.	♩ = 32–40; ♩ = 64–80	Contemplative, gospel style	3 and 8

Accompaniment
Unaccompanied singing in four-part harmony or gospel piano accompaniment is preferred. Guitar would also be successful.

Additional Information
Leading hint: Strive for rhythmic accuracy in measures 3, 6, and 7.

753   Dona nobis pacem

DONA NOBIS PACEM

Pulse	Tempo	Style	Chpt Ref
The quarter note receives the pulse. Feel a slight emphasis on the first beat of each measure.	♩ = 86–100	Warm, peaceful, moving	3 and 6

Accompaniment
This canon can be lightly supported by piano or organ.

Additional Information
Teaching hint: This canon consists of three eight-measure melodies that can be sung simultaneously. Consider having the assembly sing the entire canon one or more times. Once the melodies are familiar, divide them into three groups. Group 1 begins; groups 2 and 3 join eight and sixteen measures later. Choral leadership, three soloists, or three treble instruments could assist the keyboardist or song leader.
Latin pronunciation: doh-nah noh-bees pah-chem.

754   Jesus, the Very Thought of You

ST. AGNES

Pulse	Tempo	Style	Chpt Ref
The dotted half note receives the pulse.	♩. = 40–46	Gentle, peacefully	3 and 5

Accompaniment
Legato organ (piano) accompaniment is preferred.

Additional Information
See pages 38–39 for help with playing repeated notes on the organ.

755 Jesus, Savior, Pilot Me

PILOT

Pulse	Tempo	Style	Chpt Ref
The quarter note receives the pulse.	♩ = 64–74	Flowing, prayerful	3 and 7

Accompaniment
Organ (piano). Singing unaccompanied in four-part harmony would work well.

756 Eternal Father, Strong to Save

MELITA

Pulse	Tempo	Style	Chpt Ref
The half note receives the pulse.	♩ = 46–54	Strong, confident, prayerful	3 and 5

Accompaniment
Organ (piano)

757 All My Hope on God is Founded

MICHAEL

Pulse	Tempo	Style	Chpt Ref
The half note receives the pulse.	♩ = 46–52	Soaring, affirmative, sturdy	3 and 5

Accompaniment
Organ accompaniment is preferred.

Additional Information
Leading hint: A legato articulation suits this grand English tune, yet keep the repeated notes and dotted rhythms clearly marked.

758 You Are the Way

DUNDEE

Pulse	Tempo	Style	Chpt Ref
The half note receives the pulse.	♩ = 48–62	Sturdy, forward-moving	3 and 5

Accompaniment
Organ (piano)

759   My Faith Looks Up to Thee

OLIVET

Pulse	Tempo	Style	Chpt Ref
The quarter or half note receives the pulse.	♩ = 52–60	Assured, confident	3 and 7

Accompaniment
Organ (piano)

Additional Information

Leading hint: One can approach this tune in two ways. At a quicker tempo with a quarter-note pulse, it has assured, strong spirit. At a slightly slower tempo with a half-note pulse, it is more meditative. A legato articulation suits either approach.

760   O Christ the Same

RED HILL ROAD

Pulse	Tempo	Style	Chpt Ref
The half note receives the pulse.	♩ = 58–62	Broad, legato, confident	3, 5, and 6

Accompaniment
Organ (piano)

761   Evening and Morning

DIE GÜLDNE SONNE

Pulse	Tempo	Style	Chpt Ref
The dotted half note receives the pulse. Sense the half-note/quarter-note pattern in each half measure.	♩. = 40–46	Lilting	3 and 5

Accompaniment
Organ (piano)

Additional Information

Unison, legato singing is preferred. Be sure to allow for clean breaths at the ends of phrases.

762   Holy, Holy, Holy, Holy

Santo, santo, santo, santo

CUÉLLAR

Pulse	Tempo	Style	Chpt Ref
The pulse shifts from the dotted quarter to the quarter every other measure. Feel 𝟔/𝟖 (two beats to the bar) and 𝟑/𝟒 (three beats to the bar) simultaneously. For example, the first full measure of the refrain has a broad, two-beat feel, while the second has a more articulate, three-beat feel. In the verses, these two feels often combine with the bass clef feeling 𝟔/𝟖 and the treble clef (the melody) feeling 𝟑/𝟒, and vice versa.	♩.= 68–80. If the assembly knows it well, this could be faster.	Very lively, joyous, dance-like	3 and 10

Accompaniment

Guitar and/or piano accompaniment with light percussion (conga drum, egg shakers, claves) is preferred.

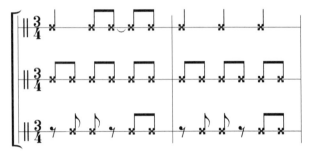

Additional Information

See also the *Soncentroamericano* and *Huapango* rhythms, examples 14 and 11, page 67.

763   My Life Flows On in Endless Song

HOW CAN I KEEP FROM SINGING

Pulse	Tempo	Style	Chpt Ref
The half note receives the pulse.	♩= 56–72	Simply on stanzas, more jubilant on refrain	3, 6, and 7

Accompaniment

Piano (organ) or unaccompanied singing is preferred.

Additional Information

Leading hint: Note the different character between the stanzas and refrain. A more reflective, legato feel characterizes the verses, while a rhythmic bounce suits the refrain.

Leading challenge: The dotted half note in the next-to- last measure ("keep") seems long in comparison to the surrounding melody. Playing the tenor line clearly can encourage the assembly to hold the full three beats.

764   Have No Fear, Little Flock

LITTLE FLOCK

Pulse	Tempo	Style	Chpt Ref
The half note receives the pulse.	♩= 72–82	Playful, simple	3 and 6

Accompaniment

Organ (piano). Consider adding a string bass on the bass line and a solo flute or recorder on the treble line.

Additional Information

A detached articulation keeps this tune light and playful.

765   Lord of All Hopefulness

SLANE

Pulse	Tempo	Style	Chpt Ref
The dotted half note receives the pulse.	♩.= 30–34; ♩.= 90–98. Find a comfortable tempo that allows the assembly to sing the longer phrase.	Flowing, simple	3 and 6

766   Lord of Our Life

ISTE CONFESSOR

Pulse	Tempo	Style	Chpt Ref
The half note receives the pulse, yet feel a broad whole note as well. A slow tempo allows one to feel the half-note pulse, but being mindful of the larger pulse helps keep the tune moving forward.	♩= 64–74	Trusting, broad	3 and 5

Accompaniment

Organ (piano)

767   Lord, Take My Hand and Lead Me

SO NIMM DENN MEINE HÄNDE

Pulse	Tempo	Style	Chpt Ref
The half note receives the pulse.	♩= 56–62	Flowing, gentle	3 and 5

Accompaniment

Organ (piano)

Additional Information

Leading hint: Feel each line leading to the half notes at the end of each phrase. Too much stress on the quarter notes can make this tune feel heavy and laborious.

768   Lead Me, Guide Me

LEAD ME, GUIDE ME

Pulse	Tempo	Style	Chpt Ref
The quarter note receives the pulse.	♩ = 66–76. Various tempos work for this gospel song. It could be played quite slowly, with a more relaxed feel. A livelier, faster interpretation may suit others. In either case, choose a tempo that does not rush the triplets.	Energetic, spirited, with fervor	3 and 8

Accompaniment
Piano, keyboard, or gospel organ is preferred. Drum set or bass could enhance this tune. Hand claps could be added on beats two and three of each measure.

769   If You But Trust in God to Guide You

WER NUR DEN LIEBEN GOTT

Pulse	Tempo	Style	Chpt Ref
The dotted half note receives the pulse. Beats three and six of each measure are light and move toward the next strong beat.	♩. = 38–42	With a gentle lilt	3 and 5

Accompaniment
Organ (piano)

770   Give Me Jesus

GIVE ME JESUS

Pulse	Tempo	Style	Chpt Ref
The half note receives the pulse.	♩ = 42–50. Due to their roots in oral tradition, many African American spirituals can be successful at a wide range of tempos. Knowing your context and your assembly is especially important when setting a tempo.	Legato, prayerful	3 and 8

Accompaniment
Organ (piano) or unaccompanied singing is preferred.

771 God, Who Stretched the Spangled Heavens

HOLY MANNA

Pulse	Tempo	Style	Chpt Ref
The half note receives the pulse.	♩ = 60–68	Declarative, joyful	3 and 7

Accompaniment

Piano or accompaniment is preferred. Other possible instruments include flute, Orff instruments, or guitar.

Additional Information

A slightly detached accompaniment helps this dance.

772 Oh, That the Lord Would Guide My Ways

EVAN

Pulse	Tempo	Style	Chpt Ref
The half note receives the pulse.	♩ = 66–86	Sturdy, declarative, forward-moving	3 and 5

Accompaniment

Organ (piano)

773 Precious Lord, Take My Hand

PRECIOUS LORD

Pulse	Tempo	Style	Chpt Ref
The quarter note receives the pulse.	♩ = 50–66	Introspective, soulful, unhurried	3 and 8

Accompaniment

Piano accompaniment is preferred. Consider singing unaccompanied.

Additional Information

Leading hint: This blues-style tune lends itself to improvisation. The eighth notes can be swung and played as relaxed triplets.

774 What a Fellowship, What a Joy Divine

Leaning on the Everlasting Arms

SHOWALTER

Pulse	Tempo	Style	Chpt Ref
The half note receives the pulse.	♩ = 50–60	Joyful, upbeat	3, 7, and 8

Accompaniment

Piano, organ, or unaccompanied singing is preferred. Singing in harmony is integral to this tune. Clapping can be added on the upbeats. A detached, punctuated articulation suits this style. See page 54.

Additional Information

Leading hint: This tune is often sung in a $\frac{12}{8}$ meter. See page 57 for a discussion of this practice.

775   Jesus, Priceless Treasure
JESU, MEINE FREUDE

Pulse	Tempo	Style	Chpt Ref
The half note receives the pulse.	$\half = 50–58$	Reverent, sturdy	3 and 5

Accompaniment
Organ (piano)

Additional Information
A legato articulation suits this chorale.

776   What God Ordains Is Good Indeed
WAS GOTT TUT

Pulse	Tempo	Style	Chpt Ref
The half note receives the pulse.	$\half = 48–56$	Lyrical, stately	3 and 5

Accompaniment
Organ (piano)

777   Come to Me, All Pilgrims Thirsty
BEACH SPRING

Pulse	Tempo	Style	Chpt Ref
The half note receives the pulse.	$\half = 76–92$	Hopeful, declarative	3 and 7

Accompaniment
Organ (piano)

Additional Information
This American tune works well sung in canon. A treble string or woodwind instrument could enhance the singing. A legato articulation with clearly articulated repeated notes is appropriate. See pages 38–39 for help with playing repeated notes on the organ.

778   The Lord's My Shepherd
BROTHER JAMES' AIR

Pulse	Tempo	Style	Chpt Ref
The half note receives the pulse.	$\half = 62–72$	Flowing	3 and 6

Accompaniment
Organ (piano)

Additional Information
This American tune works well sung in canon. A treble string or woodwind instrument could enhance the singing. Allow the articulation to bring out the rhythmic character of two quarter notes followed by two half notes.

779   Amazing Grace, How Sweet the Sound

NEW BRITAIN

Pulse	Tempo	Style	Chpt Ref
The quarter note receives the pulse. Early American tunes from the Southern Harmony tradition have a rugged quality. A quarter-note pulse helps to convey this quality.	♩ = 78–100. Pay attention to the context when selecting a tempo. A more contemplative setting calls for a tempo slower than a joyous one.	Moving, assured, thankful	3 and 7

Accompaniment

Organ (piano)

Additional Information

This classic American tune is commonly song unaccompanied. Be careful to keep the tempo flowing.

780   Shepherd Me, O God

SHEPHERD ME

Pulse	Tempo	Style	Chpt Ref
The half note receives the pulse.	♩ = 42–46	Lyrical, flowing	3, 6, and 9

Accompaniment

Piano accompaniment is preferred; guitar optional. If playing on the organ, consider soloing out the melody. See pages 26–27 for help with soloing out on the organ.

781   Children of the Heavenly Father

Tryggare kan ingen vara

TRYGGARE KAN INGEN VARA

Pulse	Tempo	Style	Chpt Ref
The quarter note receives the pulse, yet feel a ♩ ♩ pattern in each measure.	♩ = 68–80	Gentle, sweet, child-like	3 and 6

Accompaniment

Organ (piano). This tune also works well when sung unaccompanied in harmony.

782 My Shepherd, You Supply My Need

RESIGNATION

Pulse	Tempo	Style	Chpt Ref
The quarter note receives the pulse. Many early American tunes have a rugged quality that is conveyed well by a quarter-note pulse.	♩= 88–104	Forward-moving	3 and 6

Accompaniment

Organ (piano)

Additional Information

This North American tune can be sung as a canon. The second voice enters on the third beat of measure two ("supply").

783 Praise and Thanks and Adoration

FREU DICH SEHR

Pulse	Tempo	Style	Chpt Ref
The pulse shifts between the dotted half note and half note: ♩. ♩. ♩ ♩ See page 37 for further guidance in leading this rhythmic tune.	♩= 56–70	Gentle, dance-like	3 and 5

Accompaniment

Organ (piano). Allow the accompaniment to emphasize the shifting pulse.

Additional Information

Unison singing is preferred.

784 Grant Peace, We Pray, in Mercy, Lord

VERLEIH UNS FRIEDEN

Pulse	Tempo	Style	Chpt Ref
As with all chant, this hymn flows according to the natural textual accents. For chant, depending on the text, the beats will be grouped in twos or threes.	A fluid tempo that neither rushes nor moves too slowly works best.	Imploring	3 and 4

Accompaniment

While it is preferable to sing chant unaccompanied, you may need to use organ or piano for support. If keyboard is needed, be sure it does not obstruct the natural rhythm. Unison singing is preferred.

785 When Peace like a River
It Is Well with My Soul

VILLE DU HAVRE

Pulse	Tempo	Style	Chpt Ref
The half note receives the pulse. This is best felt in an easy two, yet never rushed.	♩= 52–60	Meditative, confident	3, 7, and 9

Accompaniment

Organ, piano, or unaccompanied singing is preferred.

786 O Holy Spirit, Enter In

WIE SCHÖN LEUCHTET

Pulse	Tempo	Style	Chpt Ref
The pulse shifts between the half note and dotted half note, producing groupings of two and three quarter notes. Keep a steady pulse.	♩= 62–74	Vigorous, trusting	3 and 5

Accompaniment

Organ accompaniment is preferred. An accompanying style that articulates the half and dotted-half groupings will aid the singers. It can also be sung unaccompanied.

Additional Information

Leading hint: Be sure to allow the assembly to breathe between phrases, particularly before the final phrase. Yet do not add extra beats or lose the pulse.

787 On Eagle's Wings

ON EAGLE'S WINGS

Pulse	Tempo	Style	Chpt Ref
The half note receives the pulse.	♩= 40–50	Gently on verses, confidently on refrains	3 and 9

Accompaniment

Piano and/or guitar accompaniment is preferred. If leading with a worship band, see #483 for further suggestions.

Additional Information

Leading hint: Consider having a soloist sing the verses, with the full assembly joining on the refrain. This practice highlights the dialogical quality of this song.

788   If God My Lord Be for Me

IST GOTT FÜR MICH

Pulse	Tempo	Style	Chpt Ref
The half note receives the pulse.	$\half$ = 52–64	Bold, confidently	3 and 5

Accompaniment
Organ (piano)

789   Savior, like a Shepherd Lead Us

BRADBURY

Pulse	Tempo	Style	Chpt Ref
The half note receives the pulse.	$\half$ = 48–54. Consider the many eighth notes when setting the tempo.	Confident, prayerful	3 and 7

Accompaniment
Organ, (piano). Unaccompanied voices would work well.

Additional Information
Leading hint: Keep the eighth notes legato but lightly detach the quarter notes.

790   Day by Day

BLOTT EN DAG

Pulse	Tempo	Style	Chpt Ref
The quarter note receives the pulse. A slower tempo allows one to feel the quarter-note pulse, but be mindful of the larger pulse as well.	$\quarter$ = 88–96	With simple devotion	3 and 6

Accompaniment
Piano (organ)

791   We Sing to You, O God

LOVE UNKNOWN

Pulse	Tempo	Style	Chpt Ref
The half note receives the pulse.	$\half$ = 54–62	Lyrical, confident, smoothly	3 and 5

Accompaniment
Organ (piano)

Additional Information
Consider soloing out the melody or adding a solo instrument. See pages 26–27 for help with soloing out on the organ.

792   When Memory Fades

FINLANDIA

Pulse	Tempo	Style	Chpt Ref
The half note receives the pulse.	♩ = 50–60	Hopeful, smooth	3 and 5

Accompaniment
Organ (piano)

793   Be Thou My Vision

SLANE

Pulse	Tempo	Style	Chpt Ref
The dotted half note receives the pulse.	♩. = 30–34; ♩ = 90–98. Find a comfortable tempo that allows the assembly to sing the longer phrase.	Flowing, simple	3 and 6

794   Calm to the Waves

CALM SEAS

Pulse	Tempo	Style	Chpt Ref
The quarter note receives the pulse. A dotted-half-note pulse is not appropriate to the meditative spirit of this hymn.	♩ = 80–88	Legato, meditative, very calm	3, 4, and 5

Accompaniment
Organ (piano). Various melody instruments could play the soprano, alto, and tenor lines in different octaves.

Additional Information
This chant, like Taizé choruses, calls for repetition (more than two or three times).

795   God, My Lord, My Strength

PÁN BŮH

Pulse	Tempo	Style	Chpt Ref
The quarter note receives the pulse.	♩ = 92–108	Dynamic, vigorous, confident	3, 5, and 6

Accompaniment
Organ (piano)

Additional Information
Leading hint: Due to the asymmetrical nature of this tune, a marcato articulation can help the assembly feel the pulse. Special attention should be given to textual accents and phrasing. The C after the first breath mark may be felt as a pickup to the second full phrase that begins on B flat.

796 How Firm a Foundation
FOUNDATION

Pulse	Tempo	Style	Chpt Ref
The half note receives the pulse.	$\half = 62\text{–}90$	Confident, energetic, with conviction	3 and 7

Accompaniment
Organ (piano). A slightly detached articulation works best. Unaccompanied voices would work well.

Additional Information
This shape-note tune can be sung as a canon at either one or two measures.

797 Blessed Be the Name
Heri ni jina

HERI NI JINA

Pulse	Tempo	Style	Chpt Ref
The quarter note receives the pulse.	$\quarter = 88\text{–}100$	Lively	3 and 11

Accompaniment
Unaccompanied singing in four-part harmony is preferred. Piano could be used for vocal support. Drums or shakers could be added on the last two systems.

Additional Information
Leading hint: Clap on each quarter note in the first two systems, but refrain from clapping on the last two systems.

798 Will You Come and Follow Me
The Summons

KELVINGROVE

Pulse	Tempo	Style	Chpt Ref
The dotted half note receives the pulse.	$\half. = 62\text{–}68$	Gentle, lilting	3 and 6

Accompaniment
Piano or guitar accompaniment is preferred. Organ is possible.

Additional Information
Leading hint: Consider singing stanzas one through four in alternation between two sections of the assembly, with all singing stanza five. This highlights the dialogical nature of the text.

799   Come, Follow Me, the Savior Spake

MACHS MIT MIR, GOTT

Pulse	Tempo	Style	Chpt Ref
Both the dotted half and the half note receive the pulse at different points.	♩ = 62–68	Gently rhythmic	3 and 5

Accompaniment

Organ accompaniment is preferred.

Additional Information

Leading hint: This chorale is very active in its rhythmic variety. Articulate the changing rhythmic structure. Allow time for a breath in measures 4, 8, and 10, without losing the half-note pulse.

800   Spirit of God, Descend upon My Heart

MORECAMBE

Pulse	Tempo	Style	Chpt Ref
The half note receives the pulse.	♩ = 50–64	Prayerful, yearning	3 and 5

Accompaniment

Organ (piano)

Additional Information

Keep this tune very legato.

801   Change My Heart, O God

CHANGE MY HEART

Pulse	Tempo	Style	Chpt Ref
The half note receives the pulse, but at this slower tempo, feeling the quarter note also will help move the melody ahead.	♩ = 40–46	Reflective, with a pop feel	3 and 9

Accompaniment

Piano or acoustic guitar accompaniment is preferred. See #334 for further suggestions.

802   Let Us Ever Walk with Jesus

LASSET UNS MIT JESU ZIEHEN

Pulse	Tempo	Style	Chpt Ref
The half note receives the pulse.	♩ = 50–58	Calm, hopeful	3 and 5

Accompaniment

Organ (piano)

803   When I Survey the Wondrous Cross

HAMBURG

Pulse	Tempo	Style	Chpt Ref
The half note receives the pulse.	♩ = 54–68	Reflective, prayerful	3 and 5

Accompaniment

Organ (piano)

804   Come Down, O Love Divine

DOWN AMPNEY

Pulse	Tempo	Style	Chpt Ref
The half note receives the pulse.	♩ = 50–60	Lyrical, serene, flowing	3 and 5

Accompaniment

Organ (piano)

Additional Information

Consider soloing out the melody. See pages 26–27 for help with soloing out on the organ.

805   Lead On, O King Eternal!

LANCASHIRE

Pulse	Tempo	Style	Chpt Ref
The half note receives the pulse.	♩ = 58–68	Victorious, confident, march-like	3 and 5

Accompaniment

Organ (piano)

Additional Information

Consider the text imagery in stanza two when selecting an organ registration for this tune.

806   O God, My Faithful God

WAS FRAG ICH NACH DER WELT

Pulse	Tempo	Style	Chpt Ref
The half note receives the pulse.	♩ = 58–66	Confident, prayerful	3 and 5

Accompaniment

Organ (piano)

Additional Information

A legato articulation suits this chorale.

807   Come, Thou Fount of Every Blessing
NETTLETON

Pulse	Tempo	Style	Chpt Ref
The quarter note receives the pulse. Feel a strong accent on the first beat of each measure.	♩ = 94–110	Energetic, jubilant, dance-like	3 and 7

Accompaniment

Unaccompanied singing is preferred. Organ or piano would work well.

Additional Information

Leading hint: Keep this tune light and detached.

808   Lord Jesus, You Shall Be My Song
Jésus, je voudrais te chanter
LES PETITES SOEURS

Pulse	Tempo	Style	Chpt Ref
The dotted half note receives the pulse.	♩. = 40–44	Quiet, reflective, lyrical	3, 6, and 7

Accompaniment

Piano or guitar accompaniment is preferred.

Additional Information

Leading hint: Be careful not to let the dotted rhythm "hiccup" and interrupt the smooth flow of the phrases.

809   Send Me, Lord
Thuma mina
THUMA MINA

Pulse	Tempo	Style	Chpt Ref
The quarter note receives the pulse.	♩ = 68–78	Prayerful, subdued	3 and 11

Accompaniment

Unaccompanied singing in four-part harmony is preferred. Piano or organ can provide vocal support if necessary. Drums are not integral to this song.

810   O Jesus, I Have Promised
MUNICH

Pulse	Tempo	Style	Chpt Ref
The half note receives the pulse.	♩ = 50–58	Flowing, with quiet confidence	3 and 5

Accompaniment

Organ (piano)

811   On My Heart Imprint Your Image

DER AM KREUZ

Pulse	Tempo	Style	Chpt Ref
The half note receives the pulse.	$\half = 50\text{–}56$	Strong, sturdy	3 and 5

Accompaniment
Organ (piano)

Additional Information
A slightly detached articulation suits this chorale.

812, 813   Faith of Our Fathers

ST. CATHERINE

Pulse	Tempo	Style	Chpt Ref
The dotted half note receives the pulse.	$\half. = 40\text{–}44$	Strong, sturdy	3 and 5

Accompaniment
Legato organ (piano) accompaniment is preferred.

814   Take, Oh, Take Me As I Am

TAKE ME AS I AM

Pulse	Tempo	Style	Chpt Ref
The quarter note receives the pulse.	$\quarter = 64\text{–}74$. A fairly slow tempo works well, taking care to move through each phrase. Each phrase relaxes as the inner voices resolve.	Reflective, prayerful	3 and 6

Accompaniment
Unaccompanied singing in four-part harmony is preferred. Piano or organ may be used for support if necessary.

Additional Information
Sing this meditative chant repeatedly (more than two or three times). Resist the temptation to resolve the final chord to the tonic; the song ends on the dominant.

815   I Want to Walk as a Child of the Light

HOUSTON

Pulse	Tempo	Style	Chpt Ref
The dotted half note receives the pulse.	♩.= 42–46	Expectant, flowing	3 and 6

Accompaniment

Articulate the repeated notes of the melody clearly. See pages 38–39 for help with playing repeated notes on the organ.

Additional Information

This hymn can be rendered in two quite different styles. It can be sung at a broader tempo in four-part harmony; envision or employ a string quartet. It can also be sung more quickly in unison, taking into account the "walking" text.

816   Come, My Way, My Truth, My Life

THE CALL

Pulse	Tempo	Style	Chpt Ref
The dotted half note receives the pulse.	♩.= 42–50	Lyrical, prayerful	3 and 5

Accompaniment

Legato organ (piano) accompaniment is preferred.
Consider soloing out the melody. See pages 26–27 for help with soloing out on the organ.

Additional Information

Leading hint: This tune can be challenging for many congregations. Consider moving along the melisma in the final line. This helps the overall flow of the melody.

817   You Have Come Down to the Lakeshore

Tú has venido a la orilla

PESCADOR DE HOMBRES

Pulse	Tempo	Style	Chpt Ref
The dotted quarter note receives the pulse.	♩.= 56–72	Lyrical, flowing	3 and 10

Accompaniment

Piano and/or guitar accompaniment with light percussion (maracas, egg shakers, bongo or conga drums).

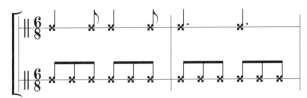

Additional Information

See also the *Balada* rhythm, example 1, page 66. Although scored for unison voices, this can be sung in thirds.

818 O Master, Let Me Walk with You

MARYTON

Pulse	Tempo	Style	Chpt Ref
The dotted half or quarter note receives the pulse. A slow tempo allows one to feel the quarter-note pulse, but being mindful of the larger pulse helps keep the tune moving forward.	♩.= 40–44	Meditative, forward-moving	3 and 5

Accompaniment

Legato organ (piano) accompaniment is preferred.

PRAISE, THANKSGIVING

819 Come, All You People

Uyaimose

UYAIMOSE

Pulse	Tempo	Style	Chpt Ref
The dotted quarter note receives the pulse.	♩.= 54–68	Joyous, celebrative	3 and 11

Accompaniment

Unaccompanied singing in four-part harmony is preferred. Hand percussion (drums, shakers, rattle, bell, clave) can be added.

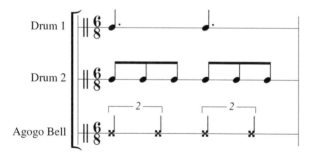

Additional Information

Leading challenge: Although the vocal harmonies are sung in $\frac{6}{8}$ (two triple beats to the bar), some part of the percussion rhythm needs to be in $\frac{4}{4}$ (two duple beats to the bar) at the same time.

820 O Savior, Precious Savior

ANGEL'S STORY

Pulse	Tempo	Style	Chpt Ref
The half note receives the pulse.	♩= 50–56	Gentle praise	3 and 5

Accompaniment

Organ (piano)

821   Shout to the Lord
SHOUT TO THE LORD

Pulse	Tempo	Style	Chpt Ref
The half note receives the pulse.	♩= 38–44	With conviction	3 and 9

Accompaniment
Worship band accompaniment is preferred. Piano is possible.

Additional Information
Leading hint: Contrast the reflective style of the verses with the bolder refrain, yet maintain the same pulse throughout.

822   Oh, Sing to the Lord
Cantad al Señor

CANTAD AL SEÑOR

Pulse	Tempo	Style	Chpt Ref
The dotted half note receives the pulse.	♩.= 50–64	Dance-like	3 and 10

Accompaniment
Guitar with percussion (conga drum, shakers, claves, tambourine, guiro) is the preferred accompaniment. This tune can be led with the compound rhythm of two against three; modified zamba, and guaracha simplificada. See pages 69–70 for a detailed description of possibilities.

823   Praise the Lord! O Heavens
AUSTRIA

Pulse	Tempo	Style	Chpt Ref
The quarter note receives the pulse.	♩= 90–108	Triumphant, joyful	3 and 5

Accompaniment
Organ (piano)

824   This Is My Father's World
TERRA PATRIS

Pulse	Tempo	Style	Chpt Ref
The quarter note receives the pulse.	♩= 98–116	Simple, joyful	3 and 5

Accompaniment
Organ (piano)

825   You Servants of God

LYONS

Pulse	Tempo	Style	Chpt Ref
The quarter note receives the pulse.	♩ = 114–124	Confident, forward-moving	3 and 5

Accompaniment

Organ (piano)

Additional Information

Although the quarter-note tactus adds a sturdy quality to this tune, also feel a strong first beat to each measure. A lightly detached articulation works well.

826   Thine the Amen

THINE

Pulse	Tempo	Style	Chpt Ref
The quarter note receives the pulse.	♩ = 64–68	Broad, smoothly	3 and 5

Accompaniment

A legato organ (piano) accompaniment is preferred.

827   Arise, My Soul, Arise!

Nyt ylös, sieluni

NYT YLÖS, SIELUNI

Pulse	Tempo	Style	Chpt Ref
The half note receives the pulse. Consider leaning into beat three and giving a slight lift before beat four.	♩ = 42–48	Sturdy, dance-like	3 and 5

Accompaniment

Organ (piano). If playing on organ, consider soloing out the melody or adding an obbligato instrument. See pages 26–27 for helping with soloing out on the organ.

828   Alleluia! Voices Raise

PRINCETON

Pulse	Tempo	Style	Chpt Ref
The quarter note receives the pulse. Note the shifting meters between $\frac{4}{4}$, $\frac{3}{4}$, and $\frac{2}{4}$.	♩ = 82–86. A moderate processional tempo works best.	Sturdy processional, flowing	3 and 5

Accompaniment

Organ (piano). A solo instrument on the melody can enhance the singing.

Additional Information

Leading hint: Notice the slightly different characters present in this tune. The measures with text are more processional-like, while the alleluias are more flowing.

829   Have You Thanked the Lord?

LAMOTTA

Pulse	Tempo	Style	Chpt Ref
The half note receives the pulse, although at a slower tempo, the quarter could be used.	♩ = 58–72	Light	3, 8, 9

Accompaniment

Piano accompaniment is preferred, perhaps with light percussion.

Additional Information

Using claves to bring out a ♩. ♩. ♩ rhythm would add vitality to the piece.

830   How Marvelous God's Greatness

DEN BLOMSTERTID NU KOMMER

Pulse	Tempo	Style	Chpt Ref
The half note receives the pulse.	♩ = 46–52	Smooth, broad, forward-moving	3 and 6

Accompaniment

Organ (piano)
Articulate the repeated notes clearly. See pages 38–39 for help with playing repeated notes on the organ.

Additional Information

Leading hint: Shape the phrases so that the many quarter notes are part of a larger phrase.

831   The God of Abraham Praise

YIGDAL

Pulse	Tempo	Style	Chpt Ref
The half note receives the pulse.	♩ = 48–62	Strong, majestic	3 and 5

Accompaniment

Organ (piano)

832   My Lord of Light

BARBARA ALLEN

Pulse	Tempo	Style	Chpt Ref
The quarter note receives the pulse.	♩ = 84–98	Flowing, direct	3, 6, and 7

Accompaniment

Organ (piano)

Additional Information

Leading hint: Consider this folk tune as two legato phrases.

833   Oh, That I Had a Thousand Voices

O DASS ICH TAUSEND ZUNGEN HÄTTE

Pulse	Tempo	Style	Chpt Ref
The half note receives the pulse.	♩= 52–60	Joyous	3 and 5

Accompaniment
Organ (piano)

Additional Information
Unison singing is preferred.

834   Immortal, Invisible, God Only Wise

ST. DENIO

Pulse	Tempo	Style	Chpt Ref
The dotted half note receives the pulse.	♩.= 38–44	Sturdy, forward-moving	3 and 5

Accompaniment
Organ (piano)

Additional Information
Articulate the repeated notes clearly. See pages 38–39 for help playing repeated notes on the organ.

835   All Creatures, Worship God Most High!

LASST UNS ERFREUEN

Pulse	Tempo	Style	Chpt Ref
The quarter note receives the pulse.	♩= 66–76	Brisk, sturdy, rhythmic	3 and 5

Accompaniment
Organ accompaniment is preferred.

Additional Information

Leading challenge: The musician needs to consider how long to hold the second melody note in the sixth full measure. One common practice is to hold the note for an extra quarter note; another is to play as written. If playing as written, consider making the A an eighth note followed by an eighth rest. In either option, clear and consistent leadership encourages the assembly's singing.

Leading challenge: The assembly may be tempted to move too soon in the next-to-last measure. Be clear and exact in encouraging them to hold the melody-note E for the full three beats.

836   Joyful, Joyful We Adore Thee

HYMN TO JOY

Pulse	Tempo	Style	Chpt Ref
The half note receives the pulse.	♩ = 56–66	Joyous	3 and 5

Accompaniment

Organ (piano)

Additional Information

Articulate the repeated notes clearly. See pages 38–39 for help with repeated notes on the organ.

837   Many and Great, O God

Wakantanka taku nitawa

LAC QUI PARLE

Pulse	Tempo	Style	Chpt Ref
Feel a strong half-note pulse throughout this hymn.	♩ = 46–72. Notice the wide range of tempo possibilities.	Strong, yet reverent	3 and 7

Accompaniment

This Native American tune is best sung unaccompanied in unison. Hand drum or flute could be added.

Additional Information

A detached articulation in voices and instruments suits this style.

838   Beautiful Savior

SCHÖNSTER HERR JESU

Pulse	Tempo	Style	Chpt Ref
The half note receives the pulse.	♩ = 44–54	Warm, devotionally	3 and 5

Accompaniment

Organ (piano)

Additional Information

This hymn lends itself to singing unaccompanied in four-part harmony.

839   Now Thank We All Our God

NUN DANKET ALLE GOTT

Pulse	Tempo	Style	Chpt Ref
The half note receives the pulse.	♩ = 64–80	Vigorous, joyful	3 and 5

Accompaniment

Organ (piano)

Additional Information

Articulate the rhythms crisply.

840   Now Thank We All Our God

NUN DANKET ALLE GOTT

Pulse	Tempo	Style	Chpt Ref
The half note receives the pulse.	♩ = 54–63.	Vigorous, joyful	3 and 5

Accompaniment

Organ (piano)

Additional Information

Leading challenge: A challenge in this hymn is taking breath at the end of the first and second lines without interrupting the tactus. Organists should lift very clearly on beat three so that the first beat of the next line (the pickup) is on time.

841   Lift Every Voice and Sing

LIFT EVERY VOICE AND SING

Pulse	Tempo	Style	Chpt Ref
The dotted quarter note receives the pulse.	♩. = 44–52	African American gospel, unhurried, joyful	3 and 8

Accompaniment

Piano accompaniment is preferred. Piano/organ combination is possible.

Unison singing is preferred. Sing as one voice.

Additional Information

Leading hint: This gospel song has a strong lilt. Feel the eighth-note upbeats on beats 2, 3, 5, and 6. Choose a tempo that allows one to clap on these beats.

842   Oh, Worship the King

HANOVER

Pulse	Tempo	Style	Chpt Ref
The dotted half note or quarter note receives the pulse. At a slower tempo, the quarter note can be the tactus while still feeling a strong downbeat at the beginning of each measure. At a brisker tempo, the dotted quarter note would be the tactus guaranteeing the strong downbeat.	♩ = 104–132; ♩. = 34–44	Confident, forward-moving	3 and 5

Accompaniment

Organ (piano)

Additional Information

A lightly detached articulation works well. For further discussion of this tune's articulation and phrasing, see page 40.

843   Praise the One Who Breaks the Darkness

NETTLETONA

Pulse	Tempo	Style	Chpt Ref
The quarter note receives the pulse. Feel a strong accent on the first beat of each measure.	♩ = 94–110	Energetic, jubilant, dance-like	3 and 7

Accompaniment

Unaccompanied singing is preferred. Organ or piano would work well.

Additional Information

Leading hint: Keep this tune light and detached.

844   Praise to the Lord

Louez l'Eternel

RICHARDSON-BURTON

Pulse	Tempo	Style	Chpt Ref
The dotted quarter note receives the pulse.	♩. = 60–72	Gentle, lilting	3 and 6

Accompaniment

Guitar accompaniment is preferred.

This folk-style song is commonly sung in unison. If the harmonies are sung, be sure to keep the texture light.

Additional Information

Leading hint: Use a light and clear articulation for the eighth notes in the third and fourth lines.

845   Voices Raised to You

SONG OF PRAISE

Pulse	Tempo	Style	Chpt Ref
The quarter note receives the pulse, yet feel the broader half note as well.	♩ = 92–112	With joyful praise	3 and 5

Accompaniment

Organ (piano)

846   Amen, We Praise Your Name
Amen siakudumisa

AMEN SIAKUDUMISA

Pulse	Tempo	Style	Chpt Ref
The quarter note receives the pulse.	♩ = 90–114	Joyful	3 and 11

Accompaniment

Unaccompanied singing in four-part harmony is preferred. Hand percussion (shaker, djembe, bell, large claves) could be added.

Additional Information

Leading hint: The leader and assembly's parts should overlap. Hold endings for their full value.

847   Come, Let Us Join Our Cheerful Songs

NUN DANKET ALL

Pulse	Tempo	Style	Chpt Ref
The half note receives the pulse.	♩ = 66–78	Spirited, strong	3 and 5

Accompaniment

Organ (piano)

848   Give to Our God Immortal Praise!

DUKE STREET

Pulse	Tempo	Style	Chpt Ref
The half note receives the pulse.	♩ = 64–70	Stately, bright, victorious	3 and 5

Accompaniment

Organ (piano)

Additional Information

This tune serves as a good example for the approaches to spacing between phrases. See pages 40–42.

849   Yours, Lord, Is the Glory

Tuya es la gloria

TUYA ES LA GLORIA

Pulse	Tempo	Style	Chpt Ref
The quarter note receives the pulse.	♩ = 88–108	Determined, confident	3 and 10

Accompaniment
Guitar accompaniment with percussion (conga drums, claves, egg shakers) is preferred. Piano accompaniment would also be successful.

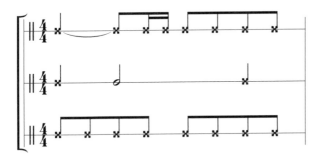

850   When in Our Music God Is Glorified

FREDERICKTOWN

Pulse	Tempo	Style	Chpt Ref
The half note receives the pulse.	♩ = 48–54	Reflective, strong, lyrical	3 and 5

Accompaniment
Organ (piano)

Additional Information
Leading hint: The opening E of the melody is the second beat of a ⁶₄ measure. Consider playing a C in the bass before the first note to start the singing.

851   When in Our Music God Is Glorified

ENGELBERG

Pulse	Tempo	Style	Chpt Ref
The half note or quarter note receives the pulse. A slow tempo allows one to feel the quarter-note pulse, but being mindful of the larger pulse helps keep the tune moving forward.	♩ = 50–60	Strong, flowing	3 and 5

Accompaniment
Consider adding a trumpet to the melody or soloing out with a reed stop on the organ. See pages 26–27 for help with soloing out.

852   Golden Breaks the Dawn

Qing zao qilai kan

LE P'ING

Pulse	Tempo	Style	Chpt Ref
The quarter note receives the pulse.	♩ = 76–88	Simple, quiet, meditative	3 and 12

Accompaniment

Unaccompanied singing is preferred. If keyboard accompaniment is needed, use the piano lightly. Organ, flute, or violin may be added to double the melody. Finger cymbals or triangle could be added after the half and whole notes; a gong could begin and end the song.

853   When Morning Gilds the Skies

LAUDES DOMINI

Pulse	Tempo	Style	Chpt Ref
The half note receives the pulse, yet the tactus can be flexible when singing in harmony.	♩ = 56–62	Joyful	3 and 5

Accompaniment

Organ (piano)

854   Blessing and Honor

AMERICAN HYMN

Pulse	Tempo	Style	Chpt Ref
The half note receives the pulse.	♩ = 62–74	Strong, boldly	3 and 5

Accompaniment

Organ (piano)

855   Crown Him with Many Crowns

DIADEMATA

Pulse	Tempo	Style	Chpt Ref
The half note receives the pulse.	♩ = 52–62	Strong, joyful	3 and 5

Accompaniment

Organ (piano)

Additional Information

Brass accompaniment can enhance this regal tune.

856   How Great Thou Art

O STORE GUD

Pulse	Tempo	Style	Chpt Ref
The quarter note receives the pulse.	♩ = 54–66	Devotional, strong	3 and 5

Accompaniment
Organ (piano)

Additional Information

Leading hint: Soloists often sing this tune in a very free manner. Many take liberty with the tempo in the last two measures. Some also swing the eighth notes on the second and sixth measures of the refrain ("Savior God, to thee"). Assemblies, however, need the rhythms to be very accurate. Consider releasing the tied quarter and half notes precisely on the following eighth note to help the assembly breathe.

Articulate the repeated notes clearly. See pages 38–39 for help with playing repeated notes on the organ.

857   Lord, I Lift Your Name on High

LORD, I LIFT YOUR NAME

Pulse	Tempo	Style	Chpt Ref
The quarter note receives the pulse.	♩ = 88–100	Driving rock style	3 and 9

Accompaniment
Worship band is preferred. See #433 for further suggestions. See also the discussion of this song on page 61.

858, 859   Praise to the Lord, the Almighty

LOBE DEN HERREN

Pulse	Tempo	Style	Chpt Ref
The dotted half note receives the pulse.	♩. = 38–46	Exuberant, praise-filled	3 and 5

Accompaniment
Organ (piano)

Additional Information

Consider using a slightly detached articulation.

860   I'm So Glad Jesus Lifted Me

JESUS LIFTED ME

Pulse	Tempo	Style	Chpt Ref
The quarter note receives the pulse, with the accent on the upbeat between each quarter note.	♩ = 70–96. Due to their roots in oral tradition, many African American spirituals can be successful at a wide range of tempos. Knowing your context and your assembly is especially important when setting a tempo.	Energetic, lively	3 and 8

Accompaniment

Piano accompaniment is preferred. Bring out the walking bass line. Drums, bass and guitar could be added.

Additional Information

See pages 56–57 for more on the articulation, instrumentation, and improvisation for this spiritual.

861   When Long before Time

The Singer and the Song

THE SINGER AND THE SONG

Pulse	Tempo	Style	Chpt Ref
The dotted half note receives the pulse.	♩. = 42–48. This ballad should not feel rushed.	Simple, smooth, flowing	3 and 6

Accompaniment

Organ, piano, or guitar accompaniment is preferred.

Additional Information

Since the interest of this tune is its simple, singable melody, it is best sung in unison. If the harmonies are sung, keep the texture light and moving forward.

862   Praise, Praise! You Are My Rock

ZACHARY WOODS ROCK

Pulse	Tempo	Style	Chpt Ref
The quarter note receives the pulse.	♩ = 90–104	Legato, joyful, buoyant	3 and 6

Accompaniment

Organ (piano)

863 My God, How Wonderful Thou Art
DUNDEE

Pulse	Tempo	Style	Chpt Ref
The half note receives the pulse.	♩ = 48–62	Sturdy, forward-moving	3 and 5

Accompaniment

Organ (piano)

864 Praise, My Soul, the God of Heaven
PRAISE, MY SOUL

Pulse	Tempo	Style	Chpt Ref
The half note receives the pulse.	♩ = 42–60	Expansive, majestic	3 and 5

Accompaniment

Organ (piano)

Additional Information

Articulate the repeated notes clearly. See pages 38–39 for help with playing repeated notes on the organ.

865 Praise, My Soul, the King of Heaven
PRAISE, MY SOUL

Pulse	Tempo	Style	Chpt Ref
The half note receives the pulse.	♩ = 42–60	Expansive, majestic	3 and 5

Accompaniment

Organ (piano)

Additional Information

Articulate the repeated notes clearly. See pages 38–39 for help with playing repeated notes on the organ.

866 We Are Marching in the Light
Siyahamba

SIYAHAMBA

Pulse	Tempo	Style	Chpt Ref
The half note receives the pulse.	♩ = 48–56	Joyous, celebrative	3 and 11

Accompaniment

Unaccompanied singing in four-part harmony is preferred. The harmony is integral to this song. Piano can provide vocal support if necessary. The use of drums is not typical.

Additional Information

Teaching hint: The notation to this tune can look daunting. Break it into sections, teach it orally, and people will learn it more easily. Encourage movement!

867 In Thee Is Gladness
IN DIR IST FREUDE

Pulse	Tempo	Style	Chpt Ref
The dotted half note receives the pulse.	𝅗𝅥. = 50–56	Energetic, dance-like	3 and 5

Accompaniment

Organ (piano)

Additional Information

Leading hint: Think of this as a madrigal or Renaissance dance. A detached articulation works best.

868 Isaiah in a Vision Did of Old
JESAIA, DEM PROPHETEN

Pulse	Tempo	Style	Chpt Ref
The quarter note receives the pulse, but also feel the underlying half-note pulse.	♩ = 108–116	Sturdy, forward-moving, majestic	3 and 5

Accompaniment

Organ accompaniment is preferred.

Additional Information

Leading hint: Consider having a choir or soloist sing this chorale with the full assembly joining on "Holy."

869 We Have Seen the Lord
Nimemwona Bwana

NIMEMWONA BWANA

Pulse	Tempo	Style	Chpt Ref
The quarter note receives the pulse.	♩ = 104–116	Joyful	3 and 11

Accompaniment

Unaccompanied singing in four-part harmony is preferred. If keyboard is necessary, keep it secondary to the assembly's voice, perhaps playing just the harmonies on the main pulses. Percussion (shaker, African drums, bell, djembe, large clave) can be added.

Additional Information

Leading hint: Call and response characterizes this Tanzanian song. While the leader parts need to be well accented, the assembly's part can be sung more smoothly.

870   We Praise You, O God

KREMSER

Pulse	Tempo	Style	Chpt Ref
Either the quarter note or dotted half note receives the pulse. Feel a half note followed by a quarter note in each measure.	$\dot{\rho}$ = 40–50	Joyful, dance-like	3 and 5

Accompaniment

Organ (piano)

871   Sing Praise to God, the Highest Good

LOBT GOTT DEN HERREN, IHR

Pulse	Tempo	Style	Chpt Ref
The dotted half note receives the pulse.	$\dot{\rho}$ = 42–50	Energetic, praise-filled	3 and 5

Accompaniment

Organ (piano)

Additional Information

A light, slightly detached articulation works best.

872   Praise Ye the Lord

CLEVELAND

Pulse	Tempo	Style	Chpt Ref
The half note receives the pulse. This is in a gospel style. Feel two kinds of upbeats: The half note on beat three and the quarter notes on beats two and four. Choose a tempo where both are comfortable.	ρ = 52–58	Joyous, exuberant	3 and 8

Accompaniment

Gospel piano accompaniment is preferred.

Additional Information

Leading hint: Sing the refrains in harmony and the verses in unison. Due to the change in tonality, a vocal ensemble/soloist/cantor could sing the verses, with the congregation joining on the refrain. Teaching hint: Note that the refrain is repeated each time.

873   Rejoice, Ye Pure in Heart!
MARION

Pulse	Tempo	Style	Chpt Ref
The half note receives the pulse.	$\quad$ = 62–76	Strong, joyful	3 and 5

Accompaniment

Organ (piano)

874   Rejoice, Ye Pure in Heart!
VINEYARD HAVEN

Pulse	Tempo	Style	Chpt Ref
The quarter note receives the pulse.	$\quad$ = 100–108	Marcato, majestic, joyful	3 and 5

Accompaniment

Organ accompaniment is preferred. The use of brass or snare drum could enhance the singing.

875   Praise, Praise, Praise the Lord!
CAMEROON PRAISE

Pulse	Tempo	Style	Chpt Ref
The quarter note receives the pulse.	$\quad$ = 70–82	Energetic, strong, a processional	3 and 11

Accompaniment

Unaccompanied singing in four-part harmony is preferred. Piano can provide vocal support if necessary. Percussion (shaker, bell, large clave, drums) can be added.

Additional Information

Leading hint: Singing in harmony is essential to this song. Note that the alto line is the melody. When teaching, begin the alto voice and add the other voices in turn (tenor, bass, then soprano).

876   Let the Whole Creation Cry

SALZBURG

Pulse	Tempo	Style	Chpt Ref
The half note receives the pulse.	♩ = 52–62	Walking tempo	3 and 5

Accompaniment

Organ (piano)

877   Praise the Almighty!

LOBE DEN HERREN, O MEINE SEELE

Pulse	Tempo	Style	Chpt Ref
The dotted half note receives the pulse.	♩. = 44–56	Spirited, joyful	3 and 5

Accompaniment

Organ (piano)

Additional Information

Slightly detaching the dotted half notes will help support the singing.

878   Soli Deo Gloria

SOLI DEO GLORIA

Pulse	Tempo	Style	Chpt Ref
The quarter note receives the pulse.	♩ = 78–84	Lyrical, strong	3 and 5

Accompaniment

Piano or organ accompaniment is preferred.

879   For the Beauty of the Earth

DIX

Pulse	Tempo	Style	Chpt Ref
The half note receives the pulse.	♩ = 52–62	Flowing	3 and 5

Accompaniment

Organ (piano)

880 O God beyond All Praising

THAXTED

Pulse	Tempo	Style	Chpt Ref
The quarter note receives the pulse, yet feel the large, soaring phrases.	♩ = 70–80	Broad, majestic, forward-moving	3 and 5

Accompaniment
Organ accompaniment is preferred.

Additional Information
Teaching hint: The length and range of this tune can be challenging for some assemblies. Consider introducing it first as a choral anthem.

881 Let All Things Now Living

THE ASH GROVE

Pulse	Tempo	Style	Chpt Ref
The dotted half note receives the pulse.	♩. = 42–50	Energetic, flowing	3, 5, and 6

Accompaniment
Organ (piano)

Additional Information
Leading hint: Keep the eighth notes light, always moving to the next downbeat.

882 My Soul Does Magnify The Lord

GOSPEL MAGNIFICAT

Pulse	Tempo	Style	Chpt Ref
The quarter note receives the pulse. Feel the upbeats on the eighth notes and on beats two and four of each measure.	♩ = 96–108	Gospel, energetic	3 and 8

Accompaniment
Piano accompaniment is preferred. Guitar, bass, and drums can be added.

883 All People That on Earth Do Dwell

OLD HUNDREDTH

Pulse	Tempo	Style	Chpt Ref
The half note receives the pulse.	♩ = 50–60	Strong, steady, confident	3 and 5

Accompaniment
Organ (piano)

884, 885   Praise God, from Whom All Blessings Flow

OLD HUNDREDTH

Pulse	Tempo	Style	Chpt Ref
The half note receives the pulse.	♩ = 50–60	Strong, steady, confident	3 and 5

Accompaniment
Organ (piano)

886   Oh, for a Thousand Tongues to Sing

AZMON

Pulse	Tempo	Style	Chpt Ref
The quarter note receives the pulse. Feel an accent on the first beat of each measure.	♩ = 88–102	Sturdy, joyful	3 and 5

Accompaniment
Organ (piano)

Additional Information
Leading hint: A rather detached articulation suits this tune.

NATIONAL SONGS

887   This Is My Song

FINLANDIA

Pulse	Tempo	Style	Chpt Ref
The half note receives the pulse.	♩ = 50–60	Aspiring, trusting	3 and 5

Accompaniment
Organ (piano)

888   O Beautiful for Spacious Skies

MATERNA

Pulse	Tempo	Style	Chpt Ref
The half note receives the pulse.	♩ = 48–58	Noble, confident	3 and 5

Accompaniment
Organ (piano). Could be sung unaccompanied in harmony.

889   The Right Hand of God

LA MANO DE DIOS

Pulse	Tempo	Style	Chpt Ref
The half note receives the pulse.	♩ = 70–78	Cheerful, joyous	3 and 10

Accompaniment

Piano accompaniment is preferred. Bass and percussion (congas, shakers, cow bell) can be added.

Additional Information

The ♩. ♩. ♩ rhythmic pattern is characteristic of Caribbean song. Note the optional stanza to be used in the Caribbean context.

890   Mine Eyes Have Seen the Glory

BATTLE HYMN

Pulse	Tempo	Style	Chpt Ref
The quarter note receives the pulse.	♩ = 80–100	March-like, crisp	3 and 5

Accompaniment

Organ (piano)

891   God Bless Our Native Land

NATIONAL ANTHEM

Pulse	Tempo	Style	Chpt Ref
The quarter note receives the pulse.	♩ = 82–98	Firm, bold	3 and 5

Accompaniment

Organ (piano)

892   O Canada

O CANADA

Pulse	Tempo	Style	Chpt Ref
The quarter note receives the pulse.	♩ = 108–120	Fervent, bold	3 and 5

Accompaniment

Organ (piano)

Additional Information

Leading hint: Be sure to play the dotted rhythms of this march in a detached, clean manner.

893 Before You, Lord, We Bow

DARWALL'S 148TH

Pulse	Tempo	Style	Chpt Ref
The half note receives the pulse.	$\half = 64$–74	Joyful, lyrical, walking style	3 and 5

Accompaniment

Organ (piano)

Additional Information

Consider playing the opening leaps as a marcato fanfare, yet keeping the stepwise motion legato.

BIBLIOGRAPHY

Music in *Evangelical Lutheran Worship*

Evangelical Lutheran Worship Hymns Audio Edition. Multiple volumes. Augsburg Fortress, 2006.

Evangelical Lutheran Worship Liturgies Audio Edition. Multiple volumes. Augsburg Fortress, 2006.

Evangelical Lutheran Worship Simplified Keyboard Accompaniment Edition, Service Music and Hymns. Augsburg Fortress, 2007.

Evangelical Lutheran Worship Guitar Accompaniment Edition, Service Music and Hymns. Augsburg Fortress, 2007.

Brugh, Lorraine, and Gordon Lathrop. *The Sunday Assembly.* Augsburg Fortress, 2007.

Bushkofsky, Dennis, and Craig Satterlee. *The Christian Life: Baptism and Life Passages.* Augsburg Fortress, 2007.

Ramshaw, Gail, and Mons Teig. *Keeping Time: The Church's Years.* Augsburg Fortress, 2007.

Farlee, Robert Buckley, Mark Mummert, and Thomas Pavlechko. *Festival Setting One.* Augsburg Fortress, 2007.

Haugen, Marty, and John Ferguson. *Festival Setting Two.* Augsburg Fortress, 2007.

Indexes to Evangelical Lutheran Worship. Augsburg Fortress, 2007.

Introductions and Alternate Accompaniments for Hymns in Evangelical Lutheran Worship. Editions for piano and for organ, ten volumes each. Augsburg Fortress, 2007—.

Principles for Worship. Evangelical Lutheran Church in America, 2002.

Skills for Leading Assembly Song

Cherwien, David. *Let the People Sing! A Keyboardist's Creative and Practical Guide to Engaging God's People in Meaningful Song.* Concordia, 1997.

Farlee, Robert Buckley, ed. *Leading the Church's Song.* Augsburg Fortress, 1998.

Parker, Alice. *Melodious Accord: Good Singing in Church.* Liturgy Training Publications, 1991.

Westermeyer, Paul. *The Church Musician.* Rev. ed. Augsburg Fortress, 1997.

Wilson-Dickson, Andrew. *The Story of Christian Music.* Fortress, 1992.

Chant

Apel, Willi. *Gregorian Chant.* Indiana University Press, 1958.

Berthier, Jacques. *Music from Taizé, vol. 1 & 2.* GIA Publications.

Gajard, Joseph. *The Solesmes Method: Its Fundamental Principles and Practical Rules of Interpretation.* The Liturgical Press, 1960.

Hiley, David. *Western Plainchant: A Handbook.* Clarendon, 1995.

Tortolano, William, tr. & ed. *Beginning Studies in Gregorian Chant.* GIA Publications, 1988.

Northern European Hymnody

Blume, Friedrich. *Protestant Church Music.* Norton, 1974.

Halter, Carl, and Carl Schalk. *A Handbook of Church Music.* Concordia, 1982.

Julian, John. *Dictionary of Hymnology, vol. 1 & 2.* J. Murray, 1907. Reprint: Kregel Publications, 1985.

Routley, Erik (edited and expanded by Paul A. Richardson). *A Panorama of Christian Hymnody.* GIA Publications, 2005.

Westermeyer, Paul. *Let the People Sing: Hymn Tunes in Perspective.* GIA, 2005.

———. *Te Deum: The Church and Music.* Augsburg Fortress, 1998.

North American Hymnody

Blumhofer, Edith L. *Singing the Lord's Song in a Strange Land: Hymnody in the History of North American Protestantism.* University of Alabama, 2004.

Rivers of Delight: American Folk Hymns from the Sacred Harp Tradition. Audio CD. Nonesuch, 1992.

Stowe, David W. *How Sweet the Sound: Music in the Spiritual Lives of Americans.* Harvard, 2004.

Walker, William, ed. Glenn Wilcox. *The Southern Harmony and Musical Companion.* Reprint. University of Kentucky, 1993.

African American Song

This Far by Faith: An African American Resource for Worship. Augsburg Fortress, 1999.

Abbington, James. *Readings in African American Church Music and Worship*. GIA Publications, 2001.

Costen, Melva Wilson. *In Spirit and Truth: The Music of African American Worship*. Westminster, 2004.

McGann, Mary. *A Precious Fountain: Music in the Worship of an African American Catholic Community*. The Liturgical Press, 2004.

Reagon, Bernice Johnson. *If You Don't Go, Don't Hinder Me: The African American Sacred Song Tradition*. University of Nebraska, 2000.

Singing in the African American Tradition: Choral and Congregational Music (book and cassette tapes) taught by Ysaye Barnwell with George Brandon. Homespun Tapes Ltd., Box 694, Woodstock, NY 12498.

Spencer, Jon Michael. *Protest and Praise: Sacred Music of Black Religion*. Fortress, 1997.

Contemporary Song

McLean, Terri Bocklund, and Rob Glover, eds. *Choosing Contemporary Music: Seasonal, Topical, Lectionary Indexes*. Augsburg Fortress, 2000.

McLean, Terri Bocklund. *New Harmonies: Choosing Contemporary Music for Worship*. Alban Institute, 1998.

Weidler, Scott, and Dori Collins. *Sound Decisions*. Evangelical Lutheran Church in America, 1997.

Worship and Praise Songbook. Augsburg Fortress, 1999.

Global Song

Africa Praise. General Board of Global Ministries of the United Methodist Church, GBG-Musik.

African Songs of Worship. World Council of Churches, 1986.

Feliciano, Francisco F. *The AILM Collection: Hymns, Psalms and Songs for Worship, Volume 1*. Asian Institute for Liturgy and Music, 2005.

Asian Institute for Liturgy and Music and the World Council of Churches. *Asian Songs of Worship*. R.R. Yan Printing Press, 1988.

Bell, John, ed. *Many and Great: Songs of the World Church, Vol. I*. GIA Publications, Inc., North American ed., 1990. Iona Community.

———. *Sent by the Lord: Songs of the World Church, Vol. II*. GIA Publications, Inc., North American ed., 1992. Iona Community.

Black, Kathy. *Worship Across Cultures: A Handbook*. Abingdon Press, 1998.

Bread for the Journey. Global Songs (3 volumes). Augsburg Fortress.

Colvin, Tom. *Come Let Us Walk This Road Together: 43 Songs from Africa*. Hope Publishing Co., 1997.

———. *Fill Us With Your Love: and Other Hymns from Africa*. Agape, 1983.

Global Praise 1. General Board of Global Ministries of the United Methodist Church, GBG-Musik, 1996.

Global Praise 2: Songs for Witness and Worship. General Board of Global Ministries of the United Methodist Church, GBGMusik, 2000.

Harling, Per. *Worshipping Ecumenically*. WCC Publications, 1995.

Hawn, Michael. *Gather into One: Praying and Singing Globally*. Eerdmans, 2003.

———. *One Bread, One Body, Exploring Cultural Diversity in Worship*. Alban Institute, 2003.

Hymns from the Four Winds: A Collection of Asian American Hymns. Abingdon Press, 1983.

Hymns of Praise. Taosheng Publishing House, 1994.

Kimbrough, S T and Carlton Young, eds. *Global Praise 1*. GBGMusik, General Board of Global Ministries, 1996, rev. 1997, and *Global Praise 2*. GBGMusik, 2000.

Libro de Liturgia y Cántico. Augsburg Fortress, 1998.

Sound the Bamboo. Second edition. Christian Conference of Asia, 2000.

Thuma Mina: International Ecumenical Hymnbook. Strube Verlag and Basileia Verlag, 1995.

INDEXES

Alphabetical Index of Tunes

Indented lines indicate names by which tunes may also be known.

Metrical Index of Tunes

8 5 8 4 7 7
Mit Fried und Freud   440

8 5 8 5 8 4 3
Castlewood   687

8 5 8 8
Vi rekker våre hender frem   690

8 5 9 5 and refrain
Stoneridge   492

8 6
Dona nobis pacem   753

8 6 6 8 6 6
Warum sollt ich   273

8 6 7 6 4 4 5
Goodness Is Stronger   721

8 6 8 6 6
Dove of Peace   482
Lobt Gott, ihr Christen   287, 304, 441, 604

8 6 8 6 7 6 8 6
St. Louis   279

8 6 8 6 8 6
Brother James' Air   778
Coronation   634
Pace mio Dio   700

8 6 8 6 8 8 and refrain
Une jeune pucelle   284

8 6 8 6 8 8 6
I himmelen, i himmelen   630

8 6 8 8 6 6
Repton   428, 580, 737

8 7 8 7
Barbara Allen   691, 832
Buckhurst Run   497
Galilee   696
Harvest Gifts   734
Jill   306
Kas dziedāja   701
Merton   246, 603
New Orleans   724
Omni die   494
Rathbun   324
Restoration   397
St. Columba   502
Stuttgart   455
The Servant Song   659

8 7 8 7 and refrain
Hanson Place   423
How Can I Keep from Singing   763

8 7 8 7 D
Abbot's Leigh   526, 579, 688
Austria   823
Beach Spring   445, 712, 777
Blaenwern   647
Bradbury   789
Camrose   469
Converse   742
Ebenezer   327, 511
Holy Manna   461, 771
Hyfrydol   392, 585, 631, 707
Hymn to Joy   836
In Babilone   522, 582, 655
Jefferson   254
Joyous Light   561
Lord, Revive Us   588
Mississippi   426

Nettleton   807, 843
Rustington   678
St. Helena   258, 587
Turnbull   383
Werde munter   501

8 7 8 7 D and refrain
Morgenlied   382

8 7 8 7 3 3 7
Michael   757

8 7 8 7 4 4 4 7 7
Bryn Calfaria   475

8 7 8 7 5 5 5 6 7
Ein feste Burg (rhythmic)   503

8 7 8 7 6
Bridegroom   403

8 7 8 7 6 6 6 6 7
Ein feste Burg (isometric)   504, 505, 509

8 7 8 7 6 7 6 7
Greensleeves   487

8 7 8 7 6 8 6 7
Greensleeves   296

8 7 8 7 7
Thomas   334

8 7 8 7 7 7
Irby   269
Unser Herrscher   533

8 7 8 7 7 7 8 8
Der am Kreuz   811
Freu dich sehr   256, 672, 783

8 7 8 7 7 8 7 4
Christ lag in Todesbanden   370

8 7 8 7 8
Verleih uns Frieden   784

8 7 8 7 8 7
Fortunatus New   356
Jennings-Houston   736
Julion   331
Nagel   329
Pange lingua   355
Picardy   490
Praise, My Soul   318, 864, 865
Regent Square   275, 417
Sicilian Mariners   545
Song of Praise   845
Surge ecclesia   548
Union Seminary   312, 470
Westminster Abbey   645

8 7 8 7 8 7 7
Cwm Rhondda   400, 618, 705
Divinum mysterium   295
Was Gott tut   776

8 7 8 7 8 7 7 8 7 7
Lasset uns mit Jesu ziehen   802

8 7 8 7 8 7 1 1
Ouimette   451

8 7 8 7 8 8
Machs mit mir, Gott   799

8 7 8 7 8 8 7
Allein Gott in der Höh   410
Aus tiefer Not   600
Es ist das Heil (isometric)   442
Es ist das Heil (rhythmic)   590

Lobt Gott den Herren, ihr   871
Mit Freuden zart   727
Nun freut euch   594

8 7 8 7 8 8 7 7
Jesu, meines Lebens Leben   339
Wżłobie leży   276

8 7 8 7 12 7
Helmsley   435

8 7 9 8 8 7
Besançon   248

8 8
Wait for the Lord   262

8 8 7 D
Alles ist an Gottes Segen   544, 589

8 8 7 8 8 7 7
Nuestro Padre nos invita   486

8 8 8 and alleluias
Beverly   662
Gelobt sei Gott   385

8 8 8 with alleluias
O filii et filiae   386, 387
Victory   366

8 8 8 6
Just as I Am   714

8 8 8 7 8 7 8 7
Come to the Table   481

8 8 8 8 6
Deep Blue   699

8 8 8 8 8
Mayenziwe   741

8 8 8 8 8 and alleluias
Lasst uns erfreuen   424, 835

8 8 8 8 8 8
Melita   597, 756
Ryburn   358
St. Catherine   812, 813
Sussex Carol   274
Vater unser   746, 747
Veni, Emmanuel   257

8 8 8 8 8 8 and alleluias
Lasst uns erfreuen   367

8 8 8 8 8 8 6 6
Macht hoch die Tür   259

8 8 8 8 8 8 8
Kirken den er et gammelt hus   652
Mit Freuden zart   368
The Solid Rock   596

8 8 8 8 8 8 8 8 7 8
Wir glauben all   411

8 8 9 and refrain
Healer of Our Every Ill   612

8 8 9 9 9 7 7 7
Dapit hapon   566

8 9 8 8 and refrain
Vårvindar friska   407

8 10 10 and refrain
Pescador de hombres   817

9 5 7 5 7
Nelson   637

9 6 7 7
Roeder 740

9 6 8 6 8 7 10 and refrain
Two Oaks 641

9 6 8 8 8 6
Lac qui Parle 837

9 6 9 6 6
Carol of Hope 252

9 7 9 6 D
Waterlife 732

9 8 8 9 and refrain
God Be with You 536

9 8 9 5 and refrain
Yisrael v'oraita 519

9 8 9 6 and refrain
Christ, Be Our Light 715

9 8 9 8
St. Clement 563, 569

9 8 9 8 and refrain
Santo Domingo 375

9 8 9 8 D
Rendez à Dieu 478

9 8 9 8 8 7 8 9
Rejoice, Rejoice 242

9 8 9 8 8 8
O dass ich tausend Zungen hätte
    833

9 8 9 8 9 6 6
Komt nu met zang 524

9 8 9 8 9 8
Den signede dag 627
Jag kan icke räkna dem alla 683
Wer nur den lieben Gott 769

9 8 9 9
Children Praying 752

9 9 9 8 and refrain
Vamos todos al banquete 523

9 9 9 9 and refrain
Break Now the Bread 474
Mfurahini, haleluya 364

9 9 9 9 9 7 7
Soli Deo gloria 878

9 9 10 9 and refrain
Tú Señor 702

9 9 10 9 9 8
Un flambeau 292

9 9 10 10 3 3 and refrain
Shine, Jesus, Shine 671

9 10 8 8 and refrain
La Crosse 593

9 10 9 9 and refrain
Assurance 638

10 4 7 5 6 5
Pán Bůh 795

10 7 9 6
Tif in veldele 240

10 7 10 6 6
Jenkins 709

10 7 10 8 and refrain
Houston 815

10 8 8 8 10
O Heiliger Geist 405

10 8 10 8 8 8 8
Lobe den Herren, O meine Seele
    877

10 9 10 9 and refrain
Showalter 774

10 9 10 9 D
Blott en dag 790

10 9 10 10 D
Gather Us In 532

10 9 11 9 4
Nun bitten wir 743

10 9 11 9 11 9
La paz del Señor 646

10 10 and refrain
Break Bread Together 471

10 10 10 and alleluias
Engelberg 546
Fredericktown 850
Sine nomine 422

10 10 10 and refrain
Fredericktown 615

10 10 10 4
Engelberg 449, 851

10 10 10 5 8
Romedal 730

10 10 10 8 8
Schneider 285

10 10 10 10
A va de 491
Adoro te devote 402, 476
Crucifer 660
Ellers 534
Eventide 629
Morecambe 800
Slane 793
Sursum corda 584
Woodlands 390

10 10 10 10 10
Old 124th 321
American Hymn 854

10 10 10 10 10 10
Song 1 463

10 10 11 11
Laudate Dominum 418
Lyons 825
Hanover 842

10 10 12 10
Gabriel's Message 265

10 10 14 10
Were You There 353

10 11 11 12
Slane 765

11 7 11 7 and refrain
Thompson 608

11 8 11 9 and refrain
Ville du Havre 785

11 10 10 11
Noël nouvelet 379

11 10 11 10
Atkinson 507
Consolator 607
Morning Star 303
Telos 626

11 10 11 10 and refrain
Angelic Songs 668
Faithfulness 733
O store Gud 856

11 10 11 10 D
Red Hill Road 760

11 10 11 10 11 10
Finlandia 792, 887

11 11 11 5
Christe sanctorum 415, 558
Herzliebster Jesu 349
Innisfree Farm 560
Iste confessor 766
Shades Mountain 342
Wojtkiewiecz 665

11 11 11 5 5
Lost in the Night 243

11 11 11 6
Lux in tenebris 307

11 11 11 11
Away in a Manger 277
Cradle Song 278
Foundation 796
St. Denio 575, 834
The Singer and the Song 861

11 11 11 11 D
Afton Water 508

11 11 12 5
Christe sanctorum 458

11 11 12 12
Toda la tierra 266

12 9 6 6 12 9
Wondrous Love 666

12 11 8 7 and refrain
LaMotta 829

12 11 12 4 and refrain
Un pueblo que camina 706

12 11 12 11
Andrew's Song 648
Kremser 870

12 11 12 11 11
El camino 725

12 12 12 and refrain
Very Soon 439

12 12 12 12 and refrain
Ubi caritas 653

12 12 12 12 12 12
Enviado 538**

12 14 12 12
Les Petites Soeurs   808

13 12 13 11
St. Catherine's Court   429

13 13 7 7 13
Kelvingrove   798

13 13 13 13 13 13
Thaxted   710, 880

14 14 4 7 8
Lobe den Herren   858, 859

14 14 15 14
Thine   826

15 14 and refrain
Miren qué bueno   649

15 15 15
Armolaulu   598

15 15 15 6 and refrain
Battle Hymn   890

Irregular
Adeste fideles   283
Amen siakudumisa   846
As the Grains   465
Balm in Gilead   614
Berthier   472
Blest Are They   728
Called to Follow   704
Calvary   354
Cleveland   872
Closer Walk   697

Cranham   294
Give Me Jesus   770
I Am the Bread   485
Jesus Lifted Me   860
Lead Me, Guide Me   768
Magnificat   882
Neither Death nor Life   622
Nicaea   413
Nimemwona Bwana   869
Now We Remain   500
O Canada   892
On Eagle's Wings   787
Precious Lord   773
Richardson-Burton   844
St. Patrick's Breastplate   450
Salve festa dies   394
Shepherd Me   780
Siyahamba   866
Sojourner   325
Spirit   396
Star of County Down   723
Stille Nacht   281
Taizé Ubi caritas   642
Taizé Veni Sancte   406
Taste and See   493
The First Nowell   300
This Far by Faith   633
This Joy   677
Thuma mina   809
Wade in the Water   459
We Are Called   720
Weary Land   333
Wet Saints   446
You Are Mine   581
Zname to, Pane Bože náš   602

PM (Peculiar Meter)
An Wasserflüssen Babylon   340
Ascension   255
Blessing, Honor, and Glory   433
Build Us Up   670
Change My Heart   801
Christ ist erstanden   372
Confitemini Domino   528
Cuéllar   762
Den store hvide flok   425
Die güldne Sonne   761
Du är helig   525
El desembre congelat   299
Go, Make Disciples   540
Good Soil   512
Gott sei gelobet und gebenedeiet
   499
Herzlich lieb   750
In dir ist Freude   867
Jesaia, dem Propheten   868
Kyrie, Gott Vater   409
Lift Every Voice and Sing   841
Lord, I Lift Your Name   857
Now   460
Nyt ylös, sieluni   827
Offering   692
Shout to the Lord   821
Somos uno   643
Stay with Me   348
Victimae paschali   371
Wachet auf   436
Wie schön leuchtet   308, 786
Wisdom's Feast   518
Wonderful Child   297

First Lines and Titles of Liturgical Music

Indented lines indicate first lines or titles by which some songs in Evangelical Lutheran Worship may also be known.

First Lines and Titles of Hymns

A

393	A hymn of glory let us sing!
340	A lamb goes uncomplaining forth
503–505	A mighty fortress is our God
539	Abide, O dearest Jesus
629	Abide with me
539	Abide with us, our Savior
691	Accept, O Lord, the gifts we bring
349	Ah, holy Jesus
337	Alas! And did my Savior bleed
375	*¡Aleluya! Cristo resucitó*
641	All Are Welcome
835	All creatures, worship God most high!
835	All creatures of our God and King
589	All depends on our possessing
266	All earth is hopeful
410	All glory be to God on high
344	All glory, laud, and honor
634	All hail the power of Jesus' name!
273	All my heart again rejoices
757	All my hope on God is founded
883	All people that on earth do dwell
565	All praise to thee, my God, this night
442	All who believe and are baptized
461	All who hunger, gather gladly
724	All who love and serve your city
375	Alleluia! Christ is arisen
377	Alleluia! Jesus is risen!
392	Alleluia! Sing to Jesus
318	Alleluia, song of gladness
828	Alleluia! Voices raise
516	Almighty God, your word is cast
644	Although I speak with angel's tongue
779	Amazing grace, how sweet the sound
846	*Amen siakudumisa*
846	Amen, we praise your name
888	America the Beautiful
275	Angels, from the realms of glory
289	Angels we have heard on high
680	*Aramos nuestros campos*
827	Arise, my soul, arise!
314	Arise, your light has come!
468	Around you, O Lord Jesus
508	As rain from the clouds
695	As saints of old
261	As the dark awaits the dawn
331	As the deer runs to the river
465	As the grains of wheat
329	As the sun with longer journey
522	As we gather at your table
302	As with gladness men of old
362	At the Lamb's high feast we sing
416	At the name of Jesus
242	Awake! Awake, and greet the new morn
378	Awake, my heart, with gladness
557	Awake, my soul, and with the sun
452	Awake, O sleeper, rise from death
277, 278	Away in a manger

B

453	Baptized and Set Free
456	Baptized in water
890	Battle Hymn of the Republic
388	Be not afraid
793	Be thou my vision
838	Beautiful Savior
457	Before I can remember
893	Before you, Lord, we bow
649	Behold, how pleasant
425	Behold the host arrayed in white
648	Beloved, God's chosen
338	Beneath the cross of Jesus
326	Bless now, O God, the journey
638	Blessed assurance
250	Blessed be the God of Israel
552	Blessed be the God of Israel
797	Blessed be the name
854	Blessing and honor
433	Blessing, Honor, and Glory
433	Blessing, honor, glory to the Lamb
728	Blest are they
656	Blest be the tie that binds
732	Borning Cry
474	Bread of life from heaven
464	Bread of life, our host and meal
515	Break now the bread of life
301	Bright and glorious is the sky
303	Brightest and best of the stars
700	Bring Peace to Earth Again
670	Build us up, Lord
652	Built on a rock
420, 421	By all your saints
626	By gracious powers
469	By your hand you feed your people

C

794	Calm to the waves
354	Calvary
822	*Cantad al Señor*
555	*Cantemos al Señor*
723	Canticle of the Turning
801	Change my heart, O God
609	Chief of sinners though I be
781	Children of the heavenly Father
715	Christ, Be Our Light
364	Christ has arisen, alleluia
389	Christ is alive! Let Christians sing
372	Christ is arisen
645	Christ is made the sure foundation
382	Christ is risen! Alleluia!
383	Christ is risen! Shout Hosanna!
662	Christ is the king!
370	Christ Jesus lay in death's strong bands
560	Christ, mighty Savior
339	Christ, the life of all the living
373	Christ the Lord is risen today!
369	Christ the Lord is risen today; Alleluia!
304	Christ, when for us you were baptized
553	Christ, whose glory fills the skies
371	Christians, to the paschal victim

299	Cold December flies away
819	Come, all you people
528	Come and fill our hearts
306	Come, beloved of the Maker
804	Come down, O Love divine
799	Come, follow me, the Savior spake
404	Come, gracious Spirit, heavenly dove
395	Come, Holy Ghost, God and Lord
412	Come, join the dance of Trinity
491	Come, let us eat
847	Come, let us join our cheerful songs
720	Come! Live in the light!
816	Come, my way, my truth, my life
247	Come now, O Prince of peace
408	Come, thou almighty King
807	Come, thou Fount of every blessing
254	Come, thou long-expected Jesus
777	Come to me, all pilgrims thirsty
481	Come to the table
687	Come to us, creative Spirit
625	Come, we that love the Lord
501	Come with us, O blessed Jesus
607	Come, ye disconsolate
693	Come, ye thankful people, come
363	Come, you faithful, raise the strain
256	Comfort, comfort now my people
528	*Confitemini Domino*
444	Cradling children in his arm
455	Crashing waters at creation
684	Creating God, your fingers trace
245	Creator of the stars of night
577, 578	Creator Spirit, heavenly dove
855	Crown him with many crowns
725	*Cuando el pobre*

D

790	Day by day
374	Day of arising
594	Dear Christians, one and all, rejoice
520	Dearest Jesus, at your word
443	Dearest Jesus, we are here
298	*Det kimer nu til julefest*
753	Dona nobis pacem
470	Draw us in the Spirit's tether
593	Drawn to the Light
525	*Du är helig*

E

252	Each winter as the year grows older
731	Earth and all stars!
472	Eat this bread
492	Eat this bread, drink this cup
664	*El cielo canta alegría*
538	*Enviado soy de Dios*
756	Eternal Father, strong to save
321	Eternal Lord of love, behold your church
402	Eternal Spirit of the living Christ
761	Evening and morning
354	Every time I think about Jesus

F

812, 813	Faith of our fathers
415	Father most holy
478	Father, we thank you

259	Fling wide the door
419	For all the faithful women
422	For all the saints
427	For all your saints, O Lord
598	For by grace you have been saved
879	For the beauty of the earth
494	For the bread which you have broken
679	For the fruit of all creation
605	Forgive our sins as we forgive
268	From heaven above

G

532	Gather Us In
484	*Gift of Finest Wheat*
770	Give Me Jesus
428	Give Thanks for Saints
428	Give thanks for those whose faith is firm
848	Give to our God immortal praise!
647	Glorious things of you are spoken
540	Go, make disciples
543	Go, my children, with my blessing
290	Go tell it on the mountain
347	Go to dark Gethsemane
536	God be with you till we meet again
891	God bless our native land
738	God created heaven and earth
486	God extends an invitation
526	God is here!
323	God loved the world
795	God, my Lord, my strength
705	God of grace and God of glory
400	God of tempest, God of whirlwind
740	God of the sparrow
736	God the sculptor of the mountains
603	God, when human bonds are broken
564	God, who made the earth and heaven
771	God, who stretched the spangled heavens
673	God, whose almighty word
734	God, whose farm is all creation
678	God, whose giving knows no ending
509	God's word is our great heritage
852	Golden breaks the dawn
288	Good Christian friends, rejoice
385	Good Christian friends, rejoice and sing!
721	Goodness is stronger than evil
401	Gracious Spirit, heed our pleading
784	Grant peace, we pray, in mercy, Lord
358	Great God, your love has called us
733	Great is thy faithfulness
618	Guide me ever, great Redeemer

H

394	Hail thee, festival day!
311	Hail to the Lord's anointed
535	*Haleluya! Pelo tsa rona*
380	Hallelujah! Jesus lives!
535	Hallelujah! We sing your praises
239	Hark, the glad sound!
246	Hark! A thrilling voice is sounding!
270	Hark! The herald angels sing
764	Have no fear, little flock
829	Have you thanked the Lord?
253	He came down
737	He comes to us as one unknown